Early Jewish Exegesis and Theological Controversy

Jewish and Christian Heritage Series

Volume 2

Early Jewish Exegesis and Theological Controversy

Studies in Scriptures in the Shadow of Internal and External Controversies

by

Isaac Kalimi

2002 ≋ ROYAL VAN GORCUM

ISBN 90 232 3713 7

Typesetting: Infobever, Nijmegen
Printing by: Royal Van Gorcum, Assen, The Netherlands

For Chava, Nisan and Etai

Psalms 128, 3b

"Have we not all one father?
Has not one God created us?
Why then are we faithless to one another,
profaning the covenant of our fathers?"

(Malachi 2, 10)

Table of Contents

Abbreviations

AB	The Anchor Bible
ABD	D.N. Freedman (Editor-in-Chief), *The Anchor Bible Dictionary* , vols. 1-6 (New York / London / Toronto / Sydney / Auckland: Doubleday, 1992)
ABRL	The Anchor Bible Reference Library
AnBib	Analecta Biblica
ASOR	American Schools of Oriental Research
ATD	Das Alte Testament Deutsch
ATDER	Das Alte Testament Deutsch Ergänzungsreihe
Athenaeum	*Athenaeum – Studi di letteratura e Storia dell'Antichita*
BASOR	*Bulletin of the American Schools of Oriental Research*
BEATAJ	Beiträge zur Erforschung des Alten Testaments und des Antiken Judentums
Beit Mikra	*Beit Mikra – Quarterly Founded by the Israel Society for Biblical Research*
BI	*Biblical Interpretation – A Journal of Contemporary Approaches*
BibOr	Biblica et Orientalia
BJS	Brown Judaic Studies
BKAT	Biblischer Kommentar Altes Testament
BN	*Biblische Notizen*
BO	*Bibliotheca Orientalis*
BR	*Bible Review*
BTB	*Biblical Theology Bulletin – A Journal of Bible and Theology*
BTZ	*Berliner Theologische Zeitschrift*
BWANT	Beiträge zur Wissenschaft vom Alten und Neuen Testament
BZAW	Beihefte zur Zeitschrift für die alttestamentliche Wissenschaft
CBK	Calwer Bibelkommentar
CBQ	*Catholic Biblical Quarterly*
CBQMS	The Catholic Biblical Quarterly Monograph Series
CCAR Journal	*The Central Conference of American Rabbis Journal – A Reform Jewish Quarterly*
CIS	Copenhagen International Seminar
DSD	*Dead Sea Discoveries*
Eretz-Israel	*Eretz-Israel – Archaeological, Historical and Geographical Studies*

EvT	*Evangelische Theologie*
ExpTim	*The Expository Times*
Henoch	*Henoch – Historical and Philological Studies on Judaism*
Horeb	*Horeb – Devoted to Research in Jewish History and Literature*
HSM	Harvard Semitic Monographs
HTR	*Harvard Theological Review*
HUCA	*Hebrew Union College Annual*
IBT	Interpreting Biblical Texts
ICC	The International Critical Commentary
IEJ	*Israel Exploration Journal*
Immanuel	*Immanuel – A Bulletin of Religious Thought and Research in Israel*
ITL	International Theological Library
JBL	*Journal of Biblical Literature*
JBTh	*Jahrbuch für Biblische Theologie*
JJS	*Journal of Jewish Studies*
JPS	*Jewish Publication Society*
JR	*The Journal of Religion*
JSJ	*Journal for the Study of Judaism in the Persian, Hellenistic and Roman Period*
JSOT	*Journal for the Study of the Old Testament*
JSOT Suppl.	*Journal for the Study of the Old Testament Supplement Series*
JSP	*Journal for the Study of the Pseudepigrapha*
JSP Suppl.	*Journal for the Study of the Pseudepigrapha Supplement Series*
KAT	Kommentar zum Alten Testament
KEKNT	Kritisch-exegetischer Kommentar über das Neue Testament
KHCAT	Kurzer Hand-Commentar zum Alten Testament
Lešonenu	*Lešonenu – A Journal for the Study of the Hebrew Language and Cognate Subjects*
MGWJ	*Monatsschrift für Geschichte und Wissenschaft des Judentums*
NCBC	The New Century Bible Commentary
NICOT	The New International Commentary on the Old Testament
NovT	*Novum Testamentum*
NTL	The New Testament Library
NTS	*New Testament Studies*
Numen	*Numen – International Review for the History of Religions*
OBO	Orbis Biblicus et Orientalis
Oriens	*Oriens – Journal of the International Society for Oriental Research*
OTL	The Old Testament Library
Qadmoniot	*Qadmoniot – Quarterly for the Antiquities of Eretz-Israel and Bible Lands*
RB	*Revue Biblique*
SBB	Simor Bible Bibliography
SBL	Society of Biblical Literature
SBLDS	Society of Biblical Literature Dissertation Series
SBLMS	Society of Biblical Literature Monograph Series

SBT	Studienbücher Theologie
SJOT	*Scandinavian Journal of the Old Testament*
SJT	*Scottish Journal of Theology*
SVTP	Studia in Veteris Testamenti Pseudepigrapha
TANZ	Texte und Arbeiten zum neutestamentlichen Zeitalter
Tarbiz	*Tarbiz – A Quarterly for Jewish Studies*
TB	Theologische Bücherei
TRE	*Theologische Realenzyklopädie*
VT	*Vetus Testamentum*
WBC	Word Biblical Commentary
WMANT	Wissenschaftliche Monographien zum Alten und Neuen Testament
WTJ	*Westminster Theological Journal*
YJS	Yale Judaica Series
ZAW	*Zeitschrift für die alttestamentliche Wissenschaft*
Zion	*Zion – A Quarterly for Research in Jewish History*
ZNW	*Zeitschrift für die neutestamentliche Wissenschaft*
ZRGG	*Zeitschrift für Religions- und Geistesgeschichte*

Illustrations

Acknowledgments

The present book is one of the products of the author's research and scholarly activities in the last ten years. Almost all the chapters are based on lectures, given upon invitation, which I was honored to deliver at international conferences sponsored by the Society of Biblical literature (San Francisco, Leuven and Helsinki), the Association for Jewish Studies (Boston), the European Association of Jewish Studies (Copenhagen), the International Organization for the Study of Old Testament (Basel), and in several distinguished universities and institutions in Western Europe and the United States of America. Among those may I mention the Boston Theological Institute; *Societas Hebraica Amstelodamensis*, University of Amsterdam; the Theological University of Kampen; *Institutum Judaicum Delitzschianum*, Westfälische Wilhelms-Universität Münster; Universität Luzern, Katholisch-Theologische Fakultät und Gesellschaft Schweiz-Israel; and Das Biblische Institut der Universität Freiburg/Schweiz. I express a deep gratitude to all those colleagues for their kind invitations as well as the invigorating and stimulating discussions which followed the lectures.

Further thanks are extended to Professors Richard J. Clifford and John S. Kselman of the Weston School of Theology (Cambridge, MA), Professor Peter Machinist of Harvard University, Professor Michael V. Fox of University of Wisconsin-Madison, and Professor Marvin A. Sweeney of Claremont School of Theology and Claremont Graduate University (Claremont, CA), who are always supportive of a friend and colleague.

It is also a pleasure to acknowledge The Catholic Biblical Association of America, especially the Executive Secretary, Rev. Professor Joseph Jensen, who generously awarded me a "Young Scholars Fellowship" during the preparation of this volume. Many thanks as well to Dr. Aaron Zeidenberg, the president of Beit Berl Academic College in Israel, for providing me with the time to advance my research on this study.

My thanks go furthermore to Ms. Barbara Wolff for her competent proof-reading of the manuscript, and to Professor M.A. Sweeney for reading the book and making helpful notations. It is also a privilege to express an appreciation to the Jerusalem Vice-Rector of Ratisbonne Pontifical Institute, Mr. Elio Passeto, who constantly opened the doors of the library for my academic inquiries. Last but not least my gratefulness goes to the editors of the journals and books as well as their publishers who allowed me to reshape, revise and use the essays which were originally published by them for the purpose of this volume; to Dr. David E. Orton director of Deo Publishing House (Leiden), for initially accepting the book for publication; and to Mr. Theo Joppe and Mr. Nathan Brinkman of Royal Van Gorcum (Assen) for publishing and producing it in an attractive format.

The book is dedicated to my kids Chava, Nisan and Etai, whom I missed very much, and by whom I had been missed while the research, writing and lecturing were being done.

Beit Berl Academic College /   Isaac Kalimi
The Hebrew University of Jerusalem /
The Leiden Institute for the Study of Religions

Prologue

This book comprises three main parts, approximately comparable in length. Although each part deals with a specifically defined topic, and it is not my intention to tie them definitely together, there are two points that draw clearly the interrelationship of all three conjointly. First, all are linked by the common discussion on early Jewish exegesis; namely, the interpretation of early Scriptures in late Biblical literature, in the Apocrypha and Pseudepigrapha, in Jewish-Hellenistic writings, in the Dead Sea Scrolls, and in a variety of Rabbinic sources, essentially the Targumim and Midrashim. Second, each chapter covers theological controversies, either among the various Jewish sects themselves (internal), and/or between Judaism and some other religious denominations, especially Christianity (external).

The first part of the book, "The *Aqedah* and the Temple: A Disputed Heritage," treats the binding of Isaac within a diversity of texts and contexts through various generations.

Chapter one, "The Land / Mount Moriah, and the Site of the Jerusalem Temple in Biblical Historical Writing,"[1] mentions the inexact location of "the land of Moriah" (Gen 22,2). The Temple Mount is identified with the site of the *Aqedah*, presumably in the beginning of the monarchic era (Gen 22,14b), while the name "Mount Moriah" (2 Chr 3,1) was linked to it through the Chronicler's interpretation in the Persian era, ca. the first quarter of the fourth century BCE. As the site both of the *Aqedah* and of the altar on Araunah's threshing floor was chosen by God, the inclusion of references to these stories in Kings would have strengthened the Deuteronomistic conception of the divine election of the Temple's site. The failure of 1 Kgs 6 to describe the precise location of the

---

[1] An earlier version of this chapter was published in 1990 as "The Land of Moriah, Mount Moriah and the Site of Solomon's Temple in Biblical Historiography", *HTR* 83, pp. 345-362.

Temple can be interpreted in terms of the genre of ancient Near Eastern construction stories, of which 1 Kgs 5,15 – 9,25 is probably a part. The exact location of the Temple, as well as the various traditions related to the site, were familiar to the audience the book was intended for. Moreover, the tradition of the divine election of Araunah's threshing floor had already been given in Deuteronomistic history, so there was no necessity to repeat it in 1 Kgs 6. The detailed reference to the Temple site to be found in 2 Chr 3,1 seems to be an effort on the Chronicler's part to "fill in the gaps" in his *Vorlage* from Kings. The references to the stories of the *Aqedah* and the Araunah's threshing floor were probably intended, first and foremost, to endow Zerubbabel's Temple with a certain degree of sanctity as it fell short of Solomon's Temple in size, wealth, and ritual accessories. Possibly, it contains a hidden polemic with some Jewish groups who negated Zerubbabel's Temple (as stated in various Biblical and post-Biblical sources), and with the Samaritans who insisted that JHWH's holy place was on Mount Gerizim.

Chapter two treats the topic, "The Affiliation of Abraham and the *Aqedah* with Zion / Gerizim in Jewish and Samaritan Sources."[2] The chapter is a continuity of the previous one in order to expose the attitude to the Temple and the Temple Mount by various Jewish writers and by an artist of Dura-Europos, as well as by those whose belief related them somehow to Jews and Judaism. Essentially it is an inquiry of the Jewish and Samaritan key texts, originating during several centuries, concerning the site of Isaac's binding. This issue became a basis of measurement – a parameter – for the attitude expressed towards the Temple and its Mount. The chapter reviews the Jewish sources, starting with Hebrew Bible and Pseudepigrapha; continuing through the Dead Sea Scrolls (Pseudo-Jubilees[a] [4Q225]; Genesis Apocryphon [1QGenAp]), Jewish–Hellenistic writers (Pseudo-Eupolemus; Josephus Flavius); Jewish art (the fresco of the *Aqedah* at the Dura-Europos synagogue) and Rabbinic literature (Targumim,

---

[2] This chapter is based on its earlier versions which were published as "Zion or Gerizim? The Association of Abraham and the *Aqeda* with Zion / Gerizim in Jewish and Samaritan Sources", in M. Lubetski, C. Gottlieb & S. Keller (eds.), *Boundaries of the Near Eastern World – A Tribute to Cyrus H. Gordon* (*JSOT Suppl.* 273; Sheffield: Sheffield Academic Press, 1998), pp. 443-457; and in V. Morabito, A.D. Crown and L. Davey (eds.), *Samaritan Researches Volume V* (Société d'Études Samaritaines & The University of Sydney – Studies in Judaica, no. 10; Sydney: Mandelbaum Publishing, 2000), pp. 32-46.

Jewish liturgy, Midrashim), and ending with Medieval Jewish exegesis. All these sources point to the Temple Mount – Zion/Moriah – as the location of Isaac's binding by his father Abraham. By contrast, the Samaritan sources, such as the Samaritan Pentateuch, Samaritan Midrashim, as well as other Samaritan discoveries, all identify the Samaritan sacred place on Mount Gerizim with the location of the *Aqedah*, and associate Abraham with their own temple (an excursus describes the location, erection, and destruction of the Samaritan temple in recent scholarship). The chapter concludes that the dispute between Jews and Samaritans regarding Moriah / Gerizim had a serious influence on the entire relationship of the two communities in *Eretz* (the Land of) Israel. This issue was and still is indeed one of the main determining criteria for who is a Jew and who is a Samaritan.

The second part, "Biblical Texts in Polemical Contexts," examines some sources in the light of their interpretation in Jewish extra-Biblical literature in general, and in classic rabbinical writings in particular. The texts are mostly from the Joseph story in the First Book of Moses and some allusions to it in the Book of Psalms. There is an attempt to uncover the presumed historical-political and socio-religious contexts of the Midrashim. It is assumed that some of them reflect internal polemics in the Jewish community, others, a dispute between Jews and Christians. Let us turn our attention to these points in some detail:

Chapter three, " 'He was Born Circumcised' – Some Midrashic Sources, Their Concept, Roots and Presumably Historical Context,"[3] deals with the rabbinic concept that to be born circumcised means to be without blemish. Being born circumcised is considered by the rabbis as a preliminary sign of a forthcoming important personality. The roots of the idea can be found already in Jubilees, in a text connected to Antiochus IV Epiphanes who prohibited circumcision. Later on, in *Liber Antiquitatum Biblicarum*, Pseudo-Philo illustrates Moses as one who was born circumcised. It can be traced, presumably, also from John's Gospel, which makes an analogy between a sick man and an uncircumcised man. The concept was, however, reinforced mostly in Midrashim which listed several famous Biblical figures, and claimed that they were born circumcised. One can better

---

[3] A slightly different version of this chapter is published in *ZNW* 93 (2002), pp. 1-12.

understand these homilies against the historical background of the
events in Palestine in the second half of the first and the first half
of the second centuries of the Common Era, that is, the dispute with
Pauline Christianity about circumcision and the Hadrianic prohibition
of circumcision.

Chapter four, "Joseph's Slander of His Brethren – Perspectives on
the Midrashic Interpretation in the Light of the Jewish – Christian
Controversy,"[4] discusses the lack of detail in the action of Joseph's
slander of his brothers, and whether or not he was punished for this
misconduct. Because of these gaps, Philo of Alexandria, Pseudo-Philo
and Josephus Flavius were not provided with the information required by them. These gaps are clarified, however, in the *Testament
of Gad*, and later on by the rabbis of the *aggadic* Midrashim. The
rabbis paid much closer attention to this subject and raised presump-
tions in several directions while showing that Joseph's slander was
a completely non-ethical deed. They determine that Joseph was
punished "measure for measure", and was imprisoned for ten years
on account of slandering his ten brothers. Midrash Psalms *Shocher-
Tov's* introduction of Joseph's slander of his brethren is contrasted
with Benjamin's silence later on. Furthermore, it emphasizes that also
in the long-run Joseph's misbehavior had negative results. God
forbids Moses to appoint a High Priest from among his offspring. In
spite of the sharp contrast between their own theological thought as
revealed in Midrash Psalms, and that of at least some verses in
Jeremiah and Ezekiel, the rabbis did not refrain from noting that
Joseph's descendants were punished. Once again, we can better
evaluate these homilies especially against the historical background
of the events in the Land of Israel around the mid-first to the mid-
second centuries CE. The strict view of the rabbis with regards to
Joseph's slander is reasonable in light of the dispute with the (Judeo-)
Christians, and the painful fight against informers and slanderers
(although we do not know for sure who they were).

Chapter five, "Joseph Between Potiphar and His Wife: The
Biblical Text in the Light of a Comparative Study on Early Jewish
Exegesis," reveals that Midrash Psalms does not reflect negatively on

---

[4] An earlier version of this chapter is published, in German, "'...und Joseph
verleumdete seine Brueder': Josephs Verrat in den Midraschim als Beitrag zur
zeitgenoessischen jüdisch-christlichen Kontroverse", *ZRGG* 54 (2002), pp. 23-
31.

Joseph in the affair of Potiphar's wife.[5] It rejects possible doubts
about the trustworthiness of the Biblical story, and stresses that God
himself testifies that Joseph did not touch her. Due to Joseph's fine
moral quality there was no need for interference of divine forces to
keep him away from Potiphar's wife.

The uncommon righteousness of Joseph in this incident is offered
as an explanation as to why the miracle, the division of the Red Sea,
occurred. By contrast, Joseph's term of imprisonment was extended
two years from that originally planned by the Almighty, because he
placed his hope and trust to be released from prison in a mortal,
Pharaoh's chief butler, rather than in God. The Sages of Midrash
Psalms presented Joseph as a perfect man physically, morally, socially
and religiously; as a model for one of the finest personalities of all
times. Nonetheless, they did not refrain from criticizing some of
Joseph's behavior. They considered him to have been like many
other Biblical figures, that is, after all, no more than a mortal, and
as such he was not excluded from the framework of the concept in
Eccl 7,20: "Surely there is not a righteous man on earth who does
good and never sins".

The third and last part deals with "Biblical theology, Judaism and
Christianity". It includes chapter six which investigates the relationship between the history of Israelite religion and Hebrew Bible /
Old Testament theology. The author concludes that both disciplines
do not exclude each other, and are beneficial and equal in merit.
There are noticeable distinctions and profound differences between
the two. Therefore, both approaches must be kept separate and
follow distinct, clearly defined methods so as to avoid confusion. It
is of interest to uncover the theological guidelines of the Biblical
writers, editors and those responsible for the formation of the Jewish
and Christian canons. One also needs to be aware of the theological
guidelines controlling the Biblical corpora; to read the Bible for
religious messages and moral values that may be derived from it.
Nonetheless, it is impractical to look for or to impose one single
idea on the whole Bible. Unfortunately, some Christian theologians
introduce anti-Jewish and anti-Semitic views into their study of the
Bible. These tendencies should be avoided in any future works.
Without any doubt, there is a Jewish interest in the theology of the

---

[5] This chapter is based on my essay originally published in *BN* 107/108
(2001), pp. 55-64.

Hebrew Bible and in Biblical theology. This originated already in the Hebrew Bible itself and continues in the many Jewish Biblical commentaries from the sages of the midrashim, Saadia Gaon, Maimonides, and Kimchi to Martin Buber, Meir Weiss, and many others. The main reasons for the seemingly moderate interest of Jewish scholars in Biblical theology are to be found in the relatively late development of modern critical scholarly Jewish Biblical research; the timely focus of Jewish-Israelis in Biblical research in the last decades, and in the formation of higher educational institutions above all in Israel as well as the establishment of some Jewish institutions of learning in America.[6]

Chapter seven, "The Task of Hebrew Bible / Old Testament Theology – Between Judaism and Christianity," originated from a response given on Rolf P. Knierim's book, *The Task of Old Testament Theology*, at the Society of Biblical Literature panel review in San Francisco, in 1997.[7] Indeed, I share many of Knierim's methodological premises for the task of Hebrew Bible / Old Testament theology; for example, a comprehensive canonical and historical range of vision as an important methodological framework, the plurality of theologies which constitutes central issues, rejection of criteriological superiority of the New Testament. I am critical of him, nevertheless, on several essential points, for instance, his view of election theology. The critical-review concludes that all in all Knierim's book shows respect for Judaism, and makes a significant contribution to Biblical scholarship in general and to Biblical theology in particular.

As indicated already in the footnotes, earlier version(s) of some chapters originally were published in a variety of international periodicals, collections and *Festschriften* in the last decade, while others are based on extracts from published articles. All the essays / chapters, however, are fully revised, enlarged, updated and improved for the purpose of this volume.

[6] Parts of this essay were originally published as "History of Israelite Religion or Old Testament Theology? Jewish Interest in Biblical Theology", *SJOT* 11 (1997), pp. 100-123.

[7] The early versions of this chapter were originally published in *Henoch* 20 (1998), pp. 225-241; and in W. Kim, D. Ellens, M. Floyd, and M.A. Sweeney (eds.), *Reading the Hebrew Bible for a New Millennium: Form, Concept and Theological Perspective, Volume 1: Theological & Hermeneutical Studies* (Studies in Antiquity & Christianity; Harrisburg, PA: Trinity Press International, 2000), pp. 230-251.

I

The *Aqedah* and the Temple:
A Disputed Heritage

1

The Land / Mount Moriah, and the Site of the Jerusalem Temple in Biblical Historical Writing

I. The Land of Moriah, Mount Moriah, and the Temple Mount

A close reading reveals that the term *"Mount* Moriah" does not appear at all in the story of the *Aqedah* ("binding") of Isaac (Gen 22,1-14.19).[1] The story opens with the divine command to Abraham to go to "the *land* of Moriah", there to sacrifice his beloved son, Isaac, "upon *one of the mountains*" which would be pointed out to him (verse 2). Later, the story tells how Abraham went to "the *place* of which God had told him" and how, on the third day, he saw "the *place* afar off" (verses 3-4). However, at no point does the story give details concerning the name of "the place" or of the mountain on which Isaac was bound.

In fact, a certain lack of precision in divine speech can be discerned also on other occasions when God revealed himself to Abraham. When God made the covenant with Abraham, he said "Know well that your offspring shall be strangers in a land not theirs, and they shall be enslaved and oppressed four hundred years; but I will

---

[1] There are thematic and stylistic differences between verses 1-14, 19 (the *Aqedah* story; mainly E source) and verses 15-18 (the promise motif, R[JE]). On the secondary and late nature of verses 15-18, see J. Skinner, *A Critical and Exegetical Commentary on Genesis* (ICC; Edinburgh: T&T Clark, 1930), pp. 328, 331 and the references there to earlier literature; J. Hoftijzer, *Die Verheissungen an die drei Erzväter* (Leiden: E.J. Brill, 1956), p. 15; G. von Rad, *Genesis – A Commentary* (OTL; 2nd edn.; London: SCM Press, 1963), pp. 237-238; E. Blum, *Die Komposition der Vätergeschichte* (WMANT 57; Neukirchen-Vluyn: Neukirchener Verlag, 1984), p. 320. On the structure of verse 14 see below, and on that of verse 19 see note 5.

execute judgment on the nation they shall serve" (Gen 15,13-14). At no stage does the author give the name either of the "land not theirs" or of "the nation they shall serve". Much of the same phenomenon may be seen in the passage in which God commands Abraham: "Go forth from your native land and from your father's house to the land that I will show you" (Gen 12,1). Abraham is not informed of the name of the land until God appears to him a second time in Canaan and says: "I will give this land to your offspring" (verse 7). The same feature is revealed as well in the story concerning Jacob in Beit El (Gen 28,10-19).

Nevertheless, it was not until after the *Aqedah* and the sacrifice of the ram that Abraham named "that place" יהוה יראה ("the Lord will see", verse 14a).[2] The name derived from the fact that this was the place where Abraham's words that "God will provide himself (אלהים יראה לו) the lamb for a burnt offering" came true (verse 8). There is no mention of whether the site had an earlier name, as there is, for example, in Gen 28,19; Judg 1,23; 18,29. Later on, the narrator or the redactor associated the phrase יהוה יראה in the ancient text (though how ancient it is hard to tell) with הר יהוה – the Temple Mount of his day (probably the First Temple period),[3] by adding the comment "whence the present saying 'On the mount of the Lord there is vision' " (verse 14b). Therefore, this verse (14b) is not an organic part of the narrative.[4] The narrator / redactor made a definite but anachronistic connection between "the mount of the Lord" known to his readers and "that site", "upon *one of the moun-*

---

[2] On the phrase *Adonai yir'eh*, see R.K. Yerkes, "The Location and Etymology of יהוה יראה, Gn. 22,14", *JBL* 31 (1912), pp. 136-139. Yerkes proposes the reading of this passage: "And Abraham named that place '*El-roi*'", following Gen 16,13. The emendation is unnecessary, however. It is worthwhile to mention that in the Qumran manuscript 4QGenExodᵃ the version is אלהים יראה. Presumably the latter kept the original version, see J.R. Davila, "The Name of God at Moriah: An Unpublished Fragment from 4QGenExodᵃ", *JBL* 110 (1991), pp. 577-582.

[3] See Isa 2,3 // Mic 4,2; Isa 30,29; Ps 24,3; Zech 8,3. The form "the Mountain of the Lord's House" is found in Isa 2,2 // Mic 4,1 and 2 Chr 33,15.

[4] On the later date of verse 14b already hinted Rabbi Abraham Ibn Ezra (Toledo 1089-1164 England), in his commentary on Deut 1,2: "And if you understand the secret... on Mount *Adonai yir'eh*... you will recognize the truth". Cf. Skinner, *Genesis*, p. 330. For other examples of this phenomenon, see Gen 19,9; 1 Sam 5,5; 10,12; 19,24.

tains" in the "land of Moriah" called by Abraham יהוה יראה. In this way he set the story in a place of some importance in the world in which he lived and even imparted to the Temple Mount an additional measure of sanctity as a place chosen for sacrifices (animal sacrifices, to be precise) in the earliest antiquity.

In fact, the oldest version of the narrative (Gen 22,1-14a.19a)[5] gives neither the name of the mountain where the *Aqedah* took place nor even a clear indication of the identity of "the land of Moriah". The narrative does say that "Moriah" was situated in a mountainous region (Gen 22,2), some three days' journey from Beer-sheba (verses 4, 19a). But a journey completed "on the third day" is a common motif in the Hebrew Bible. For example, Josh 9,17 reads: "So the Israelites set out, and *on the third day* they came to their towns". And 1 Sam 30,1 reads: "By the time David and his men arrived in Ziklag, *on the third day*". The number three, then, is a typological number when used in connection with travel, as may be seen by its use in other, related contexts in the Hebrew Bible: "Now therefore, let us go a distance of *three days* into the wilderness to sacrifice to the Lord our God" (Ex 3,18; 5,3); "they traveled *three days* in the wilderness and found no water" (Ex 15,22; cf. Num 33,8; 10,33). Thus, the use of the expression "on the third day" in the *Aqedah* story, then, is not necessarily meant as an accurate description of the length of the journey. A final point complicating the identification of the "Land of Moriah" is the failure of the narrative to relate in which direction Abraham traveled from Beer-Sheba.

---

[5] Verse 19a, "Abraham then returned to his servants, and they departed together for Beer-Sheba", seems to have concluded the original story of verses 1-14a. Here the journey of Abraham, which began with the words "and [he] arose and went to the place..." (verse 3), comes to its end. This literary feature of the Biblical story is known also elsewhere, see, for example, 1 Sam 16,4.13; 28,8.25; 1 Kgs 3,4a.15b. Verse 19b, "and Abraham stayed in Beer-Sheba", appears to be an editorial interpolation. Beer-Sheba was the place from which Abraham set out on his journey and to which he returned at its end. Cf. Skinner, *Genesis*, p. 328; von Rad, *Genesis*, p. 233.
Gen 21,34: "And Abraham sojourned many days in the land of the Philistines", which stands directly between the aetiological legend about Beer-Sheba (Gen 21,22-33) and the *Aqedah* story, is also an editorial interpolation, cf. Skinner, *Genesis*, p. 327.

"The land of Moriah" is mentioned only once in the Hebrew Bible and does not appear in epigraphic sources. Indeed, "inscription B" from the wall of the burial cave near Ḥurvat Beit Lei was originally read by Naveh, המריה אתה חננת יה יהוה "the Moriah you have favored, the dwelling of Yah, Yahweh".[6] However, re-examination of the inscription reveals that this is not so.[7] The inscription is so blurred that it is impossible to suggest a reading with any confidence.[8] Thus, it seems that there is no point also to the readings proposed by Cross and Lemaire, though none of these propose the reading מריה "Moriah" in the inscription in question.[9] The location of the land of Moriah, then, remains hidden in the mists of time. Generation after generation has wrestled with the problem of the location of this region: in the Septuagint version of Gen 22,2 and in Jub 18,2 the word "Moriah" was taken as referring to the

[6] See J. Naveh, "Old Hebrew Inscriptions in a Burial Cave", *IEJ* 13 (1963), pp. 85-86.

[7] See J. Naveh, "A Collection of Inscriptions – Canaanite and Hebrew Inscriptions", *Lešonenu* 30 (1966), pp. 65-80 esp. 73 (Hebrew).

[8] Professor Naveh pointed this fact out to me in a conversation. I would like to thank him for his help in this matter.

[9] See F.M. Cross, "The Cave Inscriptions from Khirbet Beit Lei", in J.A. Sanders (ed.), *Near Eastern Archaeology in the Twentieth Century: Essays in honor of Nelson Glueck* (Garden City, NY: Doubleday, 1970), pp. 299-306 esp. 302; A. Lemaire, "Prières en Temps de Crise: Les Inscriptions de Khirbet Beit Lei", *RB* 83 (1976), pp. 560-561. Williamson rejects Naveh's 1963 reading of Inscription B, which, he argues, "should now most probably be read and dated differently", and refers to the studies of Cross, Lemaire and Gibson (the reference to Gibson is most surprising as he adopts the very Naveh reading rejected by Williamson himself), see H.G.M. Williamson, *1 and 2 Chronicles* (NCBC; Grand Rapids, MI: Eerdmans / London: Marshall, Morgan & Scott, 1982), p. 203. Both Gibson's and Cogan's proposals (see below) are to be rejected, as they are based on Naveh's 1963 reading. Gibson includes this inscription among the corpus of Hebrew inscriptions discovered in the Land of Israel and even tries to date all the Khirbet Beit Lei inscriptions using, among other things, the paleography(!) of Inscription B, see J.C.L. Gibson, *Textbook of Syrian Semitic Inscriptions, Volume 1: Hebrew and Moabite Inscriptions* (Oxford: Clarendon Press, 1973), pp. 57-58. Cogan mentions the inscription and notes: "If the reading proposed by J. Naveh is correct... the name 'Moriah' was understood as referring to Jerusalem as early as the sixth century BCE", see M. Cogan, "'The City that I Chose' – The Deuteronomistic View of Jerusalem", *Tarbiz* 55 (1986), pp. 301-309 esp. 307 note 21 (Hebrew).

topographical nature of the region τὴν γῆν τὴν ὑψηλήν "a high land". The Syriac version identifies ארץ המריה "the land of Moriah" with ארעא דאמוריא "the land of the Amorites" mentioned in Num 21,31; Josh 24,8; Judg 10,8 and 11,21, among other places. This was probably due to the similarity in the pronunciation of the two names, and is not a testimony for an original version.[10] The same identification was also made by Rabbi Samuel ben Meir (Rashbam; 1080-1160), as well as by various modern commentators and scholars[11] who held that the name "Moriah" as found in the Masoretic Text was a corruption. Julius Wellhausen, too, felt that it was a corruption, but determined (probably under the influence of the Samaritan tradition) that the Elohist (E) did not write ארץ המריה "the land of Moriah" but ארץ חמרים "land of asses" as is to be found in the region around Shechem (cf. Gen 33,19).[12] Other scholars have kept to the Masoretic Text, proposing (probably under the influence of the Jewish tradition) that "the land of Moriah is an ancient name for the mountainous region in which Jerusalem lies".[13] In contrast, Nelson Glueck wanted to identify Moriah in a different region altogether:

> It would not have been necessary for Abraham... to drag a supply of kindling with him for the altar fire had his mission been to the wooded hills of Judah. God's revelation, which is a free translation of what

[10] Contra C. Westermann, *Genesis – 2. Teilband, Genesis 12-36* (BKAT 1,2; Neukirchen-Vluyn: Neukirchener Verlag, 1981), p. 437.

[11] See, e.g., A. Dillmann, *Genesis* (Edinburgh: W.B. Stevenson, 1897), p. 142; Skinner, *Genesis*, p. 329; L.H. Vincent, "Abraham à Jerusalem", *RB* 58 (1951), pp. 366-371; von Rad, *Genesis*, p. 235; Westermann, *Genesis 12-36*, p. 437.

[12] J. Wellhausen, *Die Composition des Hexateuchs und der historischen Bücher des Alten Testaments* (Berlin: Georg Reimer, 1889), p. 19. On Samaritan tradition, see the next chapter in this book.

[13] S.E. Loewenstamm, "Moriah, the Land of Moriah", *Encyclopaedia Biblica* (Jerusalem: Bialik Institute, 1968), vol. 5, p. 460 (Hebrew); cf. U. Cassuto, "Jerusalem in the Pentateuch", *Biblical and Oriental Studies, Volume 1: Bible* (Jerusalem: Magnes Press, 1973), pp. 71-78 esp. 74-76. The later Jewish tradition, as seen in Gen 22,14b and 2 Chr 3,1 (and see below), is also reflected in the rabbinic literature. See the references in M.M. Kasher, *Torah Shelemah (Complete Torah) – Talmudic-Midrashic Encyclopaedia of the Pentateuch* (New York: American Biblical Encyclopaedia Society, 1949), vol. 3 Tome 4 (*Genesis*), pp. 870-872.

Moriah means, is pictured as having taken place in the severe and treeless ranges of Sinai.[14]

A number of scholars have argued that the name "Moriah" was introduced into Gen 22,2 following 2 Chr 3,1: It presents a late Jerusalemite redaction of the text.[15] It seems more likely, however, that the name is part of the original text; this is most clearly to be seen from the fact that the narrative derives the name from the root רא"ה, which is used no less than five times in the story (verses 4,8,13,14).[16] In addition, it is difficult to suppose that the author of the Book of Chronicles in the Persian period did not have this story in some form in front of him.[17] In the Chronicler's era, the Torah was already canonized. It means, at that time it was impossible to insert any word into the text of Gen 22, and certainly at the time after the composition of Chronicles.[18]

The term "Mount Moriah" appears only once in the Hebrew Bible – in the late historiography. When the Chronicler added the precise location of Jerusalem's Temple to his reworking of the text of the Book of Kings (where it is not mentioned at all, see below), he found a clear connection between the site of the Temple Mount and the place where Isaac was bound (Gen 22,14b). He transferred the name "Moriah" from being that of a land to being that of a

---

[14] N. Glueck, *Rivers in the Desert: A History of the Negev* (New York: Farrar, Straus and Cudahy, 1959), p. 60; cf. N.M. Sarna, *Understanding Genesis* (2nd edn.; New York: Schocken, 1970), pp. 159-160.

[15] For example, Skinner, *Genesis*, pp. 328-29; von Rad, *Genesis*, p. 190; Westermann, *Genesis 12-36*, p. 437; J.A. Montgomery, "Paronomasias on the Name Jerusalem", *JBL* 49 (1930), pp. 277-282 esp. 279; R. Kilian, *Isaaks Opferung: Zur Überlieferungsgeschichte von Gen. 22* (Stuttgart: Katholisches Bibelwerk, 1970), pp. 31-37 esp. 31; F.W. Golka, "The Aetiologies in the Old Testament", *VT* 26 (1976), pp. 423-424; G.J. Wenham, *Genesis 16-50* (WBC 2; Dallas, TX: Word, 1994), p. 104.

[16] Not *seven* times, as claimed by Cassuto, "Jerusalem in the Pentateuch", p. 16.

[17] Cf. Williamson, *Chronicles*, p. 205.

[18] On this issue, see I. Kalimi, *Zur Geschichtsschreibung des Chronisten: Literarisch-historiographische Abweichungen der Chronik von ihren Paralleltexten in den Samuel- und Königsbüchern* (BZAW 226; Berlin & New York: Walter de Gruyter, 1995), pp. 336-337 esp. 337; idem, *The Book of Chronicles: Historical Writing and Literary Devices* (The Biblical Encyclopaedia Library XVIII; Jerusalem: Bialik Institute, 2000), p. 373 (Hebrew).

mountain on which the Temple was later constructed, as if to imply that the region was named after the holy mountain found on it.[19] In this way, the Chronicler was able to connect the story of the *Aqedah* with his own account of the construction of the Temple. Moreover, just as the narrative in Genesis derived the name from the root ה"רא in Abraham's naming the spot יהוה יראה "the Lord will see / appear", so the Chronicler derived it from the same root: "on Mount Moriah, where [the Lord][20] had seen / appeared to (נראה) his father, David" (2 Chr 3,1).

It comes into view, then, that the Temple Mount was identified with the site of the *Aqedah* during the period of the first Temple (Gen 22,14b). However, as far as can be inferred from the sources, the name "Mount Moriah" seems to have been given to the site only at the instigation of the Chronicler, in the Second Temple period. In the light of this, the use of the term "Mount Moriah" by certain scholars when referring to the *Aqedah* story, or the site of the Temple during the United Monarchy,[21] seems to be imprecise.

---

[19] In similar fashion, the Neofiti version of Gen 22,2 combines the "*land* of Moriah" of Masoretic Text Genesis 22,2, and "*Mount* Moriah" of 2 Chr 3,1. The translator reads ואזל לך לארע טור מורייה "and go to the *land* of *Mount* Moriah", see A. Díez Macho, *Neophyti 1 – Tomo I: Génesis* (Madrid & Barcelona: Consejo Superior de Investigaciones Científicas, 1968), p. 125. On the gloss in the margin of this Targum's manuscript, see in the next chapter of this volume, p. 45.

[20] The context here demands the addition of the word "the Lord". The Greek version has κύριος here, and see also the Aramaic version.

[21] Cogan, "The City that I Chose", p. 301, comments on the *Aqedah* story: "It is well known that it was on Mount Moriah that God tested Abraham by requiring him to offer his son as a burnt offering". He continues to conclude (pp. 306–307): "it was in this period [i.e., the United Monarchy, I.K.] that the site of the Jerusalem Temple was identified with Mount Moriah". The same lack of precision may be seen in Williamson, *Chronicles*, p. 203: "First, and most striking, is his [i.e., the Chronicler's, I.K.] identification of the temple site with *Mount Moriah*, referred to elsewhere in the OT only at Gen 22,2 as the site where Abraham was commanded to offer up Isaac". *Mount* Moriah is not mentioned at all in Gen 22,2!

II. The Site of the Jerusalem Temple in Biblical Historical Writing

1. The Deuteronomistic History

The failure of the Book of Kings to give the location of the Temple, in general, and to identify it with the site of the *Aqedah* and/or the altar erected by David on Araunah's threshing floor, in particular, seems somewhat surprising, all the more so when one considers the central role played by Jerusalem and its Temple in Deuteronomistic literature. This failure to identify the site of the Temple in Jerusalem with Mount Moriah in Deuteronomistic literature has been examined by Mordechai Cogan. He concludes:

> The members of the Deuteronomistic school consistently applied the fundamental doctrine of the law [of the centralization, I.K.] of worship found in Deut 12,5: 'But look only to the site that the Lord your God will choose amidst all your tribes as his habitation, to establish his name there; there you are to go'. The site of the Temple was chosen by God and not by man. It was impossible, then, to use an historical event [to explain this, I.K.], since it would have detracted from the Deuteronomistic conception of divine selection.[22]

Later, Cogan has to deal with the question of the erection of the altar on Araunah's threshing floor:

> While 2 Sam 24,25 tells how David built an altar to the Lord on a threshing floor, properly purchased from Araunah the Jebusite, the account of the construction of the Temple in 1 Kings 6-7 does not mention anything of David's altar at all... [it] has disappeared altogether – or following my line of argument, it has been removed from the Book of Kings by the author for the same doctrinal reasons involved in the description of the site of the Temple: the selection of the site for the altar could not be connected with an historical event of any kind (even if, in 2 Sam 24,18, the instruction to erect the altar was given by the prophet Nathan).[23] There was no room in Deuteronomistic ideology for

---

[22] Cogan, "The City that I Chose", p. 307.

[23] In fact Nathan the prophet is not mentioned in 2 Sam 24; it is "the prophet *Gad*, David's seer" who appears in verses 11,13,14,18.

the involvement of human agencies in the process of sanctification taking place in a world at whose center stood God.[24]

If Cogan was right, however, we might have expected the Deuteronomistic historian to have emphasized the divine nature of the election of Jerusalem and/or the site of the Temple. We might also have expected him to have stressed the divine election of the Temple's site by describing (in the plainest possible terms) how the sites of the rival royal temples at Dan and Beit El were chosen by a man, be he a contemporary or a historical figure. Yet in 1 Kgs 6 and 12,28-29 he did none of these things.[25] In fact, a close reading of the *Aqedah* (Gen 22,1-14a.19a) and the census (2 Sam 24) stories demonstrate that had the Deuteronomist made use of these "historical events" in his account, far from detracting from the "Deuteronomistic conception of divine selection", they would have gone not a little way towards strengthening it:

It is clearly stated in the *Aqedah* story that God commanded Abraham to "go to the land of Moriah, and offer him [= Isaac] there as a burnt offering upon one of the mountains of *which I shall tell you* (אשר אמר אליך)" (verse 2). Obedient to the divine com-

---

[24] Cogan, "The City that I Chose", p. 307.

[25] According to Judg 18,30, the site of Dan had been considered holy from the time that the region was settled by the tribe of Dan: "The Danites set up the sculptured image for themselves; and Jonathan son of Gershom, son of Moses (another reading – a scribal correction – is Manasseh), and his sons were priests to the tribe of the Danites until the day of the captivity of the land". It is, on the other hand, very difficult to determine precisely when and by whom this temple was established. Beit El, too, presents a number of problems: 1 Sam 10,3 mentions "three men making a pilgrimage to God at Beit El". However, it is not clear whether this passage is referring to a temple or an open holy area with an altar / high place, since the three men are described as making a pilgrimage "to God" and not "to *the house of* God". 1 Kgs 12,31: "He [= Jeroboam] made cult places...", is not sufficient to attribute the establishment of the Beit El temple to Jeroboam, the son of Nebat, see M. Haran, *Temples and Temple-Service in Ancient Israel: An Inquiry into Biblical Cult Phenomena and the Historical Setting of the Priestly School* (Winona Lake, IN: Eisenbrauns, 1985), p. 28 note 27. The text in 2 Kgs 23,15, too, refers only to an altar or a high place established by Jeroboam, the son of Nebat, cf. 1 Kgs 12,33, "Jeroboam ascended the altar which he had made in Beit El". Haran, *Temples and Temple-Service,* p. 30, may be right, however, in arguing that Jeroboam enlarged the altar in the already functioning Beit El temple.

mand, Abraham rose early, and went "to the place of *which God had told him* (אֲשֶׁר אָמַר לוֹ הָאֱלֹהִים)" (verse 3). As if to drive the point home, the text repeats the phrase a third time: "They arrived at the place of *which God had told him* (אֲשֶׁר אָמַר לוֹ הָאֱלֹהִים)" (verse 9a). Abraham built an altar there; he laid the wood in order; and bound his son Isaac, etc. (verse 9b). Thus, the site of the *Aqedah* on one of the mountains of the land of Moriah was chosen, not by a man, but by God himself.

The story of the census in 2 Samuel 24, at the end of which Araunah's threshing floor is chosen as the site of the altar, seems also to display a similar approach. There is a hint of God's special purpose for the site when he prevents the destructive angel from continuing his operation precisely at that place: "The Lord renounced further punishment and said to the angel who was destroying the people, 'Enough! Stay your hand!' The angel of the Lord was then by the threshing floor of Araunah the Jebusite" (verse 16). The Jewish Hellenistic writer Eupolemus (ca. 157 BCE) was quick to identify this as a clear sign that God had chosen the place: "Since David wanted to build a temple for God, he asked God to show him a place for the altar. Then an angel appeared to him standing above the place where the altar is set up in Jerusalem".[26] In verses

---

[26] Fragment 2, Alexander Polihistor, "On the Jews", in Eusebius, *Praeparatio Evangelica*, 9,30,5. I am following here the translation of F. Fallon, "Eupolemus", in J.H. Charlesworth (ed.), *The Old Testament Pseudepigrapha* (ABRL; New York / London / Toronto / Sydney / Auckland: Doubleday, 1985), vol. 2, pp. 861–872 esp. 866. Later in the parallel passage in 1 Chr 21,15, the Targum is quick to make use of the opportunity to connect Araunah's threshing floor with the site of the *Aqedah*: "God has sent the Angel of Pestilence to Jerusalem in order to destroy it. However before [it could carry out] the destruction, He took notice of the ashes of Isaac's *Aqedah* which were in the base of the altar. He then considered his covenant with Abraham which He had made with him on the Mount of Divine Worship; [He also considered] the Sanctuary Above, where the souls of the righteous [rested] and the image of Jacob was engraved on the Throne of Glory. He decided against the evil which he had determined to do and said to the Angel of Death, 'This is enough for you! Now take Abishai their leader from among them and stop tormenting the rest of the people'. But the Angel sent before God remained on the land of Araunah, the Jebusite". The translation here follows R. Le Déaut and S. Robert's French edition, *Targum des Chroniques (cod. Vat. Urb. Ebr. 1)*, (AnBib 51; Rome: Biblical Institute Press, 1971), vol. 1, pp. 86–87. This passage of the Targum finds a parallel in the Babylonian Talmud, *Berakot 62b*: "*And He said to the Angel that*

18-19, the Biblical text gives the clearest possible indication that the threshing floor had been chosen by God: "Gad came to David the same day and said to him, 'Go and set up an altar to the Lord on the threshing floor of Araunah the Jebusite'. David went up, following Gad's instructions, *as the Lord had commanded*". And indeed, the purchase of the threshing floor, the construction of the altar, and the offering of sacrifices on it brought the plague to an end: "The Lord responded to the plea for the land, and the plague was averted from Israel" (verse 25). This, then, may be seen as the final proof of God's choice of, or at least approval of and intentions for, that place. Thus, the author of the Book of Chronicles in the Second Temple period had good reason to expand the text of the passage from the Book of Samuel (1 Chr 21,26 – 22,1). A new element was added to the story – the descent of heavenly fire onto the altar, showing that both its construction on Araunah's threshing floor and the offering of sacrifices there were the will of God: "He [= David] invoked the Lord, who answered him with fire from heaven on the altar of burnt offerings. The Lord ordered the angel to return his sword to its sheath" (1 Chr 21,26-27). This precisely parallels the

destroyed the people, It is enough [*rab*; 2 Sam 24,16], Rabbi Eleazar said: The Holy One, blessed be He, said to the angel: take *a great man* [= *rab*] among them, through whose death many sins can be expiated for them. At that time there died Abishai son of Zeruiah, who was [singly] equal in worth to the greater part of the Sanhedrin. *And as he was about to destroy, the Lord beheld, and He repented Him.* What did He behold? – Rab said: He beheld Jacob our ancestor, as it is written, *And Jacob said when he beheld them*. Samuel said: He beheld the ashes of [the ram of] Isaac, as it says, *God will see for Himself the lamb* [Gen 22,8]... R. Jochanan said: He saw the Temple, as it is written, *On the mount of the Lord it shall be seen* [Gen 22,14b]...". For English translation, compare M. Simon, *Berakoth – Translated into English with Notes, Glossary and Indices* (London: Soncino Press, 1948), p. 393. On "the ashes of the binding of Isaac", which were supposed to have remained on the Temple Mount for generations, see Mekhilta de-Rabbi Ishmael, *dePaseḥa, Bo, Parasha* 7 (H.S. Horovitz' edition, pp. 24-25); Midrash Hagadol on Gen 22,13 (M. Margoliot's edition, p. 358). For other sources and a discussion on them, see B. Grossfeld, "The Targum to Lamentations 2,10", *JJS* 28 (1977), pp. 60-64 (Grossfeld does not discuss the parallel between the Targum to 1 Chronicles and the Babylonian Talmud). On later treatments of the legend of Isaac's ashes, see S. Spiegel, "From the *Aqedah* Legends: A Piyyut on the Slaughtering of Isaac and his Resurrection by Rab Ephraim of Buna," *The Alexander Marx Jubilee Volume* (New York: The Jewish Theological Seminary, 1950), pp. 471-547 esp. 483-497 (Hebrew section).

account of the dedication of the altar / Tabernacle in the desert (Lev 9,24), and of the dedication in the altar / Temple in Jerusalem (2 Chr 7,1, see also verse 9).[27]

The explanation proposed by Cogan for the failure of the Book of Kings to identify the site of the Temple, then, is not consistent with the narratives of the *Aqedah* and the census. Both these texts clearly describe the divine election of the place identified as the site of the Temple. Therefore, the solution to the problem must be sought elsewhere.

The thematic structure of the account of the Temple's construction in 1 Kgs 5,15 – 9,25 is very similar to that of parallel Mesopotamian (in particular Assyrian) and northwest Semitic traditions.[28] A detailed comparison of the Biblical construction story with other extra-Biblical construction stories reveals that it is "a typical ancient Near-Eastern construction story".[29] One of the features of these ancient Near Eastern construction stories discovered so far is the failure to give the precise location of the Temples (and even the palaces and other royal or public buildings) described. The exception which proves this rule is the inscription from Kultepe in Cappadocia in which Erišum I, vice-regent of Assyria (ca. 1939-1900 BCE), tells of its construction to the god Ashur in the city of Ashur: "I reserved land for Ashur, my lord, from the Sheep Gate to the People's Gate. I built all of the temple area".[30] Thus, when the author of the account in the Book of Kings failed to give the precise location of Solomon's Temple, he was following the rules of the same genre as

---

[27] See also the descent of heavenly fire as the Divine reply to Elijah on Mount Carmel, in 1 Kgs 18,36-39.

[28] On this subject, see V. (A.) Horowitz, *I Have Built You an Exalted House – Temple Building in the Bible in the Light of Mesopotamian and Northwest Semitic Writing,* (JSOT Suppl. 115; Sheffield; Sheffield Academic Press, 1992), pp. 32-128, 311-316, esp. 126, 312.

[29] Horowitz, *I Have Built You an Exalted House,* pp. 126, 311. It seems that Yadin may be right in holding that "the plan of the Temple, the vessels [used] there, the decorative motifs that graced it, as well as the building methods – all are thoroughly grounded in ancient Middle Eastern tradition", see Y. Yadin, "The First Temple", in M. Avi-Yonah (ed.), *The Book of Jerusalem* (Jerusalem & Tel Aviv: Bialik Institute and Dvir, 1956), vol. 1, pp. 176-190 esp. 190.

[30] See A.K. Grayson, *Assyrian Royal Inscriptions: Volume I – From the Beginning to Ashur-resha-ishi I* (Wiesbaden: Otto Harrassowitz, 1972), inscription no. 9, p. 12; see also inscription no. 7, pp. 10-11.

his colleagues throughout the fertile crescent.[31] Furthermore, although Solomon's Temple is the only permanent temple in which the construction is described in detail in the Hebrew Bible,[32] no detailed information is given for the site of any of the other temples mentioned in the *early* historical books. The site of (or mountain, hill, etc. on which was built or stood) the Canaanite temple "Beit Baal-Berith" // "Beit El-Berith" in Shechem (or in "Migdal Shechem," Judg 9,4.46; cf. verse 27),[33] of the Temple of the Lord at Gilgal in the Heights of Ephraim (1 Sam 11,15; 13,8-9; 15,12-21.33),[34] and of the temple of Mizpah Benjamin (Judg 20,1-3; 21,1.5.8; 1 Sam 7,6.9; 10,17.25) is not given. The same is true of the temple of

---

[31] This, then, is another point of similarity between the Biblical construction story and ancient Near Eastern construction stories to add to Horowitz's list.

[32] There is another precise description of the construction of a sanctuary in the Hebrew Bible – that of the portable temple in the desert, the Tabernacle (Ex 25-32; 35-40). This is not a realistic description, however, see Haran, *Temples and Temple-Service*, pp. 194-204.

[33] Scholarly opinion differs as to whether this temple was located in the fortified part of the city, or in a nearby settlement called "Migdal Shechem". For a detailed discussion, see N. Na'aman, "Migdal-Shechem and the House of El Berith", *Zion* 51 (1986), pp. 260-265 (Hebrew). A contrary view is taken by G.E. Wright, *Shechem – The Biography of a Biblical City* (New York: McGraw-Hill, 1965), pp. 136-38; idem, "The Biblical Traditions of Shechem's Sacred Area", *BASOR* 169 (1963), pp. 30-32. The temple under discussion should probably not be confused with the "Temple of the Lord" which was situated outside Shechem (Josh 24,26 and cf. verse 1: "Joshua assembled all the tribes of Israel... and they presented themselves *before God*"). On this point, see Haran, *Temples and Temple-Service*, p. 51; Na'aman, "Migdal Shechem", pp. 279-280.

[34] On the Gilgal's temple, see also Hos 12,12. Both Hosea and Amos denounced this temple together with that at Beit El (Hos 4,15; 9,15; Amos 4,4; 5,2). The references in Josh 4,19; 5,8-12; 7,6; 9,6.19 are to a different settlement, situated between Jericho and the Jordan river. There seems to have been no temple building at this place but only an open-air cultic precinct with an altar and so on, see Haran, *Temples and Temple-Service*, pp. 31-32. De Vaux confused the verses from Joshua which refer to this open-air cultic precinct near Jericho with those referring to the Temple of the Lord on Mount Ephraim. He failed to discern that the texts refer to two different regions and to two quite distinct types of cultic institution, see R. de Vaux, *Ancient Israel: Its Life and Institutions* (2nd edn.; London: Darton, Longman & Todd, 1965), pp. 302-303.

Mizpah Gilead to the east of the Transjordan (Judg 11,11),[35] the temple of Shiloh (Josh 18,1.8; 19,51; 21,2; 22,19.29; Judg 18,31; 21,19; 1 Sam 1,7.9.24; 3,3.15), the temple at Hebron (2 Sam 5,3; 15,7), and the Temple of God at Bethlehem in Judah (1 Sam 20,6; Judg 19,18). The small temples that may have stood at Nob (1 Sam 21,1-10 esp. verses 7 and 10), at Beit Micah on Mount Ephraim (Judg 17-18 and esp. 17,5), at Ophrah (Judg 8,27), and on Gibeah of Saul (2 Sam 21,6 [LXX reads: "on the Mount of the Lord"], 9) are also mentioned without any detailed identification of their sites.[36] Even the sites of the two famous temples of Dan and Beit El are not described anywhere in the Bible.[37] The conclusion to be drawn

---

[35] Haran (*Temples and Temple-Service*, pp. 33, 39) argues that there was an open-air precinct in Mizpah Gilad, but no temple. There is no reason, however, not to accept the verse, "...And Jephthah repeated all these terms *before the Lord* at Mizpah" (Judg 11,11), at face value. "Before the Lord" is generally a technical term designating the use of a temple. The context here is of all the children of Israel gathering and appointing Jephthah "commander and chief" – a procedure normally carried out in a temple (see, for example, 1 Sam 10,19.24-25; 2 Sam 5,3; 2 Kgs 11,11-12). The fact that this is the only evidence in the Hebrew Bible for the existence of a temple at Mizpah Gilad does not justify Haran's claim that the use of the expression "before the Lord" was caused by the confusion of Mizpah Gilad with Mizpah Benjamin (where there quite definitely was a temple). The Mizpah Gilad temple was probably not the only one to be found in eastern Transjordan. The Mesha stone provides some evidence that there was a temple at Nebo: ואקח משם את כֹלי יהוה ואסחב הם לפני כמש "And I took from there the vessels of YHWH and dragged them before Kemosh", see H. Donner – W. Röllig, *Kanaanäische und Aramäische Inschriften* (3rd edn.; Wiesbaden: Otto Harrassowitz, 1971), vol. I: *Texte*, p. 33, no. 181, lines 17-18. The restoration is accepted by the vast majority of scholars, see for example, H. Donner – W. Röllig, *Kanaanäische und Aramäische Inschriften* (3rd edn.; Wiesbaden: Otto Harrassowitz, 1973), vol. II: *Kommentar*, pp. 169, 177; Gibson, *Textbook of Syrian Semitic Inscriptions, Volume 1*, pp. 75-76. There may have been some connection between this temple and the traditions concerning Moses' death on Mount Nebo (Deut 32,49-50; 34,1-5), see A. Rofé, "Moses' Blessing, the Sanctuary at Nebo and the Origin of the Levites", in Y. Avishur and J. Blau (eds.), *Studies in Bible and the Ancient Near East Presented to S.E. Loewenstamm on His Seventieth Birthday* (Jerusalem: E. Rubinstein's Publishing House, 1978), vol. I, pp. 409-424 esp. 414-417 (Hebrew).

[36] For the list of temples, cf. Haran, *Temples and Temple-Service*, pp. 34-37.

[37] On the Beit El temple during the period of the Monarchy, see also 1 Kgs 13,1; 2 Kgs 23,13; Hos 3,14; 4,4; 5,5-6; Amos 4,15; 7,13; Jer 48,13.

from this is that the sites of the various temples, either under construction or already functioning, were so well known to the Israelite people that there was no need to mention them – either in the context of their construction or in any other context.

It is extremely likely that attempts were made during the Monarchic period to endow the site of the Temple in Jerusalem with an early Israelite background. In this context, it is noteworthy to mention not only Gen 22,14b and 2 Sam 24, but also Gen 14,17-24, which seems to imply that Jerusalem was already a holy city in the distant past.[38] A similar attempt seems also to have been made for the temple of Beit El (Gen 28,10-12.16-22; 35,7; and cf. Hos 12,5),[39] and for that of Dan (Judg 18,30). The various traditions concerning the site and other aspects of Jerusalem's Temple were so well known to the potential audience of the Book of Kings that there was no need to repeat them in the text. Furthermore, it seems that the Book of Kings was not an independent composition, to be read on its own; rather, it formed the final part of the complex of Deuteronomistic history, which began with the Book of Deuteronomy and covered all the books of the Former Prophets.[40] The divi-

---

[38] See Cassuto, "Jerusalem in the Pentateuch", pp. 71-74; B. Mazar, "The Historical Background of the Book of Genesis", *The Early Biblical Period – Historical Studies* (Jerusalem: The Israel Exploration Society, 1986), pp. 49-62 esp. 51-52; and see also above.

[39] See, too, Judg 20,18.26-27; 21,2-4. There is a school of thought that these verses originally referred to Shiloh, but this seems unlikely, see U. Cassuto, "Beit El in the Bible", *Encyclopaedia Biblica* (Jerusalem: Bialik Institute, 1954), vol. 2, pp. 63-67 (Hebrew).

[40] This idea was first presented by M. Noth, *Überlieferungsgeschichtliche Studien* (Tübingen: Max Niemeyer Verlag, 1957), pp. 12-18 (English translation, idem, *The Deuteronomistic History* [JSOT Suppl. 15; Sheffield: JSOT Press, 1981], pp. 12-17). It has been accepted, in one form or another, by a broad spectrum of scholarly opinion, see for example, F.M. Cross, "The Themes of the Book of Kings and the Structure of the Deuteronomistic History", *Canaanite and Hebrew Epic – Essays in the History of the Religion of Israel* (Cambridge, MA: Harvard University Press, 1973), pp. 274-289 esp. 287-289; R.D. Nelson, *The Double Redaction of the Deuteronomistic History* (JSOT Suppl. 18; Sheffield: JSOT Press, 1981), pp. 13-14, 128 (Cross and Nelson stress the double redaction of the deuteronomistic work); T.E. Fretheim, *Deuteronomic History* (IBT; Nashville, TN: Abingdon Press, 1983), pp. 15-18; B. Peckham, *The Composition of the Deuteronomistic History* (HSM 35; Atlanta, GA: Scholars Press, 1985), p. 1. These scholars believe that the Deuteronomistic history follows the "Tetrateuch"

sion of this complex into "books" is only secondary due to the extraordinary length of the composition.[41] This being so, the story of the census (2 Sam 24), which describes the divine election of the threshing floor of Araunah the Jebusite for the erection of an altar in Jerusalem, was already a part of the Deuteronomistic history,[42] and so there was no need to repeat it when the construction of the Temple was described in 1 Kgs 6. In fact, there is some reason to suppose that the story of the census and the erection of the altar was not originally in its present place in the Book of Samuel, but was to be found elsewhere in the description of David's kingdom.[43] Its

(Genesis – Numbers), which is essentially a priestly composition. Others hold that the Deuteronomistic history includes only Judges – 2 Kings; Genesis – Joshua making up a "Hexateuch", so A. Kuenen, *An Historico-Critical Inquiry into the Origin and Composition of the Hexateuch* (London: MacMillan, 1886), pp. 2-16 esp. 3; J. Wellhausen, *Prolegomena zur Geschichte Israels* (6th edn.; Berlin & Leipzig: Walter de Gruyter, 1927), pp. 223-360 esp. 291-293, 358-360 (= idem, *Prolegomena to the History of Ancient Israel* [Gloucester, MA: Peter Smith, 1973], pp. 228-362, esp. 293-294, 360-362); S.R. Driver, *An Introduction to the Literature of the Old Testament* (ITL; 9th edn.; Edinburgh: T&T Clark, 1913), pp. 4-5. All agreed that the book of Samuel forms a part of the Deuteronomistic history.

[41] Cf. Noth, *The Deuteronomistic History*, pp. 4-5. Noteworthy to mention that the Masoretic books of Samuel and Kings were named in the Septuagint (ἡ βίβλος) Βασιλειῶν α-δ ('[the book of] 1-4 Kings'). The Vulgate follows the LXX division, naming them *Liber Regum*.

[42] This is not to say that the census story has Deuteronomistic elements.

[43] Though where exactly is the place of 2 Sam 24 in the description of Davidic Monarchy still is in question. Budde stresses between 2 Sam 24 and 2 Sam 21,1-14, and argues that in the early stage of the book the order of the chapters was as follows: 2 Sam 8 + 21,1-14 + 24 + 9,1 – 20,22, see K. Budde, *Die Bücher Richter und Samuel ihre Quellen und ihr Aufbau* (Gießen: J. Ricker, 1890), p. 256; idem, *Die Bücher Samuel erklärt* (KHCAT 8; Tübingen / Leipzig: J.C.B. Mohr [Paul Siebeck], 1902), pp. 304, 326. Eißfeldt is of the opinion that 2 Sam 21,1-14 is a preparation for the story of 2 Sam 9, and originally chapter 24 was located after chapter 9. According to him the earlier order was: 2 Sam 21,1-14 + 9 + 24, see O. Eißfeldt, *Einleitung in das Alte Testament* (3rd edn.; Tübingen: J.C.B. Mohr [Paul Siebeck], 1964), pp. 370-371 esp. 271 (English translation: idem, *The Old Testament – An Introduction* [New York / Hagerstown / San Francisco / London: Harper & Row, 1965], pp. 277-278 esp. 278). McCarter is also of the opinion that 2 Sam 24 is a continuation of chapter 21,1-14. According to him, in the early version of the book these passages came after the story concerning the conquest of Jerusalem

positioning in its present place seems to have been made at a certain literary stage of the book, probably at the time the Deuteronomistic history was formed.[44] The intention was presumably to place the story of the construction of the altar by David as close as possible to the account of the construction of the Temple by Solomon, in order to establish some literary proximity and connection between them.[45] Second Samuel 24 is therefore an ἱερὸς λόγος for the God's Temple in Jerusalem as related in 1 Kgs 5-9.[46] Indeed, a clear and direct connection between the two has been done by the Chronicler: "At that time when David saw that the Lord answered him at the threshing floor of Ornan the Jebusite, then he sacrificed there... and David said, '*Here will be the House of the Lord and here the altar of burnt offerings for Israel*'" (1 Chr 21,28-22,1). Following this, the Chronicler immediately goes on to relate David's preparations for the construction of the Temple (1 Chr 22,2ff).[47]

2. The Chronistic History

Although the location of the Temple is not mentioned at all in the account of its construction in the Deuteronomistic history (1 Kgs 5,15-9,25), it is described in the greatest detail in the parallel text in the Chronistic history:

> Then Solomon began to build the House of the Lord
> in *Jerusalem*
> on *Mount Moriah*, where [the Lord] had appeared to his father, David,

---

(2 Sam 5,5-10), see P.K. McCarter, Jr., *II Samuel – A New Translation with Introduction, Notes and Commentary* (AB 9; New York / London / Toronto / Sydney / Auckland: Doubleday, 1984), pp. 516-517.

[44] As opposed to Noth's view, *The Deuteronomistic History*, pp. 124-125 note 3.

[45] On this point, see McCarter, *II Samuel*, pp. 516-517.

[46] Compare Budde, *Samuel*, p. 326; W.K.A. Caspari, *Die Samuelbücher* (KAT 7; Leipzig: Deichter, 1926), p. 662; H.W. Herzberg, *Die Samuelbücher – Übersetzt und erklärt* (ATD 10; 2nd edn.; Göttingen: Vandenhoeck & Ruprecht, 1960), pp. 338-339 (English translation: idem, *I & II Samuel – A Commentary* [OTL; London: SCM Press, 1964], pp. 410-411; McCarter, *II Samuel*, p. 517.

[47] Cf. also 2 Chr 3,1 and the discussion above. This connection may also be seen in an addition to 2 Sam 24, 25, made by the LXX: καὶ προσέθηκεν Σαλωμων ἐπὶ τὸ θυσιαστήριον ἐπ᾿ ἐσχάτῳ ὅτι μικρὸν ἦν ἐν πρώτοις "And after this, Solomon enlarged the altar, for it had been too small at first".

> at *the place which David had designated,*[48] at *the threshing floor of Ornan the Jebusite* (2 Chr 3,1).

The description of the location is given in a tripartite form that moves from the general to the particular. In the first is given the name of the city in which the Temple was built – "Jerusalem"; next, the name of the mountain in Jerusalem is given – "on Mount Moriah"; and finally, the exact location on the mountain is specified – "at the place which David had designated, at the threshing floor of Ornan the Jebusite".[49] The notice of the site of the Temple forms a natural part of the account of its construction, which not only gives three different times for the date of its construction (once, counting from the Exodus, 1 Kgs 6,1a – probably a priestly addition, and twice counting from the beginning of Solomon's reign, verses 1b and 37), but also describes its size, the materials needed for its erection, the vessels used in it, etc. Thus, it is of little surprise that the Chronicler noticed that this item of information was "lacking" in his *Vorlage*, in the text of Kings (obviously he was not aware of the ancient Near Eastern construction story genre), and decided to add it himself,[50] as he did in a number of other passages parallel to texts in Samuel-Kings.[51]

---

[48] The translation here follows the LXX, Vulgate and Peshiṭta, rather than the confused Masoretic Text: אֲשֶׁר הֵכִין בִּמְקוֹם דָּוִיד.

[49] This explanation does away with Williamson's problem (*Chronicles*, p. 204) that the verse "involves the absurd implication of identifying the whole of Mount Moriah with the threshing floor".

[50] That the books of Samuel and Kings were used as *Vorlage* for the Chronicler, see Kalimi, *Zur Geschichtsschreibung des Chronisten*, pp. 2-6; idem, *The Book of Chronicles: Historical Writing and Literary Devices*, pp. 3-8; contra A.G. Auld, *Kings Without Privilege: David and Moses in the Story of the Bible's Kings* (Edinburgh: T&T Clark, 1994). For the implausibility of Auld's arguments, see also S.L. McKenzie, "The Chronicler as Redactor," in M.P. Graham and S.L. McKenzie (eds.), *The Chronicler as Author: Studies in Text and Texture* (JSOT Suppl. 263; Sheffield: Sheffield Academic Press, 1999), pp. 70-90; Z. Talshir, "The Reign of Solomon in the Making: Pseudo-Connections between 3 Kingdoms and Chronicles", *VT* 50 (2000), pp. 233-249.

[51] Thus, for example, 2 Kgs 16,3; 21,6 mentions Kings Ahaz and Manasseh consigning their sons to the fire, without giving details of the place, while the parallel passages in 2 Chr 28,3; 33,6 add that it happened in "the Valley of Ben-hinnom". This phenomenon is discussed at length by Kalimi, *Zur Geschichtsschreibung des Chronisten*, pp. 73-79; idem, *The Book of Chronicles: Historical Writing and Literary Devices*, pp. 80-86.

The use of the words "Moriah" and "at the place which David had designated, at the threshing floor of Ornan the Jebusite" draws analogies to both, of the story of the *Aqedah* (see the first section above),[52] and to the account of the construction of an altar on the threshing floor of Ornan the Jebusite (1 Chr 21,1-22,1 // 2 Sam 24).[53] The purpose of these analogies might have been to add to the sanctity of the Jerusalem Temple at the time of the composition of Chronicles[54] by connecting it with traditions deeply rooted in the history of the ancient Israelites.[55] It was certainly true that the Second Temple, constructed as it was on the ruins of Solomon's Temple,[56] was in need of such support. It was not of an impressive size and was poorly built, especially when compared to the First Temple. As Haggai put it: "Who is there left among you who saw this House in its former splendor? How does it look to you now? It

---

[52] The story of the binding of Isaac is not retold in Chronicles. The Chronicler refers to it here on the grounds that it is familiar to his readers. A similar assumption underlies the text of Chronicles in other places too, see for example, 1 Chr 2,7: "The sons of Carmi: Achar, the troubler of Israel, who committed a trespass against the proscribed thing". This is a reference to Josh 7, although the story is not retold in Chronicles. 1 Chr 10,13 is a reference to 1 Sam 13,13-14; 15; 28. Chapters 13, 15 and 28 have no parallels in Chronicles. For these phenomena see in detail Kalimi, *Zur Geschichtsschreibung des Chronisten*, pp. 172-190; idem, *The Book of Chronicles: Historical Writing and Literary Devices*, pp. 191-210.

[53] The Chronicler's line of thought was developed later on in Rabbinic literature, see, for example, the Targum of 2 Chr 3,1; and perhaps most extensively it was developed by Maimonides, *Mishneh Torah*, Temple Laws, chapter 2,1-2. Similarly told by the Samaritans about the site of their temple on Mount Gerizim, see for instance, *Tibåt Mårqe* (= *Memar Marqah*) 2,10; and chapter two of this book.

[54] For the dating of the Book of Chronicles, see I. Kalimi, "Die Abfassungszeit der Chronik – Forschungsstand und Perspektiven", *ZAW* 105 (1993), pp. 223-233; idem, "Könnte die aramäische Grabinschrift aus Ägypten als Indikation für die Datierung der Chronikbücher fungieren?", *ZAW* 110 (1998), pp. 79-81; idem, "The Date of Chronicles: The Biblical Text, the Elephantine Papyri and the El-Ibrahimia's Aramaic Grave Inscription", in J.H. & D. Ellens, I. Kalimi and R.P. Knierim (eds.), *Hebrew Bible and Related Literature – S.J. De Veries Commemorative Volume* (Harrisburg, PA: Trinity Press International, 2002), forthcoming.

[55] For a similar approach, cf. Williamson, *Chronicles*, p. 205.

[56] See, e.g., Hag 1,4.8-9.14; 2,3; Ezra 2,68; 3,3.12; 6,3; 9,9; and also the tradition mentioned in the Babylonian Talmud, *Zebachim* 62b.

must seem like nothing to you" (2,3; cf. Ezra 3,12-13). Haggai even went as far as to make promises concerning the future wealth and splendor of the Second Temple: "I will shake all the nations. And the precious things of all the nations shall come [here], and I will fill this House with glory, said the Lord of Hosts. Silver is mine and gold is mine — says the Lord of Hosts. The glory of this latter House shall be greater than that of the former" (2,6-9).

The inferior nature of the Second Temple is also reflected in a relatively late source — the speech attributed by Josephus to King Herod before the latter reconstructed and enlarged Zerubbabel's Temple:

> For this was the temple which our fathers built to the Most Great God after their return from Babylon, but it lacks sixty cubits in height, the amount by which the first temple, built by Solomon, exceeded it... I will try to remedy the oversight caused by the necessity and subjection of that earlier time... (*Antiquitates Judaicae* 15,385-387).[57]

Furthermore, the Second Temple was also lacking a number of the more sacred ritual accessories such as the Ark of the Covenant, its two tablets of stone, and the cherubs, all of which had been in the Holy of Holiness in the First Temple (1 Kgs 8,1-9 // 2 Chr 5,2-10). Since it was placed in the Holy of Holiness, no more was heard of the Ark of the Covenant.[58] It is included neither among the Temple vessels that went with the Judeans to the Babylonian exile (2 Kgs 25,13-17; Jer 52,17-23), nor among those that were returned with them to Jerusalem (Ezra 1,7-11; cf. 5,14-15; 6,5).[59] There was no Ark in the Holy of Holiness in the Second Temple (Mishnah, *Yoma* 5,2). Indeed, when the Roman general, Pompey (Gnaeus Pompeius

---

[57] See R. Marcus, *Josephus* (The Loeb Classical Library; Cambridge, MA: Harvard University Press / London: William Heinemann, 1963), vol. VIII, pp. 187-189.

[58] The text in 2 Chr 35,3 is not a reliable historical source for the existence of the Ark in the Temple at the time of Josiah, King of Judah; see M. Haran, "The Disappearance of the Ark", *IEJ* 13 (1963), pp. 46-58. Haran assumed that the Ark was removed from the Holy of Holiness and replaced with a statue of Asherah by Manasseh, King of Judah. Since then all trace of it is lost.

[59] On this issue see in detail I. Kalimi and J.D. Purvis, "King Jehoiachin and the Vessels of the Lord's House in Biblical Literature", *CBQ* 56 (1994), pp. 449-457 esp. 452-456.

Magnus), broke in there in 63 BCE, he found the inner sanctuary empty (*Bellum Judaicum* 1,152-153).[60]

The inferiority of the Second Temple is also reflected in rabbinic literature, as, for example, may be seen in the Babylonian Talmud, *Yoma* 21b:

> Rav Samuel the son of Inia said: What is the meaning of the scriptural verse: 'And I will take pleasure in it [ואכבד] and I will be glorified' [Hag 1,8]? The traditional reading is ואכבדה, then why is the [letter] ה [its numerical equivalent is five] omitted [in the text]? To indicate that in *five* things the First Sanctuary differed from the Second: in the ark, the ark-cover, the Cherubim, the fire, the *Shechinah*, the Holy Spirit [of Prophecy], and the *Urim-we-Thummim*.[61]

The attitude so strongly attacked by the prophet Haggai was not forgotten in the course of time, and traces of it are preserved in the Book of Tobit, which was presumed to have been composed some-time close to the time of Chronicles.[62] According to the Book of Tobit, the Second Temple, so inferior to its predecessor, was only temporary until a permanent, magnificent Temple could be built:

> And God shall again have mercy on them, and bring them back into the land, and they shall build the house, but like to the former house, until

---

[60] See H.St.J. Thackeray, *Josephus in Nine Volumes* (The Loeb Classical Library; Cambridge, MA: Harvard University Press / London: William Heinemann, 1961), vol. II, p. 73. In fact, there were various legends concerning the whereabouts of the Ark of the Covenant, see Eupolemus 35,9; 2 Macc 2,4-8; 2 Baruch 6,7, The Lives of the Prophets 2,11-12; Mishnah, *Šeqalim* 6,1-2; Babylonian Talmud, *Yoma* 53b-54a; see I. Kalimi and J.D. Purvis, "The Hiding of the Temple Vessels in Jewish and Samaritan Literature", *CBQ* 56 (1994), pp. 679-685.

[61] For the English translation, cf. L. Jung, *Yoma – Translated into English with Notes, Glossary and Indices* (London: Soncino Press, 1938), p. 94.

[62] See Y.M. Grintz, *The Book of Judith* (Jerusalem: Bialik Institute, 1957), pp. 22-23 ([Hebrew], "the middle of the Persian period"); D. Flusser, "Tobit, The Book of Tobit", *Encyclopaedia Biblica* (Jerusalem: Bialik Institute, 1958), vol. 3, pp. 370-371 ([Hebrew], "the first half of the Second Temple period"); W.F. Albright, Review of E. Täubler, *Biblische Studien: Die Epoche der Richter* (Tübingen: J.C.B. Mohr, 1958), *BO* 17 (1960), pp. 242-243 esp. 242 (the fifth-fourth centuries BCE). For other datings of the book, see C.A. Moore, "Tobit, Book of", *ABD*, vol. 6, pp. 585-594 esp. 591.

the times of that age be fulfilled and afterward they shall return from the places of their captivity, and build up Jerusalem with honor, and the House of God shall be built in it forever with a glorious building, even as the prophets speak concerning it (14,5).

It seems, therefore, that the Chronicler gave the precise location of and various traditions concerning Solomon's Temple in order to boost the sanctity of the small, poorly built Temple of his own day. However, despite his efforts, certain sections of the population were still dissatisfied with the Second Temple. In 1 (Ethiopic Apocalypse of) Enoch, the author expresses the wish that "the old House" – i.e., the Zerubbabel's Temple – with all its accouterments, be cast "to a place in the south of the land" and that in its place the Lord would build "a great new House, higher than the first" (90,28-29).[63] The Second Temple did win a great deal of praise only in the late first century BCE, after Herod's enlargement and refurnishment of it,[64] as described by Josephus Flavius:

> The exterior of the building wanted nothing that could astound either mind or eye. For, being covered on all sides with massive plates of gold, the sun was no sooner up than it radiated so fiery a flash that persons straining to look at it were compelled to avert their eyes, as from the solar rays. To approaching strangers it appeared from a distance like a snow-clad mountain; for all that was not overlaid with gold was of purest white (*Bellum Judaicum* 5,222-224).[65]

---

[63] This section of 1 Enoch (dream visions, chapters 83-90) probably composed at the beginning of the Hasmonean period, see D. Flusser, "Enoch", *Encyclopaedia Biblica* (Jerusalem: Bialik Institute, 1958), vol. 3, pp. 203-210 esp. 207 (Hebrew); E. Isaac, "1 (Ethiopic Apocalypse of) Enoch", in Charlesworth, *The Old Testament Pseudepigrapha*, vol. 1, pp. 6-7.
The Epistle of Aristeas, from that period, continues the Chronicler's line and praises the Temple. It is possible that it is derived from the idealization of the Jew from the Diaspora who visited the homeland.

[64] For the date of the Herodian Temple, its size, and the extent of its construction, see D.W. Roller, *The Building Program of Herod the Great* (Berkeley / Los Angeles / London: University of California Press, 1998), pp. 176-178.

[65] See H.St.J. Thackeray, *Josephus in Nine Volumes* (The Loeb Classical Library; Cambridge, MA: Harvard University Press / London: William Heinemann, 1976), vol. III, p. 269.

In the same vein, Josephus writes later:

> Deeply as one must mourn for the most marvelous edifice which we have ever seen or heard of, whether we consider its structure, its magnitude, the richness of its every detail, or the reputation of its Holy Places... (*Bellum Judaicum* 6,267).[66]

There is also a famous rabbinic saying: "He who has not seen (the) Herodian building, has never seen a beautiful building" (Babylonian Talmud, *Baba Batra* 4a).

Beyond this, it is also not impossible that the Chronicler's identification of the site of the Temple with the *Aqedah* hides a polemic with the rival Samaritans' sacred place on Mount Gerizim. They claim this site as the location where Abraham bound his beloved son Isaac onto the altar.[67]

III. Conclusion

There is a clear distinction between "the land of Moriah" mentioned in the *Aqedah* story (Gen 22,2) and "Mount Moriah" in late historiography (2 Chr 3,1). The Temple Mount seems already to have been identified with the site of the *Aqedah* in the First Temple period (Gen 22,14b), while the name "Mount Moriah", as far as can be determined, was only linked to the site through the interpretation of the Chronicler's account (2 Chr 3,1) in the Second Temple period.

As the site both of the *Aqedah* and of the altar on the threshing floor of Araunah the Jebusite was chosen by God, the inclusion of references to these stories in the Book of Kings would have strengthened the Deuteronomistic conception of the divine election of the Temple's site. The failure of 1 Kgs 6 to describe the precise location of the Temple can be understood in terms of the genre of ancient Near Eastern construction stories, of which 1 Kgs 5,15-9,25 is an inseparable part. The exact location of the Temple, as well as the various traditions connected with the site, were familiar to the audience for whom the book was intended. Furthermore, the tradi-

---

[66] See Thackeray, *Josephus in Nine Volumes*, vol. III, p. 453; and compare *Antiquitates Judaicae* 15,380.

[67] See the next chapter in this volume, pp. 33-34, 48-54, 56-58.

tion of the divine election of Araunah's threshing floor had already been given in the Deuteronomistic history, and there was no need to repeat it in 1 Kgs 6.

The detailed reference to the Temple site to be found in the parallel passage in the Book of Chronicles seems to be a result of the Chronicler's desire to "fill in the gaps" in the Book of Kings. The references to the stories of the *Aqedah* and the census (Araunah's threshing floor) were probably intended, first and foremost, to endow Zerubbabel's Temple with a special degree of sanctity as it fell short of Solomon's Temple in size, wealth, and ritual accessories. Possibly, it contains also a hidden polemic with the Samaritan sacred place on Mount Gerizim.

2

The Affiliation of Abraham and the *Aqedah* with Zion / Gerizim in Jewish and Samaritan Sources

In John 4,20 it is related that the woman of Samaria said to Jesus: "Our fathers worshipped on this mountain; but you say, that in Jerusalem is the place where people ought to worship". Unquestionably, there was a bitter dispute between the followers of the Jerusalem Temple and those of the Samaritan's holy site on Mount Gerizim. Each side claimed the superiority and the sanctity of its shrine and attempted to strengthen its argument by relating its different legends and Biblical verses, sometimes changing their versions and their authentic meanings. It appears that the Zion community as well as the Gerizim community, were each frightened by the existence of the rival sanctity of the other. This dispute throws a heavy shadow on the entire relationship between the two communities. It played the role of a conditional principle in the way of the recognition of the legitimate existence of one by the other.

Indeed, it is possible that some of the following Jewish sources, such as the one in the Book of Jubilees (see below), contain a hidden argument not only with the Samaritan holy site on Mount Gerizim, but also with the temple of Onias IV at Leontopolis in Egypt (ca. 150 BCE-73 CE). However, it seems that the Zion community was concerned about the older rival sanctity of the Samaritans, which geographically was located nearby, much more than the younger isolated JHWH's center which was far away in the Land of the Nile.

Since the exact location of ארץ המריה "the land of Moriah" (Gen 22,2), on which one of its mountains Isaac was bound by his father, is shrouded in a thick fog,[1] the verse was used to argue the holiness and the lawfulness of both the Temple Mount in Jerusalem and Mount Gerizim: Jews associated Abraham and, particularly, the site where he bound his promised and beloved son, Isaac, with the site of the altar on the Jerusalem Temple Mount; the Samaritans argued that the binding of Isaac was on their holy place, Mount Gerizim. This sharp polemic is revealed through various Jewish and Samaritan sources from different eras, written in different literary genres.

I. The Jewish Sources

1. Hebrew Bible and Pseudepigrapha

In order to emphasize the sanctity and the great antiquity of the Temple Mount in Jerusalem, as the chosen place for sacrifices from the earliest times, the Mount was identified (apparently during the First Temple era or even already in the time of David and Solomon) as the mountain upon which Abraham bound his son Isaac (Gen 22,14).[2] Later on, in the Persian period, the Chronicler (ca. 400-375 BCE)[3] attached the name הַר הַמּוֹרִיָּה "Mount Moriah" to the Temple Mount, and connected more clearly the site of the Temple with the site of the binding of Isaac (2 Chr 3,1, an addition to the earlier text in 1 Kgs 6,1).[4] The Chronicler's identification of the site of the Temple with that of the *Aqedah*, may conceal – among other purposes[5] – a hidden polemic against the rival site holy to the Samaritans on Mount Gerizim.[6]

---

[1] See above, chapter one, pp. 9-15.

[2] For further discussion on this issue, see above, chapter one, pp. 14-15.

[3] For the dating of the Book of Chronicles, see Kalimi, "Die Abfassungs-zeit", pp. 223-233; idem, "die aramäische Grabinschrift", pp. 79-81; idem, "The Date of Chronicles: The Biblical Text, the Elephantine Papyri and the El-Ibrahimia's Aramaic Grave Inscription".

[4] See in detail, above, chapter one, pp. 25-31.

[5] For the other possible purposes, see in detail the discussion on pp. 27-31.

[6] For the Chronicler's argument against the "Separatists" in the Northern Kingdom (for example, 2 Chr 13,4-12), the group that came to comprise the Samaritans, as well as his Samaritan polemic, see, for example, Noth, *Überlieferungsgeschichtliche Studien*, pp. 174-175 (English version, idem, *The Chronicler's History* [translated by H.G.M. Williamson, JSOT Suppl. 50; Shef-field: JSOT Press, 1987], pp. 100-101); M. Oeming, *Das wahre Israel: Die*

The connection that had been made between the Temple Mount and the Mount of the *Aqedah* in Gen. 22,14, "Abraham named that place 'the Lord will see', as it is said to this day 'on the mount of the Lord it shall be seen'," was no longer sufficient for the author of the Book of Jubilees (which was probably written between 170-140 BCE).[7] In order not to leave any room for doubt that "on the mount of the Lord it shall be seen" means no other place than the *Jewish* Temple Mount in Jerusalem, and not Mount Gerizim (or even, certainly not the site of Onias' temple at Leontopolis), he added to the text from Genesis the words: "that is Mount Zion" (Jub 18,13b).

This author is also known for his anti-Beith El polemic (Jub 32,22). Beith El was perhaps an alternative cultic site in the second century BCE, and endangered the Jerusalem YHWH cultic monopoly. However, in the case under discussion, the lack of information does not allow us to assume – with any degree of certainty – whether Jub 32,22 concerns a Samaritan group or not.[8]

2. Dead Sea Scrolls

(1). Pseudo-Jubilees[a] (4Q225)

In *Discoveries in the Judaean Desert XIII* three fragments which have a narrative like that of the Abraham section of the Book of Jubilees (4Q225, 4Q226 and 4Q227) were published, and named by J.[C.] VanderKam and J.T. Milik 'Pseudo-Jubilees'.[9] In 4Q225 ('Pseudo-Jubilees[a]', paleographically dated ca. 30 BCE – 20 CE) col. I, line 13 the editors read:

"*genealogische Vorhalle*" *1 Chronik 1-9* (BWANT 128; Stuttgart, Berlin & Köln: Verlag W. Kohlhammer, 1990), pp. 45-47, 207-208, 217-218. For more literature on this issue, see Kalimi, *A Classified Bibliography*, pp. 106-107, 109-110, items 739-749, 771-779; and see also below, p. 66.

[7] For the time of the book, see J.C. VanderKam, "Jubilees, Book of", *ABD*, vol. 3, pp. 1030-1032 esp. 1030.

[8] Cf. J.C. Endres, *Biblical Interpretation in the Book of Jubilees*, (CBQMS 18; Washington, DC: The Catholic Biblical Association of America, 1987), pp. 167-168 note 18.

[9] See J.[C.] VanderKam and J.T. Milik, in *Qumran Cave 4, VIII* (Discoveries in the Judaean Desert XIII; Oxford: Clarendon Press, 1994), pp. 141-155 esp. 146-147.

...וֵיקֻ[ם וִיֵ]לֵֿ[ךְ] מִן הַבְּאַרֹות אֶל הַ[ר מֹורִיֹּה]

And he ro[se up and we]n[t] from the wells[10] to Mo[unt Moriah].[11]

In the light of 2 Chr 3,1 the reconstruction "to Mo[unt Moriah]" seems reasonable. The identification of "on one of the mountains that I will point out to you" (Gen 22,2) by the author of 4Q225 directly with "Mount Moriah", sounds like a continuity of the interpretative line of the Chronicler's thought as well as that of the author of Jubilees 18,13b. In other words, here is a hidden polemic with the Samaritans' identification of the site of the *Aqedah*.

(2). Genesis Apocryphon (1QGenAp)

In Genesis 14,17-18 it is related that the king of Sodom met Abram at "the Valley of Shaveh, that is the King's Valley", and Melchizedek, king of Salem, welcomed him with bread and wine and blessed him. The Aramaic scroll uncovered in cave 1 at Qumran and designated as *Genesis Apocryphon* (1QGenAp), and which has been dated paleographically and linguistically to the last century BCE or the first century CE,[12] deals with this issue. Here we read that Abram came to "Salem, that is Jerusalem" (column XXII, verse 13), and there he was welcomed by Melchizedek, king of Salem:

ואתה לשלם היא ירושלם ומלכיצדק מלכא דשלם אנפק מאכל
ומשתה לאברם ולכול אנשא די עמה והוא הוא כהן לאל עליון
וברך לאברם ואמר בריך אברם לאל עליון מרה שמיא וארעא
ובריך אל עליון די סגר שנאיך בידך

---

[10] "The wells", that is, Beer-Sheba, that according to Gen 21,33; 22,19 was where Abraham was then residing. Probably, the author interprets "Beer-Sheba" as "seven wells". Compare VanderKam and Milik, *Qumran Cave 4, VIII*, p. 149; G. Vermes, "New Light on the Sacrifice of Isaac", *JJS* 47 (1996), pp. 140-146 esp. 142 note 8.

[11] For detailed discussion on this fragment, see also Vermes, "New Light on the Sacrifice of Isaac", pp. 140-146.

[12] Cf. N. Avigad and Y. Yadin, *A Genesis Apocryphon – A Scroll from the Wilderness of Judaea* (Jerusalem: Magnes Press & Heikhal Ha-Sefer, 1956), p. 38; R.T. White, "Genesis Apocryphon", *ABD*, vol. 2, pp. 932-933 esp. 932.

And he came to Salem, that is Jerusalem. And Melchizedek, the king of Salem, brought out food and drink[13] for Abram and for all the men who were with him; he was a priest of the Most High God and he blessed Abram and said: 'Blessed be Abram by the Most High God, the Lord of heaven and earth. Blessed be the Most High God who delivered your enemies into your hand' (col. XXII, vs. 13-17).[14]

The identification "Salem, that is Jerusalem" in *Genesis Apocryphon* could be done according to Ps 76,3 which drew a parallel between "Salem" and "Zion": ויהי בשלם סכו / ומעונתו בציון "In Salem is his abode / his dwelling is in Zion".[15] "Zion" appears in the Hebrew Bible as synonymous with Jerusalem (for example, Isa 2,3; 4,3; 62,1; 64,9; Jer 26,18; Ps 147,12). But also, Mount Zion is synonymous with the Temple Mount (for example, Isa 10,32; 18,7; 24,23; Joel 4,17; Ps 2,6; 74,2). It is worthwhile to note that we do not have any evidence that "Salem" was used as an earlier name for Jerusalem.[16] However, this identification is common in other Jewish sources, after the destruction of the Second Temple, for example, in Josephus (*Antiquitates Judaicae* 1,180; 7,67), *Targumim* and *Midrashim*.[17]

---

[13] The author of 1QGenAp made obvious changes in the Biblical version: instead of the specific items "*bread* and *wine*" in Genesis, he used general words "*food* and *drink*". Is he concerned about the "Gentile bread and wine" which were forbidden by the Jews already according to the *Halacha* of his time? See, however, e.g., Mishnah, *Aboda Zara* 2,6; Tosefta, *Aboda Zara* 4,11 (M.S. Zuckermandel [ed.], *Tosephta Based on Erfurt and Viena Codices* [Trier 1881; reprinted: Jerusalem: Wahrmann Books, 1963], p. 467); Jerusalem Talmud, *Aboda Zara* 2,3 (41b); Babylonian Talmud, *Aboda Zara* 35b.

[14] The citation and the translation are according to J.A. Fitzmyer, *The Genesis Apocryphon of Qumran Cave I – A Commentary* (BibOr 18; 2nd edn., Rome: Pontifical Biblical Institute, 1971), pp. 72-73; cf. Avigad and Yadin, *A Genesis Apocryphon*, p. 47 (English), p. [מ] (Hebrew), and in between are located the facsimile and transcription.

[15] Cf. Fitzmyer, *Genesis Apocryphon*, pp. 12-13.

[16] In the Egyptian documents of 19th-18th century BCE the name of the city – and / or the land – is *Urušalimum*; in Tel El-Amarna letters (the first half of the 14th century BCE) it appears as *Urusalim*. For discussion on these names, see B. Mazar, "Jerusalem in Biblical Period", *Cities and Districts in Eretz-Israel* (Jerusalem: Bialik Institute & Israel Exploration Society, 1975), pp. 11-44 esp. 11-12 (Hebrew).

[17] See *Targum Onkelos* and *Targum Pseudo-Jonathan* on Gen. 14,18; A. Sperber

Some scholars, like Paul Winter and Matthew Black[18] concluded that the identification of Salem with Jerusalem in *Genesis Apocryphon* has an anti-Samaritan purpose. Winter explained this point, as follows: "At the time when the *Genesis Apocryphon* was written the region around Shechem was inhabited by the Samaritans. To concede that Melkizedek, priest of the Most High God, had worshipped God in a place in Samaritan territory, would have been tantamount to admitting doubts on the exclusive claim of Jerusalem".[19] Joseph A. Fitzmyer does not accept this conclusion unless "it could be shown that the Salem – Jerusalem identification does not antedate the Samaritan schism".[20]

Obviously, the author of *Genesis Apocryphon* did not write for Greeks or other foreigners, but rather exclusively for Jews. If the identification of Salem with Jerusalem was well known among the Jews, as proved from Psalms 76,3 (as well as from later sources), why did he bother at all identifying Salem as Jerusalem? If, in spite of this, the author under discussion did so, it is possible that he had an anti-Samaritan polemic purpose. Moreover, it is interesting to note that the story in Genesis 14,18, as reflected in *Genesis Apocryphon*, stands in opposition to that which was composed by *Pseudo-Eupolemus*.

(ed.), *The Bible in Aramaic, Vol. I: The Pentateuch According to Targum Onkelos* (Leiden: E.J. Brill, 1959), p. 20; E.G. Clark et al., *Targum Pseudo-Jonathan of the Pentateuch: Text and Concordance* (Haboken: NJ, Ktav Pulishing House, 1984), p. 15. In these *Targumim* were written directly ומלכי צדק מלכא דירושלים without mentioning שלם at all. See also *Genesis Rabbah* 43,6; 56,14 (J. Theodor [ed.], *Bereschit Rabba mit kritischem Apparat und Kommentar* [Veröffentlichungen der Akademie für die Wissenschaft des Judentums; Berlin: H. Itzkowski, 1903]; 2nd edn. with additional corrections by Ch. Albeck, Jerusalem: Wahrmann Books, 1965], pp. 420, 607-608; English translation, H. Freedman and M. Simon [translators], *The Midrash Rabbah – Volume One: Genesis* [London / Jerusalem / New York: Soncino Press, 1977], pp. 356, 500). It is noteworthy to mention that in the Epistle of Paul to the Hebrews *Salem* is interpreted as שלום "peace", see Heb 7,2.

[18] P. Winter, "Note on Salem – Jerusalem", *NovT* 2 (1957/58), pp. 151-152; M. Black, "The Recovery of the Language of Jesus", *NTS* 3 (1956/57), pp. 305-313 esp. 312; idem, *The Scrolls and Christian Origins* (Toronto & New York: Thomas Nelson, 1961), p. 196.

[19] Winter, "Salem – Jerusalem", p. 151.

[20] Fitzmyer, *Genesis Apocryphon*, p. 173.

3. Pseudo-Eupolemus

Pseudo-Eupolemus – "a designation used to identify two fragments about Abraham preserved by Eusebius".[21] This anonymous author, presumably a Samaritan, lived probably in the first half of the second century BCE.[22] In Fragment one, 15-18, it is accounted:

ξενισθῆναί τε αὐτὸν ὑπὸ πόλεως ἱερὸν Ἀργαριζίν, ὅ εἶναι μεθερμηνευόμενον ὄρος ὑψίστου. παρὰ δε τοῦ Μελχισεδὲκ ἱερέως ὄντος τοῦ θεου καὶ βασιλεύοντος λαβεῖν δῶρα

He [= Abram] was treated as a guest by the city at the temple of Argarizin;[23]

---

[21] See C.R. Holladay, "Eupolemus, Pseudo-", *ABD*, vol. 2, pp. 672-673 esp. 672.

[22] For the dating of the fragment, see N. Walter, *Fragmente jüdisch-hellenistischer Historiker,* in W.G. Kümmel (ed.), *Jüdische Schriften aus hellenistisch-römischer Zeit* (Gütersloh: Gütersloher Verlaghaus Gerd Mohn, 1976), Band I, Lieferung 2, pp. 139-140; C.R. Holladay, *Fragments from Hellenistic: Jewish Authors, Vol. I: Historians* (Chico, CA: Scholars Press, 1983), pp. 159-160; idem, "Eupolemus, Pseudo-", *ABD*, vol. 2, p. 672.

[23] The contraction of הר with גריזים as one word appears also in the Samaritan Pentateuch (see, for example, Deut 27,4.12), in the Samaritan *Targum*, in the Samaritan Greek version of the Torah (from which only a few fragments remained), as well as in other Samaritan sources, such as *Tibåt Mårqe* and liturgical texts. It also appears in the papyrus from Masada הרגרייזים, and on the two Greek inscriptions which are found on the island of Delos, and refer to "the Israelites from Delos who donated to Hargerizim". Pummer showed that the name "Mount Gerizim" as one word appears also in some non-Samaritan sources (for instance, *Vetus Latina* on 2 Macc. 5,23; 6,2). Moreover, there are some manuscripts of the Samaritan Pentateuch and a Samaritan inscription in which the words הר and גריזים are separated. On the other hand, Pummer exemplified a few contractions of the word הר with other typonyms following it in Septuagint (for example, הר שפר in Num 33,23.24; הר שעיר in Josh 15,10). Thus, the spelling הרגרייזים or its Greek form (or variants of it) cannot be used as a definite indication for recognizing the Samaritan source, writer or tradition, cf. R. Pummer, "*ARGARIZIN*: A Criterion for Samaritan Provenance?", *JSJ* 18 (1987), pp. 18-25; contra H.G. Kippenberg, *Garizim und Synagoge – Traditionsgeschichtliche Untersuchungen zur samaritanischen Religion der aramäischen Periode* (Religionsgeschichtliche Versuche und Vorarbeiten 30; Berlin & New York: Walter de Gruyter, 1971), pp. 54-55 note 121; S. Talmon, "Fragments of Scrolls from Masada", *Eretz-Israel* 20 (1989), pp. 278-286 esp. 283-285 (Hebrew).

which means 'the mountain of the Most High'. He received gifts from
Melchizedek, who was a King and Priest of God.[24]

The author of this Fragment explained the name "Salem" found in
Gen 14,18 as referring to Shechem,[25] where the Mount Gerizim temple
had been standing since the days of antiquity, when Abram was
Melchizedek's welcome guest.[26] This is a testimony to the connection
between Abra(ha)m and the Mount Gerizim temple, and the Samaritans'
dispute with the Jews over the sanctity of the Jerusalem Temple, as
we will see below (see section II). Thus, the story of *Pseudo-Eupolemus*
strengthens the assumption that the identification of Salem with
Jerusalem in *Genesis Apocryphon*, and the story of the meeting between
Abram and Melchizedek — which is expressly placed in Jerusalem —
is the result of an anti-Samaritan polemic.

4. Josephus Flavius

In his *Antiquitates Judaicae* 1,226 Josephus Flavius describes the sacrifice
of Isaac on the mountain whereon "King David [should be: Solomon,
I.K.] afterwards erected the Temple".[27] Since the Second Temple was

---

[24] For this source, see Y. Gutman, *The Beginning of Jewish-Hellenistic Literature*,
vol. II (Jerusalem: Bialik Institute, 1963), pp. 95-108 (discussion), p. 159 (text;
Hebrew); B.Z. Wacholder, "Pseudo-Eupolemus — Two Greek Fragments on
the Life of Abraham", *HUCA* 34 (1963), pp. 83-113 esp. 106-107; Holladay,
Fragments from Hellenistic: Jewish Authors, pp. 157-165 (discussion), pp. 172-173
(text); R. Doran, "Pseudo-Eupolemus", in Charlesworth, *The Old Testament
Pseudepigrapha*, vol. 2, pp. 873-879 (discussion), p. 880 (text).

[25] Apparently on the basis of Gen 33,18: וַיָּבֹא יַעֲקֹב שָׁלֵם עִיר שְׁכֶם
"And Jacob came to Salem, to the city of Shechem". It is interesting that the
Samaritan Pentateuch reads, "And Jacob came שָׁלוֹם *in peace* (or *safely*) to
Shechem", like the interpretation of the word in classical Jewish exegesis.

[26] Heinemann is of the opinion that it was possibly for this reason that
Rabbi Ishmael said concerning Melchizedek, "He was a priest, but his descendants were not priests" (Babylonian Talmud, *Nedarim* 32b). According to him,
some Sages went "much farther than Rabbi Ishmael in their anti-Samaritan
polemical fervour, and would not rest until they had slandered Melchizedek
and painted him as a son of a whore", as told in a legend that reached us
through Christian sources, see J. Heinemann, *Aggadah and its Development —
Studies in the Transmission of Traditions* (Jerusalem: Keter Publishing House,
1974), pp. 99-102 (Hebrew).

[27] See also *Antiquitates Judaicae* 1,224.

erected on the site of the First Temple,[28] reasonably this identification by Josephus contains a hidden polemic with those who identified the location of the *Aqedah* with Mount Gerizim.

At another place (*Antiquitates Judaicae* 13,74-79), Josephus relates the open dispute between the Jews and Samaritans in Alexandria, which in all likelihood took place at the time of Ptolemy VI Philometor (180-145 BCE).[29] The Jews claimed that the Temple in Jerusalem is the real Temple, and offered "proofs from the Torah". The Samaritans, "who bow down in the temple that is on [Mount] Gerizim", of course made their claim for the superiority and holiness of Mount Gerizim. Although Josephus did not specify the "proofs from the Torah" that Alexandria's Jews offered, the texts of Gen 14,18-20; 22,14 and Gen 22,2, in the light of 2 Chr 3,1, were most probably not lacking among them.

Figure 1   A face of Bar-Kochba's silver coins (132-134/5 CE): The Jerusalem Temple

[28] See above, the first chapter of this volume, p. 27.

[29] For the dating of this source in Josephus, see A. Momigliano, "Flavius Josephus and Alexander's Visit to Jerusalem", *Athenaeum* 57 (1979), pp. 442-448 esp. 445-446 (= idem, *Settimo Contributo alla storia degli studi classici e del mondo antico* [Edizioni di Storia e Litteratura 161; Roma 1984], pp. 319-329 esp. 324-325). On the relationship between this story and that in *Antiquitates Judaicae* 12,10 (i.e., both stories are about the same debate), see also U. Rappaport, "The Samaritans in the Hellenistic Period", *Zion* 55 (1990), pp. 373-396 esp. 378 note 19 (Hebrew). Mor argues that the two stories are about two different debates, see M. Mor, "Samaritans and Jews in the Ptolemaic Period and the Beginning of the Seleucid Rule in Palestine", *Studies in the History of the Jewish People and the Land of Israel* 5 (Haifa: University of Haifa, 1980), pp. 71-81 esp. 71 (Hebrew).

5. The Fresco of the *Aqedah* at the Dura-Europos Synagogue

Among the large number of frescos at the Dura-Europos synagogue (244-245 CE), there is one on the central west wall,[30] which exhibits at the left the symbolic items from the Temple – a large seven branched *menorah* (candlestick, 1 Kgs 7,49 // 2 Chr 4,20), as well as a *lulav* (palm branch) and an *etrog* (citrus) at the base of it which are associated with the *Temple* festival – Sukkot.[31] In the center is represented a Hellenistic styled Jerusalem Temple,[32] similar to those on Bar-Kochba's silver coins from the years 132-134/5 CE.[33] At the right is described, in a vertical direction, the sacrifice of Isaac: Abraham is illustrated in a Hellenistic *pallium* (white robe) with a knife in his right hand, ready to perform the divine command and sacrifice his son, who lies upon the altar (precisely as described in Gen 22,9). On the left side of the scene appears a heavenly open *hand* (but not the *"angel of the Lord"* as said in Gen 22,11) which prevents him to fulfill his plan. At the bottom to the left there is a ram *standing by a* small *tree* (but

---

[30] For the exact location of the fresco, see below.

[31] See Zech 14,16. The combination of *lulav*, *etrog* and *menorah* appears in many Jewish decorations from Palestine and the Diaspora. So, for example, on the mosaic floor of the synagogue at Hammat Tiberias, *lulav*, *etrog* and *menorah* accompanied the Torah Shrine. Compare, E.L. Sukenik, *The Synagogue of Dura-Europos and its Frescoes* (Jerusalem: Bialik Institute, 1947), p. 52 (Hebrew).

[32] Sukenik described this picture as "a representation of the Torah shrine", see E.L. Sukenik, *Ancient Synagogues in Palestine and Greece* (The Schweich Lectures of the British Academy, 1930; London: Oxford University Press, 1934), p. 83. However, later on, in his book *The Synagogue of Dura-Europos and its Frescoes*, pp. 32,52,53, he defines the same picture as "a (pattern of the) Temple". Indeed, it is most likely that the painter represented the Temple facade, as observed also by E.R. Goodenough and M. Avi-Yonah, "Dura-Europos", *Encyclopaedia Judaica* (Jerusalem: Keter Publishing House, 1971), vol. 6, pp. 279-280, 285, 293; L.I. Levine, "The Synagogue of Dura-Europos", in *idem* (ed.), *Ancient Synagogues Revealed* (Jerusalem: The Israel Exploration Society, 1981), pp. 172-177 esp. 174. Sonne described this picture as following: "a stylized picture of the Solomonic temple which represent at the same time the Ark of Covenant and the Torah shrine", see I. Sonne, "The Paintings of the Dura Synagogue", *HUCA* 20 (1947), pp. 225-362 esp. 357.

[33] Compare Sukenik, *The Synagogue of Dura-Europos*, p. 52. It is worthwhile to note that the reverse of the same coin shows a *lulav* and an *etrog*, see A. Kindler, *Thesaurus of Judaean Coins* (Jerusalem: Bialik Institute, 1958), coin no. 19a-19b, and p. 11 (Hebrew; in English summary: p. 10).

his horns are not *caught in the thicket* of a tree, as related in Gen 22,13b)[34] to be sacrificed instead of Isaac.[35]

Figure 2 Dura-Europos synagogue: The Aqedah and the Temple, a fresco on the west wall, above the Torah niche (244-245 CE)

As of today the scene of the *Aqedah* in the Dura Synagogue is the oldest one known in ancient Jewish art. The same story is presented once again a few centuries later, on the mosaic floor of the synagogue at Beth-Alpha (sixth century CE).[36] Nonetheless, the painting at the

[34] Contra E.R. Goodenough, *Jewish Symbols in the Greco-Roman Period: Volume One – The Archeological Evidence from Palestine* (Bollingen Series 37; New York: Pantheon Books, 1953), p. 231.

[35] For detailed discussion on the differences between the Biblical story of Genesis and the fresco from Dura-Europos, see J. Gutmann, "The Sacrifice of Isaac: Variations on a Theme in Early Jewish and Christian Art", in D. Ahrens (ed.), *Thiasos ton Mouson: Studien zu Antike und Christentum, Festschrift für Josef Fink zum 70. Geburtstag* (Köln & Wien: Böhlau Verlag, 1984), pp. 115-122.

[36] On Beth-Alpha synagogue, see Sukenik, *Ancient Synagogues in Palestine and Greece*, pp. 31-35; A. Kloner, "Ancient Synagogues in Israel: An Arch[a]eologic-

synagogue of Dura-Europos is the only one which brings, side by side, the Jerusalem Temple and the *Aqedah* within a single artistic picture, and creates a connection between both. As such, the fresco may be considered as a link in the chain of the Jewish sources associating Abraham and the *Aqedah* with the Temple place, thus confirming that the binding of Isaac by his father took place on the Temple Mount in Jerusalem. Moreover, the fresco is located at the most focal point of the synagogue – in the middle of the west and most important wall which faces towards Jerusalem, just above the niche, the Torah shrine, opposite the main entrance, that is, the central place on which the whole congregation's eyes are focused. This fact can certainly instruct about the centrality of the issue under discussion in the religious thought of the Dura-Europos Jewish community around the mid-third century BC.[37]

6. Rabbinic Literature

In the rabbinic literature very obvious connections have been drawn between the site of the *Aqedah* and the Temple Mount of Jerusalem. This feature could be found in different Jewish Aramaic translations – *Targumim* – of several Biblical books, in the Jewish liturgy, as well as in the rabbinic exegesis – *midrashim* – and Medieval Jewish commentaries:

(1). Targumim

The name מן[ו]ריה is derived from the root רא"ה in the story of the *Aqedah* (Gen 22,2.4.8.13.14) and in 2 Chr 3,1.[38] But *Targum Onkelos*, which is generally based on the verbal translation of the Hebrew Text, translated ארץ המריה in Gen. 2,2 as ארע פלחנא that is, the "land of worship", which can be none other than Jerusalem.[39] He derived the name מריה from the root יר"א, that is, awe, worship. One can find the same translation also

---

al Survey", in Levine, *Ancient Synagogues Revealed*, pp. 11–18 esp. 15–16.

[37] The synagogue is almost the *only* – the main and the most important – source for our knowledge about the Jewish community of Dura-Europos.

[38] See above, chapter one, pp. 15, 25–26; I. Kalimi, "Paronomasia in the Book of Chronicles", *JSOT* 67 (1995), pp. 27–41 esp. 38–39.

[39] The Targum version according to Sperber, *The Pentateuch*, p. 31.

in *Targum Pseudo-Jonathan* to Gen 22,2;[40] as well as in a *midrashic* addition of the *Targum* to 2 Chr 3,1:

בטור מוריה באתר דפלח וצלי אברהם תמן
בשמא דיהוה הוא אתר ארע פלחנא

On the *Mount Moriah*, on the spot where Abraham had worshipped and prayed in the Name of the Lord, *that place is the land of worship*.[41]

A very obvious association between the Temple Mount and the site of the *Aqedah* has been made in Targum Neofiti to Gen 22 and in Targum Pseudo-Jonathan to Gen 22,9.14; the Fragment-Targums (= Targum Yerushalmi) to Gen 22,14 as well as in the Targum to the Song of Songs.

In Targum Neofiti of Gen 22,1 we read that Abraham replied to God בלשון בית מקדשא "in the language of the sanctuary", that is, Hebrew, and said הנני "here I am".[42] The Temple related to the *Aqedah* most clearly in the next verse. In the margin of the manuscript, immediately after the word "Moriah" in Gen 22,2, there is a gloss: דתמן עתיד די יתבני בית מקדשא "where the Temple was later to be built".[43]

It is noteworthy to cite here also Pseudo-Jonathan on Gen 22,9. The Targumist expounds aggadically the word המזבח stressed with an article "*the* altar" which Abraham built. He relates the Temple

---

[40] The Pseudo-Jonathan version is according to Clark, *Targum Pseudo-Jonathan*, p. 23.

[41] The Aramaic version is according to A. Sperber (ed.), *The Bible in Aramaic – Vol. IV A: The Hagiographa* (Leiden: E.J. Brill, 1968), p. 34. For the English translation, cf. J.S. McIvor, *The Targum of Chronicles* (The Aramaic Bible 19; Edinburgh: T&T Clark, 1994), p. 146.

[42] Compare, for example, Neofiti on Gen 2,19 (Díez Macho, *Neophyti 1 – Tomo I: Génesis*, pp. 11, 125); The Fragment-Targums on Gen 22,11 (M.L. Klein, *The Fragment-Targums of the Pentateuch. Volume I: Texts, Indices and Introductory Essays* [AnBib 76; Rome: Biblical Institute Press, 1980], p. 54); and see A. Shinan, "The Language of the Sanctuary in the Targumim of the Pentateuch", *Beit Mikra* 21 (1976), pp. 472-474 (Hebrew); M. McNamara, *Targum Neofiti 1: Genesis – Translated, with Apparatus and Notes* (The Aramaic Bible 1A; Edinburgh: T&T Clark, 1992), p. 58 note 23.

[43] See Díez Macho, *Neophyti 1 – Tomo I: Génesis*, p. 125.

Mount not only with Abraham and the binding of Isaac, but also
with the well known world ancestors – Adam and Noah:[44]

ובנא תמן אברהם ית מדבחא דבנא אדם ואיתפכר במוי דטובענא ותב
נח ובנייה ואיתפכר בדרא דפלוגתא וסדר עילוי ית קיסיא וכפת ית
יצחק בריה ושוי יתיה על מדבחא לעיל מן קיסין

> And there Abraham [re]built the altar that had been built by Adam, but
> had been destroyed by the waters of the Flood; and Noah rebuilt it, but
> it was destroyed in the generation of the Division; and he [= Abraham,
> rebuilt it and] set upon it the wood, and bound Isaac his son, and put
> him on the top of the wood which were upon the altar.

Among the other Targumim, a good example could be found in the
Targum of the Song of Songs. In Cant 3,6 is written: "Who is this
coming up from the wilderness, like a column of smoke, from the
burning of myrrh and frankincense...". The *Targumist* furnished the
Biblical text with midrashic material, and wrote:

מא היא דא אומא בחירא דסלקא
מן מדברא מתגמרא מן קטורת בוסמין וסעידא בזכותא
דאברהם דפלח וצלי קדם ייי בטור מוריה ומתמרקא משח רבותא
בצדקיה דיצחק דאתעקד באתר בית מקדשא דאתקרי טור דלבונתא

> What chosen people is this coming up from the wilderness, perfumed with
> sweet-smelling incense, supported by the merit of Abraham, who worshipped
> and prayed before the Lord on Mount Moriah; anointed with the oil used
> by exalted personages, namely, with the righteousness of Isaac, bound as
> he was in the place of the Temple where was called the Mountain of
> Frankincense.[45]

---

[44] The Aramaic text is according to Clark, *Targum Pseudo-Jonathan*, p. 24.
Cf. this Targum with Genesis Rabbah 34,9 (Theodor – Albeck, *Bereschit Rabba*,
p. 317; Freedman – Simon, *Midrash Rabbah: Genesis*, p. 272); Pirke de Rabbi
Eliezer 23 and 31 (M. Higger, "Pirke Rabbi Eliezer", *Horeb* 9 [1946/47], pp.
153-154; 10 [1948], p. 195 [Hebrew]; English translation: G. Friedlander, *Pirke
de-Rabbi Eliezer* [2nd edn.; New York: Hermon Press, 1965], pp. 171, 226-227).

[45] The *Targum* version is according to Sperber, *Hagiographa*, p. 132. For the
English translation cf. H. Gollancz, "The Targum to the Song of Songs", in
B. Grossfeld (ed.), *The Targum to the Five Megilloth* (New York: Hermon Press,
1973), p. 206. See also the same Targum on Cant 1,13; 2,17; Sperber, *ibid.*,
pp. 129, 132.

(2). Jewish Liturgy

The paragraph which concludes the section זכרונות "Remembrance verses", one of the highlights of the Rosh Hashanah (the New Year) *Mussaf* service, relates clearly Abraham and the *Aqedah* with the Temple Mount:

> Remember for us, Lord, our God, the covenant, the *chesed*, and the oath that you swore to our father, Abraham, on the Mount Moriah. Let there appear before You the *Aqedah* when Abraham, our father, bound Isaac, his son, upon the altar....

Although all three special benedictions of *Mussaf* Rosh Hashanah – *Malkhuyot* ("Kingship verses"), *Zikhronot* ("Remembrance verses"), and *Shofarot* ("Shofar verses") – are old, and probably used already in the Second Temple era, it is not certain if the paragraph concerning the *Aqedah* was a part of the original "Remembrance verses" or is an addition to it after the Second Temple time.[46] Nonetheless, the "Remembrance verses" are mentioned in the Mishnah, *Rosh Hashanah* 4,5.6.[47] A close version of the prayer appears as well in the midrashic addition of the Targum Neofiti, Pseudo–Jonathan and of the Fragment-Targums to Gen 22,14, and in Genesis Rabbah 56,14.[48]

(3). *Midrashim* and Medieval Exegesis

In *Genesis Rabbah* 55,7 we read: "*And get you into the land of Moriah* [Gen 22,2] – Rabbi Hiyya the Elder and Rabbi Jannai discussed this. One said: To the place whence instruction (הורייה) went forth to the world.[49] While the other explained it: To the place whence religious

---

[46] See J. Heinemann, "The Ancient 'Orders of Benedictions' for New Year and Fasts", *Tarbiz* 45 (1976), pp. 258-267 esp. 258-259, 264-267 (= idem, *Studies in Jewish Liturgy* [edited by A. Shinan; Jerusalem: Magnes Press, 1981], pp. 44-53 esp. 44-45, 50-53; both in Hebrew).

[47] See also Jerusalem Talmud, *Rosh Hashanah* 4,7 (59c); Babylonian Talmud, *Rosh Hashanah* 16a; 32b; 34b.

[48] See Clark, *Targum Pseudo-Jonathan*, p. 24; Klein, *The Fragment-Targums*, p. 54; Theodor – Albeck, *Bereschit Rabba*, pp. 607-608. For the English translation, see Freedman – Simon, *Midrash Rabbah: Genesis*, p. 500. It is noteworthy to mention, that later on, as a result of the Kabbalistic masters' influence, it appears also in the majority of prayer-books as a preliminary supplication to the recitation of the *Aqedah* in the everyday morning service.

[49] "It was the spot where in later times the Chamber of Hewn Stones in the Temple stood and the Great Sanhedrin sat and sent forth religious teaching

awe (יראה) went forth to the world".[50] Other opinions stated there: "Rabbi Shimon Bar Yochai said: To the place that corresponds (ראוי) to the Heavenly Temple; ... The Rabbis said: To the place where incense would be offered, as you read *I will get me to the mountain of myrrh* [מור; Cant 4,6]".[51]

All these explanations are plays on the word מוריה and the words which sound phonetically close to it (folk etymologies): הורייה יראה, ראוי, מור. All of them make a clear connection between the site of the *Aqedah* and the Temple Mount.[52]

This connection was followed in the Jewish exegeses in the Middle Ages, for example in the commentaries of Rashi (Rabbi Solomon Yitzchaki, 1040-1105), Rabbi Abraham Ibn Ezra (1089-1164) and Nachmanides (Rabbi Moshe ben Nachman, Ramban, 1194-1274) on Genesis 22,2. It is worthwhile to mention that it was adopted also by some church fathers, for instance Saint Jerome (Sophronius Eusebius Hieronymus, ca. 340-420).[53]

II. The Samaritan Sources

1. Samaritan Pentateuch

As mentioned above, the sanctity of Mount Gerizim was (and is) one of the main principles of the Samaritan belief.[54] It is also a central

---

to all Israel", see Freedman – Simon, *Midrash Rabbah: Genesis*, p. 487 note 3.

[50] The Hebrew edition according to Theodor – Albeck, *Bereschit Rabba*, pp. 591-592. For the English translation, cf. Freedman – Simon, *Midrash Rabbah: Genesis*, pp. 487-488.

[51] Cf. above the *Targum* on Cant 3,6; and on 4,6 (For the Aramaic version, see Sperber, *Hagiographa*, p. 134; the English translation is according to Gollancz, *Targum*, p. 213).

[52] See also *Genesis Rabbah* 56,10 (Theodor – Albeck, *Bereschit Rabba*, pp. 607-608; for English translation, see Freedman – Simon, *Midrash Rabbah: Genesis*, pp. 500-501); Babylonian Talmud, *Berakot* 62b; Midrash Tanchuma (Buber), *Parashat Wayyera*, 22,1 (English translation, J.T. Townsend, *Midrash Tanḥuma – Translated into English with Introduction, Indices and Brief Notes: Volume I – Genesis* [Hoboken, NJ: Ktav Publishing House, 1989], pp. 127-128).

[53] See M. Rahmer, *Die hebräischen Traditionen in den Werken des Hieronymus*, Erster Teil (Breslau: H. Skutsch, 1861), pp. 34-35 (Die "Quaestiones in Genesin").

[54] See I. Ben-Zvi, *The Book of the Samaritans* (2nd edn.; Jerusalem: Yad Izhak Ben-Zvi, 1970), pp. 140-141 (Hebrew). The commandment to respect Mount Gerizim as a holy place is planted amongst the most important com-

point in their dispute with the Jews. The Samaritans expended a great deal of literary effort to form a connection between their holy site on Mount Gerizim by Shechem[55] and the site of the *Aqedah*. A hint of this argument can be seen in the Samaritan Torah (probably from the Hasmonean times).[56] In Gen 22,2 they wrote:

לך לך אל ארץ המוראה והעלהו שם
עלה על אחד ההרים אשר אמר אליך

Go to the land of Mora'a and offer him there as a burnt offering on one of the mountains which I will point out to you.[57]

mandments of the Torah, namely the Ten Commandments in the book of Exodus (following Ex 20,17) and in the book of Deuteronomy (following Deut 5,18). In other words, the Samaritans raised this to the level of an important commandment. For other places where the Samaritans altered the Torah, see for example, Deut 12,5 במקום אשר בחר "in the place which he *chose*", instead of במקום אשר יבחר "the place which he *will choose*" (and thus too in the remaining suggestions of the choice of the sacred place in Deuteronomy); Deut 27,4 בהרגרזים "on Mount Gerizim" instead of בהר עיבל "on Mount Ebal". Cf. M. Gaster, *The Samaritans: Their History, Doctrines and Literature* (The Schweich Lectures of the British Academy, 1923; London: Humphrey Milford, Oxford University Press, 1925), pp. 23-24; S. Isser, *The Dositheans – A Samaritan Sect in Late Antiquity* (Leiden: E.J. Brill, 1976), pp. 9-10, 19, 54.

[55] The site on Mount Gerizim was sanctified by the Samaritan community, apparently in the fifth century BCE, see S. Talmon, "Biblical Traditions on the Early History of the Samaritans", in J. Aviram (ed.), *Eretz Shomron – The Thirtieth Archaeological Convention – September 1972* (Jerusalem: Israel Exploration Society, 1973), pp. 19-33 esp. 23, 32-33 (Hebrew). On the issue of the temple on Mount Gerizim, see below, section II, 4. *Excursus: The Temple on Mount Gerizim*.

[56] On the dating of the Samaritan Torah to Hasmonean times, see J.D. Purvis, *The Samaritan Pentateuch and the Origin of the Samaritan Sect* (HSM 2; Cambridge, MA: Harvard University Press, 1968), pp. 16-87. For a recent survey on the Samaritan Pentateuch, see I. Hjelm, *The Samaritans and Early Judaism – A Literary Analysis* (JSOT Suppl. 303 & CIS 7; Sheffield: Sheffield Academic Press, 2000), pp. 76-93.

[57] The Samaritan version of the Torah cited in this article is according to A.F. von Gall (ed.), *Der Hebräische Pentateuch der Samaritaner* (Giessen: Verlag Alfred Töpelmann, 1918).

The alteration from the Masoretic Text "Moriah" to "Mora'a" makes this verse analogous with the Samaritan version of Deut 11,29-30: ונתת את הברכה על הרגרזים... אצל אלוני מורא מול שכם "and you shall put the blessing upon Mount Gerizim... by the oaks of Mora'a in front of Shechem" (this is instead of the Masoretic Text אצל אלוני מרה "by the oaks of Moreh").[58] Furthermore, in order not to leave any space for doubt about the meaning of this analogy, the Samaritans added the words מול שכם "in front of Shechem" to Deut 11,30.[59] Therefore, the analogy and the addition cause the reader to identify the Mount Gerizim by Shechem with the Mount of the *Aqedah*.

2. Samaritan *Midrashim*

We already pointed out the association of Abraham with Mount Gerizim which had been done by the presumed anonymous Samaritan writer, so called Pseudo-Eupolemus (Fragment one, 15-18).[60] A clear identification of the site of the *Aqedah* on Mount Gerizim is to be found, however, much later in the Samaritan *midrashim*. In *Tibât Mârqe* (= *Memar Marqah*)[61] the exegete asks:

> He said to Abraham '*In the land which I shall show you*' [Gen 12,1]. And
> what could he have shown him if not the Good Mountain? Again he

---

[58] Compare this to the Samaritan version of Gen 12,6 עד מקום שכם עד אלון מורא "unto the place of Shechem, unto the oak of *Mora*", as opposed to the Masoretic עד מקום שכם עד אלון מורה "unto the place of Shechem, unto the oak of *Moreh*".

[59] Therefore, Rabbi Elazar son of Rabbi Shimon was incorrect in maintaining that the Samaritans were not serving their case in any way by this addition to their Torah: "Rabbi Elazar son of Rabbi Shimon said: I was debating with the scholars of the Kuthites (= Samaritans): "You have falsified your Torah and not helped yourself at all, in writing in your Torah 'by the terebinths of Mamre [facing] Shechem'..." (Jerusalem Talmud, *Sotah* 7,3 [30b]). As mentioned above, the addition "facing Shechem" creates an analogy with other passages in the Samaritan Torah and directs the reader to a certain religiously motivated perspective which the Samaritans were attempting to achieve.

[60] See above, section I, 3.

[61] On *Tibât Mârqe* see A. Tal, "Samaritan Literature", in A.D. Crown (ed.), *The Samaritans* (Tübingen: J.C.B. Mohr [Paul Siebeck], 1989), pp. 462-465; idem, "*Tibât Mârqe*", in A.D. Crown, R. Pummer and A. Tal (eds.), *A Companion to Samaritan Studies* (Tübingen: J.C.B. Mohr [Paul Siebeck], 1993), pp. 235-236.

stated to him, at the time of his testing, when He demanded Isaac from him and revealed His holiness. He said 'in the Land of Vision' (**ארעה** **מחזיה**) [Gen 22,2],[62] the good and the blessed. Abraham knew it and ran to it immediately. Now, hear a question on the theme of what was said to Abraham. What was His point when He demanded from him the sacrifice of Isaac '*upon one of the mountains of which I shall tell you*' [Gen 22,2], when he [Abraham] knew it from the beginning of His [God] speech? Let your mind be at ease, O questioner, and hear now an answer, for which you need no special knowledge: While he [Abraham] maintained righteousness and truth, he sought the place that God showed him from afar, turned to it and prayed, and when he finished praying – '*he lifted his eyes*' [Gen 22,4]. And indeed, when he lifted his eyes, he was prostrate, for it was morning, and so he stood and prayed. And in what direction was his prayer if not towards Mount Gerizim? When he prayed wholeheartedly, he saw clearly.[63]

In another Samaritan work, *Sefer ha'Otot laMårqe*, the exegete says: "Mount Gerizim is the chosen place, since the day the Lord created it as his everlasting holy place, until the Day of Revenge. It has thirteen names in the Torah. Each one of these names states its honor".[64] This exegete recounts the last two names in connection with the scriptural story of the *Aqedah*:

השני עשר 'אחד ההרים' באחד השבטים...
השלישי עשר מקרתה אברהם שם המקום ההוא 'יהוה יראה'
הודיע הן כל מדרש דידרש עליו לא מסחנה ריק

The twelfth name: '*One of the mountains*' [Gen 22,2], in the territory of one of the tribes... and the thirteenth: The naming by Abraham of the name of that place 'YHWH will see' [Gen 22,14]. He informed that any request which is made upon it will not go unfulfilled.[65]

---

[62] Cf. the Samaritan Targum (Manuscripts J and A) on Gen. 22,2 **ארע** **חזיתה** "the land of Vision". For Samaritan Targum editions, see A. Tal, *The Samaritan Targum of the Pentateuch – A Critical Edition, Part I – Genesis and Exodus* (Tel Aviv: Tel Aviv University Press, 1980), pp. 74, 76 (MS J); 75, 77 (MS A).

[63] The translation based on Z. Ben-Hayyim, *Tibåt Mårqe – A Collection of Samaritan Midrashim* (Jerusalem: The Israel Academy of Sciences and Humanities, 1988), pp. 143-144, 145 (Hebrew).

[64] See Ben-Hayyim, *Tibåt Mårqe*, pp. 148, 149.

[65] See Ben-Hayyim, *Tibåt Mårqe*, pp. 150, 151.

3. Other Samaritan Sources

In the final third of the fourth century CE, the Pilgrim of Bordeaux conveyed some information, which presumably he had heard from the Samaritans: "There [that is by the city Neapolis, present day Nablus] is the mount Agazaren. There – say the Samaritans – Abraham offered the sacrifice".[66]

In fact, as of today, the flat rock on Mount Gerizim which the Samaritans called אבן השתיה "the Foundation Stone",[67] bears precisely the same name as the rock on Mount Moriah in Jerusalem, on which the Jews (and also the Muslims)[68] believe that Abraham bound his son Isaac.[69]

---

[66] See *Corpus Christianorum: Series Latina* 175 (1965), p. 13.

[67] J.A. Montgomery, *The Samaritans – The Earliest Jewish Sect: Their History, Theology and Literature* (Philadelphia 1907; reprinted New York: Ktav Publishing House, 1968), p. 237; Z. Vilnay, "Gerizim", *Ariel – The Encyclopaedia of the Land of Israel* (Tel Aviv: Sifriyat ha-Sadeh, 1974), pp. 1432, 1433-1434 (Hebrew). Y. Magen, "Mount Gerizim – A Temple-City", *Qadmoniot* 23 (1990), pp. 70-78 esp. 70 (Hebrew), mentions the existence of מזבח עקדת יצחק "altar to which Isaac was bound" on Mount Gerizim. However, see on this already R. Pummer, *The Samaritans* (Iconography of Religions 5; Leiden: E.J. Brill, 1987), pp. 24, 45 and Plate XLVI a & b.

[68] On some other Islamic legends related to this rock in Jerusalem, see C.D. Matthews, *Palestine – Mohammedan Holy Land* (Yale Oriental Series Researches 24; New Haven: Yale University Press, 1949), pp. 6, 14-15, 17, 18 (Mohammed's first *qiblah*; door to paradise); 29 (center of the world); 32 (first disclosed from the Flood); 63, 105, 118 (source of waters).

[69] Several rabbinic sources developed a mythology on this place of the Temple, see the list in J.Z. Smith, *To Take Place – Toward Theory in Ritual* (Chicago Studies in the History of Judaism; Chicago & London: The University of Chicago Press, 1987), pp. 84-85 and references on pp. 165-166 note 48. For another tradition on the Foundation Stone in Jerusalem's Temple, see Mishnah, *Yoma* 5,2.
It is noteworthy that the Christians who interpreted the sacrifice of Isaac in Gen 22 as symbolic of Christ's own sacrifice, associated the site of Isaac's binding with Golgotha, see C. Coüasnon, *The Church of the Holy Sepulcher in Jerusalem* (The Schweich Lectures of the British Academy, 1972; London: Oxford University Press, 1974), pp. 52-53.

Figure 3   The mosaic floor of the synagogue at Beth-Alpha (6th century CE): The last panel showing the binding of Isaac

Over the span of time, the Samaritans connected diverse legends to Mount Gerizim,[70] but the association with the story of the *Aqedah* remained among the most important for them.[71]

4. Excursus: The Temple on Mount Gerizim

In *Antiquitates Judaicae* 11,302-311. 321-325. 340-346, Josephus Flavius tells about the circumstances which led to the founding of the Samaritan temple on Mount Gerizim by Sanballat II, the last Persian governor of Samaria, in the fourth century BCE. According to Josephus, Alexander the Great authorized the erection of the temple, after his invasion of Palestine (332 BCE).

Some scholars, like F.M. Cross and E.J. Bickerman,[72] accepted the credibility of Josephus' story. Others, like L.L. Grabbe and M. Mor, do not give credence to the story in general, but, as Grabbe put it: "the only aspect of it now demonstrated to be correct is the origin of the Samaritan temple in the late fourth century".[73] Contrary to these scholars, there are historians who discredit the historical reliability of the whole story in Josephus.[74]

As of today, there is no archaeological evidence for the story of Josephus about the erection of the Samaritan temple.[75] Y. Magen

[70] For example, the hiding of the tabernacle and everything in it and pertaining to it in Mount Gerezim, see Kalimi – Purvis, "The Hiding of the Temple Vessels", pp. 679-685 esp. 682-685.

[71] See Ben-Hayyim, *Tibât Mårqe*; Isser, *The Dositheans*, pp. 9-10, 19, 54; J. Macdonald, *The Theology of the Samaritans* (NTL; London: SCM Press, 1964), pp. 16-21, 139 notes 1 and 2, 281, 339.

[72] See F.M. Cross, "A Reconstruction of the Judean Restoration", *JBL* 94 (1975), pp. 4-18 esp. 5-6; E.J. Bickerman, *The Jews in the Greek Age* (Cambridge, MA: Harvard University Press, 1988), pp. 10-11.

[73] See L.L. Grabbe, "Josephus and the Reconstruction of the Judean Restoration", *JBL* 106 (1987), pp. 231-246 esp. 244; and the articles of M. Mor mentioned below.

[74] See, for example, B. Bar-Kochva, *Judas Maccabaeus – The Jewish Struggle Against the Seleucids* (Cambridge: Cambridge University Press, 1989), p. 131 note 3; D.R. Schwartz, "On Some Papyri and Josephus' Sources and Chronology for the Persian Period", *JSJ* 21 (1990), pp. 175-199.

[75] See Y. Magen, "A Fortified Town of the Hellenistic Period on Mount Gerizim", *Qadmoniot* 19 (1986), pp. 91-101 esp. 101 (Hebrew); idem, "The Samaritans in Shechem and the Blessed Mount Gerizim," in Z.Ch. Ehrlich (ed.), *Shomron and Benyamin – A Collection of Studies in Historical Geography*

assumed that the Samaritan temple was located at the place where the Byzantine church stood. According to him, the Samaritan temple was erected at the time of the construction of the Hellenistic city, which started at the beginning of the second century BCE, in the days of Antiochus III, after the land was conquered from the Ptolemies.[76] Magen claimed also that he found the remains of the Samaritan *temnus* – the gates and the walls – during his excavations on Mount Gerizim.[77]

H. Eshel argues for two Samaritan temples at two different sites and two different periods: The first in Samaria in the middle of the fourth century BCE; the second at Mount Gerizim in the beginning of the second century BCE (compare Magen, above).[78]

A sharp opposition to this assumption was expressed by M. Mor.[79] Without taking sides between Mor and Eshel, I would like to note that from the methodological viewpoint, at least some of Eshel's arguments seem extremely weak as they are founded on several hypotheses which are far from certain.[80] It is apparent that the whole issue requires further investigation.

Nevertheless, there is an agreement among the scholars about the time of the destruction of the Samaritan temple as related by Josephus (*Antiquitates Judaicae* 13,254-256; *Bellum Judaicum* 1,63). The destruction was carried out by John Hyrcanus I, the Hasmonean king and high priest of Judea, who conquered and annexed Samaria to his realm.[81] The twenty-three coins of this king found in the archaeological excavations on Mount Gerizim support Josephus' account.

(Ophra [Israel]: haChevra leHaganat haTeva and Ophra's Sadeh School, 1987), pp. 177-210 esp. 207-208 (Hebrew); idem, "Temple-City", p. 83.

[76] See Magen, "A Fortified Town", p. 101; idem, "Temple-City", p. 83.

[77] See Magen, "Temple City", pp. 70-78.

[78] See H. Eshel, "The Prayer of Joseph, a Papyrus from Masada and the Samaritan Temple on *APGAPIZIN*", *Zion* 56 (1991), pp. 125-136 esp. 131-132 (Hebrew).

[79] See M. Mor, "The Samaritan Temple on Mount Gerizim", *Beit Mikra* 38 (1993), pp. 313-327 (Hebrew); but also Eshel's reply, "The Samaritan Temple on Mount Gerizim and the Historical Research", *Beit Mikra* 39 (1994), pp. 141-155 (Hebrew); and Mor's reaction, "The Samaritan Temple Once Again: Josephus Flavius and the Archaeological Find", *Beit Mikra* 40 (1994), pp. 43-64 (Hebrew).

[80] See, for example, Eshel, "The Samaritan Temple", pp. 146-147, 151-152, 155.

[81] See below, section III in this chapter.

Generally, the destruction of the Samaritan temple is dated 128 BCE.[82] Since some of the coins date from the years 115-114 and 112-111, the destruction was not before 112-111 BCE.[83]

III. Perpetuation of the Dispute

The dispute between the Jews and Samaritans concerning the "true temple" and its precise location affected the quality of the relationship between the two communities. This is revealed, indeed, in several sources: at the beginning of the second century BCE, for example, Ben-Sira considered the Samaritans not only as non-Israelites, but even as no nation at all! He called them "mean people who dwell in Shechem", even without mentioning the name "Samaritans" (Ben-Sira 50,25-26). Indeed, the Hasmonean king and high priest, John Hyrcanus I, destroyed the Samaritans' temple.[84] Moreover, in the Talmudic tradition it is related that the Sages made the day of the destruction of the Samaritan temple a feast day, and decided that "the twenty-fifth of the month [Tevet] is the day of Mount Gerizim, when mourning is forbidden" (Babylonian Talmud, *Yoma* 69a).[85]

If we turn our attention to the story in the Fourth Gospel, we will see, once again, the depth of the hostility between Jews and Samaritans (or at least between groups of them), as shown by the Samaritan woman's words to Jesus: "How is it that you, a Jew, are asking for a drink from me, a Samaritan woman?" (John 4,9a). This story may prove that in the first century CE[86] it was impossible even

---

[82] See, for instance, Bickerman, *Jews in the Greek Age*, p. 12.

[83] Cf. Magen, "Temple-City", pp. 87, 90, 96.

[84] For the destruction of the Samaritan temple, see above, section II, 4. *Excursus: The Temple on Mount Gerizim.*

[85] *Megillat Ta'anit*, line 24, mentions a different month from that which is mentioned in the Talmud: "On the twenty-first of the month [Kislev] is the day of Mount Gerizim when mourning is forbidden". The citation is according to H. Lichtenstein, "Die Fastenrolle – Eine Untersuchung zur jüdisch-hellenistischen Geschichte", *HUCA* 8-9 (1931/32), pp. 257-351 esp. 320 (text) and the discussion on p. 288.

[86] For the date of the final written form of John, see R.E. Brown, *The Gospel According to John* (AB 29; Garden City, NY: Doubleday, 1966), pp. LXXX-LXXXVI.

to imagine that either of these people could even request water from each other![87]

The last part of the verse from the Gospel of John, "For Jews have no dealings with Samaritans" (verse 9b), is missing in some manuscripts. Thus, there are scholars who considered it as a late gloss.[88] It seems more accurate to say that this comment is not of the Samaritan woman but of the Evangelist,[89] who attempted to explain the story. Nevertheless, the verse expresses the hostility between the Jews and the Samaritans at least at the time of its composition.

The antagonism between Jews and Samaritans may also be evident in John 8,48 when the Jews accuse Jesus: "Are we not right in saying that you are a Samaritan and have a demon?". Here, a "Samaritan" is mentioned in the same breath with "demon". It has, probably, also a connotation of heterodoxy,[90] and shows the intolerance which existed between these peoples.[91] Indeed, at the end of the second chapter of the extra-canonical Tractate *Kuttim* (that is, Samaritans),[92] we read that the Samaritans are not welcome into the Israelite community

---

[87] "There was nothing strange in asking a *woman* for water, as it was women who generally drew it from the wells, cf. Gen. 24,17", see J.H. Bernard, *A Critical and Exegetical Commentary on the Gospel According to St. John* (ICC; Edinburgh: T&T Clark, 1928), vol. I, p. 137.

[88] See, for example, R. Pummer, "New Testament and the Samaritans", in Crown, Pummer and Tal, *A Companion to Samaritan Studies*, p. 170; see also Brown, *John*, p. 170. Daube assumed that the impure rituals of the Samaritans form the background to the text, and proposed the translation: "Jews and Samaritans do not use vessels in common", see D. Daube, "Jesus and the Samaritan Woman: The Meaning of *sygchraomai*", *JBL* 69 (1950), pp. 137-147; reprinted as "Samaritan Women", in idem, *The New Testament and Rabbinic Judaism* (London: The Athlone Press, 1956), pp. 373-382. This assumption is not acceptable, see Pummer, *ibid.*, p. 170; G.R. Beasley-Murray, *John* (WBC 36; Waco, TX: Word Books, 1987), p. 58.

[89] See Bernard, *St. John*, p. 138.

[90] Cf. R. Bultmann, *Das Evangelium des Johannes* (KEKNT; 16th edn., Göttingen: Vandenhoeck & Ruprecht, 1959), p. 225.

[91] See also Luke 9,52-53; Mtt 10,5; but cf. Acts 8,25.

[92] This Talmudic minor book is located, along with other extra-canonical tractates, after the tractates of *Nezikin* in the Babylonian Talmud.

unless "they recant [their belief in] Mount Gerizim and accept [the holiness of] Jerusalem,[93] and the resurrection of the dead".

[93] See also Midrash Tanchuma (Buber), *Parashat Wayykra*, 3 (English transla-tion, J.T. Townsend, *Midrash Tanḥuma – Translated into English with Indices and Brief Notes: Volume II – Exodus and Leviticus* [Hoboken, NJ: Ktav Publishing House, 1997], pp. 187-188). It is worthwhile to mention that the Samaritans recognized the Tabernacle as the only legitimate sanctuary in the history of Israel, see Kalimi – Purvis, "The Hiding of the Temple Vessels", p. 682; R. Pummer, "Samaritan Tabernacle Drawings", *Numen* 45 (1998), pp. 30-68 esp. 30-31.

II

Biblical Texts in Polemical Contexts

3

"He was Born Circumcised"

Some Midrashic Sources, Their Concept, Roots and Presumably Historical Context

I. Introduction

The purpose of this chapter is to clarify the rabbinical concept to be born circumcised, and follow the roots of the idea from the earliest Jewish and Christian sources until its appearance in midrashim which claim that several Biblical figures were born circumcised. The aim is not to discuss the Christian controversy over circumcision, but the possible connection between this controversy and the midrashim under discussion on the one hand, and the Hadrianic ban on circumcision on the other.

II. The Biblical Figures Who Were Born Circumcised

Midrash Psalms 9,7 accounts thirteen people in the Biblical period who were born circumcised. Although there is no allusion in the Hebrew Bible that these men were born in such a condition or even that they were (or were not) circumcised by their fathers or anyone else, the rabbis deduced this from several verses:

> *And two peoples shall be separated from your bowels* (Gen 25,23), one circumcised, and the other not circumcised. From this verse you can learn that Jacob was born circumcised.[1] He was one of thirteen who were born

---

[1] See below, in which the rabbis related this also to Gen 25,27. However, the rabbis expounded here the word יפרדו "shall be *separated*" as "shall be *distinguished*" immediately when they were born.

circumcised, namely: Adam,[2] Seth, Enoch, Noah, Shem, Terach, Jacob, Joseph, Moses,[3] Samuel, David, Isaiah and Jeremiah.[4]

The earliest version of the list of thirteen men born circumcised appears already in Avot de-Rabbi Nathan, version A, chapter 2.[5] And it seems that the list in Midrash Psalms 9,7 is based on it. While the list in Avot de-Rabbi Nathan included non-Jews like Job, "Balaam the wicked", and one post-exilic leader, namely Zerubbabel, Midrash Psalms ignored these men and replaced them by Enoch – who "walked with God" (Gen 5,24), Terach – the father of Abraham (Gen 11,26), and the distinguished prophet, Isaiah. Thus, contrary to the later midrash, Tanchuma (Buber), *Parashat Noah*, 6 which accounts (without listing the names) ten men only (or even seven as in some manuscripts) who were born circumcised, Midrash Psalms continues to keep the framework of the "thirteen" men.

---

[2] Compare Babylonian Talmud, *Sanhedrin* 38b. In fact, regarding Adam one can only infer that he was *created* circumcised. However, according to Genesis Rabbah 11,6 (see Theodor – Albeck, *Bereschit Rabba*, pp. 94-95; an English translation: Freedman – Simon, *Midrash Rabbah: Genesis*, pp. 84-85), Adam was not circumcised at all.

[3] See also Babylonian Talmud, *Sotah* 12a; Exodus Rabbah 1,12; and below in this chapter.

[4] See S. Buber, *Midrash Tehillim* (Vilna: Reem, 1891; reprinted in Jerusalem: Ch. Wagschal, 1977), p. 84 (Hebrew); for the English translation compare W.G. Braude, *The Midrash on Psalms* (YJS 13; New Haven: Yale University Press, 1976), vol. I, p. 139. The list appears in manuscripts nos. 2, 4, 7 and in all the printed editions of Midrash Tehillim since that of the Venice edition, see Buber, *ibid.*, note 58. In Genesis Rabbah the rabbis deduced, too, from the same verse that Jacob was born circumcised. Nonetheless, there is no additional list, see Genesis Rabbah 63,7 (Theodor – Albeck, *Bereschit Rabba*, p. 685; Freedman – Simon, *Midrash Rabbah: Genesis*, p. 561).

[5] See S. Schechter (ed.), *Avot de-Rabbi Nathan* (Wien 1889; reprinted New York & Jerusalem: The Jewish Theological Seminary of America, 1997), p. 12; for an English translation, see J. Goldin, *The Fathers According to Rabbi Nathan* (YJS 10; New Haven: Yale University Press, 1955), pp. 22-23. Could the absence of this source from version B of Avot de-Rabbi Nathan be considered as an omission? – it is very hard to say. For details about the date of Avot de-Rabbi Nathan, see below.

III. The Rabbinical Concept of Being (Un)circumcised

"Greeks considered a bare glans so repugnant, perhaps indecent, that those born with a defectively short foreskin frequently submitted to epispasm, surgery designed to restore the foreskin to its natural shape".[6] Contrarily, according to the rabbis' concept, the flesh of the foreskin is considered a defect; one who is uncircumcised, is one who is imperfect or blemished.[7] Therefore, to circumcise the foreskin is to eliminate the defect, and become a perfect man physically. So it is derived from a different sort of early exegesis. For instance, in the opening verse of the command about circumcision, the Lord says to Abraham: "I am God Almighty, walk before me, and היה תמים *be perfect*" (Gen 17,1). Already in Mishnah, *Nedarim* 3,11 we read:

> Rabbi says: Great is circumcision, for despite all the religious duties which Abraham our father fulfilled, he was not called 'perfect' until he was circumcised, as it is written, *Walk before me and be perfect.*[8]

Accordingly, Targum Pseudo-Jonathan translated in Gen 17,1: והוי שלים בבישרך "be complete in your body";[9] and the

---

[6] See R.G. Hall, "Circumcision", *ABD*, vol. 1, pp. 1025-1031 esp. 1027 (and there references to the Greek sources); cf. idem, "Epispasm and the Dating of Ancient Jewish Writings", *JSP* 2 (1988), pp. 71-86.

[7] On circumcision in Ancient Israel and its Near Eastern context, as well as the presumed concepts behind it, see, for example, the reviews of de Vaux, *Ancient Israel*, pp. 46-48; J.M. Sasson, "Circumcision in the Ancient Near East", *JBL* 85 (1966), pp. 473-476. See also D. Flusser and S. Safrai, "Who Sanctified the Beloved in the Womb", *Immanuel* 11 (1980), pp. 46-55; Hall, "Circumcision", pp. 1025-1027.

[8] The English translation is according to H. Danby, *The Mishnah* (Oxford: Oxford University Press / London: Geoffrey Cumberlege, 1954), p. 268. See also Tosefta, *Nedarim* 2,5 (Zuckermandel, *Tosephta*, p. 277); Babylonian Talmud, *Nedarim* 32a; Piyyute Yannai, see S. Spiegel, *The Fathers of Piyyut — Texts and Studies* (Selected from his Literary Estate and edited by M.H. Schmelzer; New York & Jerusalem: The Jewish Theological Seminary of America, 1996), pp. 52-53 esp. 52 (Hebrew); and later on, in Rashi's commentary on Gen 17,1.

[9] The citation of the Targum is according to Clark, *Targum Pseudo-Jonathan*, p. 17. See also Genesis Rabbah 43,14 (Theodor — Albeck, *Bereschit Rabba*, p. 420; Freedman — Simon, *Midrash Rabbah: Genesis*, p. 356): "*King of Shalem* (Gen 14,18, I.K.) — Rabbi Isaac the Babylonian said: This (i.e., *Shalem* = complete, I.K.) implies that he (Melchizedek, I.K.) was born *circumcised*"! How-

Peshiṭta: וההוי דלא מום "be without defect."[10] Indeed, this view was stated most clearly in Genesis Rabbah 46,1:

> And the Holy One, blessed be He, said to Abraham: 'You have no defect in you but the foreskin, remove it and the defect ceases', hence *Walk before me and be perfect.*[11]

Consequently, Noah, who was איש... תמים "a perfect... man" (Gen 6,9), according to the rabbis was born circumcised. Indeed, in Midrash Psalms a variety of Biblical verses is cited concerning each of those men to show that they were born circumcised. Another example, the rabbis learned from Gen 25,27 and 46,2 that Jacob was born circumcised. Moreover, they deduced from Gen 37,2 that Joseph resembled his father particularly in this case:

> Jacob, for it is said Jacob was איש תם *a perfect man* (Gen 25,27, i.e., he was born circumcised, I.K.), and it is further *said God spoke unto Israel... and said Jacob, Jacob* (Gen 46,2);[12] Joseph, for the verse *These are the generations of Jacob: Joseph* (Gen 37,2) hints that Joseph, like Jacob, was born circumcised (Midrash Psalms 9,7).[13]

---

ever, Melchizedek is not counted among those who were born circumcised on the list of Avot de-Rabbi Nathan and Midrash Psalms.

[10] It is worthwhile to note that the words דלא מום in Peshiṭta do not necessarily mean a physical defect. Therefore, this translation / interpretation in Peshiṭta is not related to Pseudo-Jonathan and / or Genesis Rabbah (see below), see Y. Maori, *The Peshiṭta Version of the Pentateuch and Early Jewish Exegesis* (Jerusalem: Magnes, 1995), p. 78 (Hebrew).

[11] The English translation is mine. Compare to the parallel version in Tanchuma (Buber), *Parashat Lech-Lechah*, 21. Symbolically, the physical change – circumcision – supplemented by spiritual change – alteration of his name: "No longer shall your name be Abram, but Abraham" (Gen 17,5). In Tanchuma (Buber), *Parashat Lech-Lechah*, 20, this act is considered also as fundamental to being complete, like the act of circumcision.

[12] According to this rabbinic method one could anticipate that the name of Abraham was included on the list as well, since his name was repeated twice "*Abraham, Abraham*" (Gen 22,11). But if the Sages did include him on the list, it would contradict the story about his circumcision which was told in Gen 17.

[13] See Buber, *Midrash Tehillim*, pp. 84-85; for the English translation compare Braude, *The Midrash on Psalms*, vol. I, p. 139.

In Genesis Rabbah 84,6[14] the midrashist expounded a little more on this point: "Rabbi Samuel bar Nachman commented: *These are the generations of Jacob: Joseph.* Surely Scripture should say, *These are the generations of Jacob: Reuben.* The reason is this: as Jacob was born circumcised, so was Joseph born circumcised, ...".[15]

Thus, according to the midrash, Jacob and Joseph were born perfect men, without any physical defect.[16]

IV.   The Roots and Continuity of the Concept

The roots of this concept are much older than the time of these midrashim, as it emerges from the following early Jewish and Christian sources:

1.1.   The Book of Jubilees

In the pseudepigraphical book, Jubilees, the angels are described as those who were created circumcised: "Because the nature of all the angels... was thus (i.e., circumcised) from the day of their creation". The author continues, "And in the presence of the angels... He sanctified Israel so that they might be with Him and with His holy angels" (Jub 15,27). In other words, the writer wished to say: when

---

[14] Theodor – Albeck, *Bereschit Rabba,* pp. 1006-1007; Freedman – Simon, *Midrash Rabbah: Genesis,* p. 773.

[15] This midrash is speaking about Joseph who resembles Jacob only in one way: he was born circumcised like his father. Contrarily, in *The Testament of Joseph* 18,4b Joseph describes himself as someone who resembles his father "in all things" (see H.W. Hollander and M. de Jonge, *The Testaments of the Twelve Patriarchs – A Commentary* [SVTP 8; Leiden: E.J. Brill, 1985], p. 404; H.C. Kee, "Testaments of the Twelve Patriarchs", in Charlesworth, *The Old Testament Pseudepigrapha,* vol. 1, pp. 775-828 esp. 823); and in Genesis Rabbah 84,6 (Theodor – Albeck, *Bereschit Rabba,* pp. 1006-1008), are listed many kinds of similarities between Joseph and his father, including the case that Joseph like Jacob was born circumcised. Indeed, it is possible that Joseph's short announcement in *The Testament of Joseph* and the detailed list in Genesis Rabbah demonstrate "two stages in the development of the same midrashic motif", see J.L. Kugel, *In Potiphar's House – The Interpretive Life of Biblical Texts* (San Francisco: Harper, 1990), p. 69.

[16] This in addition to Gen 39,6b which describes Joseph as a handsome man: "And Joseph was of beautiful form, and fair to look upon", precisely like his mother, Rachel (Gen 29,17b).

the Israelites practiced the act of circumcision, they were resembling God's holy angels who had been created circumcised, that is, perfect!

1.2. The Historical Context of Jub 15

The book of Jubilees was composed some time between 170 and 140[17] or even 161-140 BCE.[18] This brings us to the time of the Seleucid emperor, Antiochus IV Epiphanes, who outlawed circumcision by imposing the death penalty (1 Macc 1,48a.60-61; 2 Macc 6,10; 4 Macc 4,25), or at least to the era during which the results of his ban still were obvious. Indeed, in the following verses the author of Jubilees speaks about the Jews who "will deny this ordinance [= circumcision, I.K.], and they will not circumcise their sons *according to all of this law* [that is, they removed only a little of the foreskin but not completely as the law in Gen 17 demands, I.K.]; ... And all of the sons of Beliar will leave their sons without circumcision just as they were born". He warns that the "great wrath from the Lord will be upon the sons of Israel because they have left his covenant... they have made themselves like the gentiles..." (Jub 15,33-34). It seems, therefore, that the author of Jubilees deals directly with the ban and/or with its results. He addresses all those Jews who could not practice circumcision at all or practiced it only partially. He encourages them to resemble God's holy angels who were created circumcised, and thus to join that high sphere.

2. Pseudo-Philo's *Liber Antiquitatum Biblicarum*

Liber Antiquitatum Biblicarum of Pseudo-Philo is dated generally from the time *before* the destruction of the Second Temple (70 CE), or, to cite Daniel Harrington, "around the time of Jesus".[19] The book describes Moses as one who "was born in the covenant of God and

---

[17] See VanderKam, "Jubilees, Book of", *ABD*, vol. 3, p. 1030.

[18] For the date of Jubilees, see O.S. Wintermute, *Jubilees — A New Translation and Introduction*, in Charlesworth, *The Old Testament Pseudepigrapha*, vol. 2, pp. 35-142 esp. 43-44.

[19] See D.J. Harrington, *"Pseudo-Philo — A New Translation and Introduction"*, in Charlesworth, *The Old Testament Pseudepigrapha*, vol. 2, pp. 297-377 esp. 299. Flusser, for instance, is of the opinion that the book was composed during the first two decades *after* the destruction of the Temple, see D. Flusser, "A New Commentary on Pseudo-Philo's *Liber Antiquitatum Biblicarum*", *Tarbiz* 67 (1997/98), pp. 135-138 esp. 136 (Hebrew; a review article on the book of H. Jacobson).

the covenant of the flesh", that is, circumcised (9,13). Later on the author repeats this point. At the time Pharaoh's daughter came down to bathe in the river, opened the cast and immediately was aware of Moses' uniqueness: "And when she saw the boy and while she was looking upon the covenant (that is, the covenant of the flesh [= the sign of his circumcision]), she said, 'It is one of the Hebrew children'. And she took him and nursed him... And the child was nursed and became glorious above all other men, and through him God freed the sons of Israel..." (*ibid.*, 15-16).[20]

3. The Gospel of John

The early roots of the rabbinic idea under discussion emerges also from a Christian source. According to John 7,21-23[21] Jesus compares the act of circumcision with that of the healing of an ill-man: "If a man on the Sabbath day receives circumcision, that the Law of Moses should not be broken;[22] are you angry at me, because I have made a whole man healthy on the Sabbath day?" (verse 23). Hence, an uncircumcised man is comparable to an ill-man! The concept behind this declaration is not so far from that of the rabbis:[23] Un-circumcised man = imperfect / blemished man = ill-man!

It appears that in the Jewish society, an angel's body as well as a man's body become perfect by being circumcised, either naturally, that is, created / was born as such, or by removing the foreskin physically.

Noteworthy to mention that later on this concept finds its way to another monotheistic religious community. Some Islamic traditions described Mohammed as one who was granted the grace of being born circumcised. Other traditions listed him among the distinguished Biblical figures such as Adam, Shith (=Seth), Nuch (= Noah), Yusuf

---

[20] The English translation from the Latin source is according to Harrington, *Pseudo-Philo*, p. 316.

[21] The final form of the Fourth Gospel is dated between 90-100 CE. However, its historical tradition goes back to a much earlier time, ca. 40-60 CE, see Brown, *The Gospel According to John*, pp. lxxx-lxxxvi esp. lxxxvi; see also R. Kysar, "John, The Gospel of", *ABD*, vol. 3, pp. 912-931 esp. 918-920.

[22] See Lev 12,3 and Mishnah, *Nedarim* 3,11.

[23] See also the commentary on these verses by C.K. Barrett, *The Gospel According to St. John* (London: SPCK, 1965), pp. 264-265.

(= Joseph), Musa (= Moses), Sulayman (= Solomon), and even 'Isa (= Jesus) who were miraculously born circumcised.[24]

V. The Meaning of Being Born Circumcised

It seems that to be born circumcised is for Pseudo-Philo as well as for the rabbis a preliminary sign of a forthcoming important national personality. Thus men who were born circumcised, that is complete, perfect, resemble a feature of God's holy angels who were created circumcised, as related in Jubilees.

This feature is comparable to the Biblical literary feature expressing the same message, by relating the great difficulties which precede the births of several national figures. So, for example, the story concerning the birth of Isaac from the infertile ninety year old Sarah (Gen 11,30; 18,11-12); the narratives on the birth of other patriarchs like Jacob (Gen 25,21-23); and Joseph who was born after seven difficult years from the formerly barren Rachel (Gen 29,31c; 30,22-24).[25]

Furthermore, Midrash Tanchuma (Buber), *Parashat Tazria*, 7, lists questions that the Roman governor of Judaea in 132 CE, Tinneius Rufus "the wicked",[26] asked Rabbi Akiva (died ca. 135 CE) concerning the circumcision. One of them is as follows:

> Tinneius Rufus said to him [= Rabbi Akiva]: Inasmuch as He [= God] finds pleasure in circumcision, why does no one emerge from his mother's belly circumcised? Rabbi Akiva said to him: And why does his umbilical cord come out on him? Does not his mother cut his umbilical cord? So why does he not come out circumcised? Because the Holy one only gave the Israelites the commandments in order to purify them....[27]

---

[24] See M.J. Kister, "... 'And He was Born Circumcised' – Some Notes on Circumcision in Hadith", *Oriens* 34 (1994), pp. 10-30 esp. 12-18, 30.

[25] See also the story concerning the births of the famous national leaders such as Samson (Judg 13) and Samuel (1 Sam 1). It seems that the same concept could be applied concerning the birth of Jesus from a virgin (Matt 1,18-25), that is, the entire birth was a great miracle.

[26] In rabbinic sources he is mentioned as "Turnus Rufus", see L. Roth, "Tinneius Rufus", *Encyclopaedia Judaica* (Jerusalem: Keter, [without date]), vol. 15, p. 1148.

[27] For the English translation, compare Townsend, *Midrash Tanhuma*, vol. II, p. 242. Townsend refers mistakenly to "*Tyrannus* Rufus" instead of "*Tinneius* Rufus".

Consequently, one may be allowed to conclude that according to the rabbis generally circumcision is one of the commandments that God furnished the Jewish people in order to purify them. However, occasionally some unique personalities were born circumcised as a preliminary sign of a forthcoming significant national character. We will return to this midrashic source once again.

VI. The Presumably Historical Context

1. Jewish – Christian Polemic?

Was the historical context of these midrashim embedded in the socio-religious situation in Judaea, in the second half of the first and the first half of the second centuries CE? In other words, are they connected somehow to the dispute with the Christians – or at least with a group of them – on the validity of circumcision during those times (e.g., Acts 15,1-29; 16,1-3; Gal 2,3; 5,2.6; 6,11-17; Rom 2,25-29; 3,1)?[28] Paul refers again and again to this issue. In the First Epistle to the Corinthians (ca. 53-55 CE), for example, he considers an uncircumcised person as equal to one who is circumcised. Both have the same merit (7,18-19)![29] In the Epistle to the Romans (ca. 56 CE), Paul justifies his negative judgment of circumcision by pointing out that Abraham's faith in God was reckoned for him as righteousness[30] while he was still uncircumcised. His faith and righteousness were not dependent on the ritual of circumcision (Rom 4,9-12).[31] Paul

---

[28] Another group of Judean-Christians found circumcision "according to the Law of Moses" a conditional stage on the way to salvation, see Acts 15,1.5 and the inner Christian dispute in Gal 5,1-5.

[29] Similarly also in Gal 5,6; 6,15; Rom 3,1.

[30] See Gen 15,6: "And he believed the Lord; and He reckoned it to him as righteousness".

[31] Flusser and Safrai assume that Paul developed his idea, that led to an unanticipated conclusion, on the basis of the Jewish blessing for circumcision, or "it may be that in addition, he knew of *midrashim* on which the blessing is based". The blessing "asserts that the descendants of Abraham were saved from destruction by virtue of circumcision, [but Abraham himself was righteous also when he was uncircumcised], because God sanctified him in the womb. From this, Paul concluded that man achieves righteousness not by circumcision but by faith". See Flusser and Safrai, "Who Sanctified the Beloved in the Womb", pp. 46-55 esp. 55 (the supplement has been done according to the earlier Hebrew version of the essay which is published in Y. Avishur and J. Blau (eds.), *Studies in Bible and the Ancient Near East Presented to S.E. Loewen-*

allegorizes the commandment concerning the physical act of circumcision and expounds it with a spiritual meaning: "And real circumcision is a matter of the heart, spiritual and not literal", he says (Rom 2,29).[32] In the letter to the Colossians (ca. 60 CE), the writer[33] considers the circumcision a sign of the old covenant, while in the new covenant it was replaced by baptism (Col 2,11-12).[34]

The Gospel of Thomas (ca. 70-80 CE)[35] accounts that as an answer to his disciples' question, "Is circumcision beneficial or not?", Jesus said to them: "If it were beneficial, their father would *beget them already circumcised* from their mother. Rather, the true circumci-

---

stamm on His Seventieth Birthday [Jerusalem: E. Rubinstein's Publishing House, 1978], vol. I, p. 336).

There is some controversy between this source which is ascribed to Paul, and the one ascribed to Jesus in John 7,21-23, as mentioned above. This phenomena, that is, inclusion of two contradictory views in a single corpus, is not uncommon in the New Testament as well as in Hebrew Bible literature, see, for example, R.P. Knierim, *The Task of Old Testament Theology: Substance, Method and Cases* (Grand Rapids, MI: Eerdmans, 1995), pp. 1-5, 8-9, 52; and below, chapter seven, pp. 140-144.

[32] Compare Philippians 3,3: "For we are the true circumcision, who worship God in spirit, and glory in Christ Jesus, and put no confidence in the flesh".

[33] Note, though Paul is mentioned as the author of Colossians (Col 1,1.23; 4,18), Pauline authorship of this Epistle is in doubt. To cite Barth and Blanke, for instance: "The substance of the preceding Sections III-IX has immediate bearing on the question whether Colossians is to be treated as a genuine Pauline product or as the work of a contemporary or later admirer [sic!] of the apostle", see in detail M. Barth and H. Blanke, *Colossians – A New Translation with Introduction and Commentary* (AB 34B; New York / London / Toronto / Sydney / Auckland: Doubleday, 1994), pp. 114-126 (the citation is from p. 114); V.P. Furnish, "Colossians, Epistle to the", *ABD*, vol. 1, pp. 1090-1096 esp. 1092-1094.

[34] Flusser and Safrai point out: "From the accounts of Josephus and the Scrolls [Josephus, *Wars* II, 138; *Manual of Discipline* (1QS 5:7-14)] we learn that those who joined the Essene covenant were then permitted to perform immersion. ... some of the sect believed that Prince Mastema leaves the man who joins the sect, and *compared entrance into the covenant of the sect to the covenant of circumcision.* Also in Christian baptism the baptized person is freed from the dominion of Satan and his angels of destruction" (italics mine, I.K.), see idem, "Who Sanctified the Beloved in the Womb", pp. 49-50. Flusser and Safrai do not refer to Col 2,11-12.

[35] K. Berger and C. Nord, *Das Neue Testament und Frühchristliche Schriften* (Frankfurt am Main & Leipzig: Insel Verlag, 1999), p. 644.

sion in spirit has become completely profitable" (*Logion* [= the Jesus' words] 53).[36]

In the Epistles of Barnabas (probably Alexandria; ca. 130-132 CE)[37] is stated that circumcision (περιτομή) does not imply a physical act on the flesh of the foreskin, as it is expounded verbatim and practiced by the Jews. Barnabas demonizes the Jewish ritual, and regards it as the work of a wicked angel (Barn 9,4). Similar to Paul (and the author of Colossians), he relates Pentateuchal law concerning the circumcision specifically with some metaphorical use of the term "circumcise" in several scriptures, such as Deut 10,16; Jer 4,3-4; 6,10; 9,24-25. Barnabas stresses that this Biblical commandment must be explained in a symbolic-allegorical method, it means, applying to the circumcision of heart and ears rather than to the flesh of the foreskin (Barn 9; see also 10,12; 13,7).[38]

Probably, the Midrashim concerning the ancestors who were born circumcised are addressed against this background as well. In other words, the rabbis wished to provide samples of Biblical figures who were considered worthy to resemble them in that they follow the law of circumcision. Let us not forget particularly that the line of thought of Jesus in his reply to his students, according to the Gospel of Thomas, is precisely the same as that behind the question that Tinneius Rufus asked Rabbi Akiva. Namely, the above cited Midrash Tanchuma is in dispute with contemporary Christians as well. One can say the same also concerning the Midrashim listing the Biblical

[36] For the text, see H. Koester and T.O. Lambdin, "The Gospel of Thomas (II,2)", in J.M. Robinson (ed.), *The Nag Hammadi Library in English* (San Francisco: Harper Collins, 1990), p. 132; Berger and Nord, *Das Neue Testament und Frühchristliche Schriften*, p. 657. The Coptic *Gospel of Thomas* from the Nag Hammadi Library was translated from the Greek language, see Koester and Lambdin, *ibid.*, p. 124.

[37] See A. Blaschke, *Beschneidung – Zeugnisse der Bibel und verwandter Texte* (TANZ 28; Tübingen & Basel: A. Francke Verlag, 1998), p. 473. For other datings of Barnabas Epistles, see for example, L.W. Barnard, "Judaism in Egypt AD 70-135", *Studies in Apostolic Fathers and their Background* (Oxford: Oxford University Press, 1966), p. 46: "the early years of the reign of Hadrian (A.D. 117-38)"; and some dated earlier by Berger and Nord, *Das Neue Testament und Frühchristliche Schriften*, p. 235: "das Ende der 1. christlichen Generation".

[38] See Blaschke, *Beschneidung*, pp. 473-481 esp. 473-474; Berger and Nord, *Das Neue Testament und Frühchristliche Schriften*, pp. 247-248; 250-251, 254.

men who were born circumcised, as a sign of distinct unique personalities that every Jew should resemble by the act of circumcision.

2. Socio-Political Situation Around the Bar-Kochba Revolt?

Did the historical context of the Midrashim under discussion also stem from the socio-political situation in Judaea, perhaps before and certainly after the Bar-Kochba revolt (132-135 CE),[39] when the Roman Emperor Hadrian(us) (117-138 CE) prohibited the practice of circumcision?[40] Are the rabbis (who remain anonymous) attempting by means of these homilies to encourage circumcision – that was considered as a proper *nota Iudaica*[41] – in their communities, in spite of all risks, as an essential ancestral tradition, without which a Jew cannot be considered a complete person? Are they trying to persuade their audience to resemble the great national personalities, similar to the author of Jubilees at the beginning of the Hasmonean era, who

---

[39] On the question if Hadrian's ban imposed on the Jews before the war and was one of the reasons for its outburst, the opinions are disputed, see the sources and discussion by M. Noth, *The History of Israel* (London: Adam & Charles Black, 1959), pp. 447-448; S. Lieberman, "On the Persecution of the Jewish Religion", in S. Lieberman and A. Hyman (eds.), *Salo Wittmayer Baron Jubilee Volume* (Jerusalem: American Academy for Jewish Research, 1974), Hebrew Section, pp. 213-245 esp. 213-217; J. Geiger, "The Ban on Circumcision and the Bar-Kokhba Revolt", *Zion* 41 (1976), pp. 139-147 (Hebrew); H. Donner, *Geschichte des Volkes Israel und seiner Nachbarn in Grundzügen* (Göttingen: Vandenhoeck & Ruprecht, 1987), pp. 463-465; L.H. Feldman, *Jew & Gentile in the Ancient World* (Princeton: Princeton University Press, 1993), pp. 158, 508 notes 82-83; P. Schäfer, *The History of the Jews in Antiquity: The Jews of Palestine from Alexander the Great to the Arab Conquest* (Luxembourg: Harwood Academic Publishers, 1995), pp. 145-148.

[40] See the paragraph from Mechilta de-Rabbi Ishmael, which is cited below. For the duration of the prohibition see G. Alon, *The History of the Jewish People in the Land of Israel in the Mishnah and Talmud Ages* (Jerusalem: Publishing House Hakibutz Hameuchad, 1977), vol. II, pp. 57-58 (Hebrew); Schäfer, *The History of the Jews in Antiquity*, pp. 145-148. In this case Hadrian resembles Antiochus IV Epiphanes, about 300 years earlier (ca. 166 BCE).

[41] See the sources listed by M. Stern, *Greek and Latin Authors on Jews and Judaism* (Jerusalem: The Israel Academy of Sciences and Humanities, 1980), vol. II, p. 41; and add to them *Targum Sheni* to Esther, 3,8; L. Ginzberg, *The Legends of the Jews* (Philadelphia: The Jewish Publication Society of America, 1968), vol. I, p. 239.

described the angels as those who were created circumcised and worthy to resemble?

As mentioned above, the list of the thirteen circumcised men in Midrash Psalms 9,7 is based, probably, on the list of Avot de-Rabbi Nathan (version A, chapter 2). The *origin* of Avot de-Rabbi Nathan is, apparently, *Tannaitic* (no *Amoraim* are quoted by it), and it is possible that "Avot de-Rabbi Nathan is so called, because it was organized as a commentary on a recension of *Avot* prepared by the Babylonian R. Nathan" (middle of the second century CE).[42] Now, a statement of this *Tanna* concerning the Hadrianic persecution is cited in the *halachic* midrash, Mechilta de-Rabbi Ishmael (*Jethro, Parasha* 6):[43]

> Rabbi Nathan says: *those who love Me and keep My commandments* [Ex 20,6 // Deut 5,10] refers to the Jews who dwell in the Land of Israel and risk their lives for the sake of the commandments: 'Why are you being led out to be decapitated?' 'Because I circumcised my son; ....'[44]

---

[42] Perhaps, we are allowed to consider this commentary a kind of "proto-Gemara" on *Avot*. For dating of Avot de-Rabbi Nathan, see J. Goldin, "Avot de-Rabbi Nathan", *Encyclopaedia Judaica* (Jerusalem: Keter, [without date]), vol. 3, pp. 984-986 esp. 984, 985. D.J. Bornstein, "Nathan ha-Bavli", *Encyclopaedia Judaica* (Jerusalem: Keter, [without date]), vol. 12, p. 861, even stated that "he [= R. Nathan, I.K.] is said to be the author of Avot de-Rabbi Nathan". M. Kister, in his *prolegomenon* to the reprinted edition of Solomon Schechter Edition of Avot de-Rabbi Nathan, pp. 10, 12, argued that the origin of Avot de-Rabbi Nathan is old but its shape as it appears before us is late. He stresses that Avot de-Rabbi Nathan used Tannaitic literature, specifically *halachic* Midrashim but also the Tosefta, although there are parallels to the *aggadic* Midrashim of the Amoraim. Even though, according to Kister version A of Avot de-Rabbi Nathan is a "post-Talmudic composition", he is not denying that there is some old material in it (see, *ibid.*, p. 13). In fact, in the paragraph under discussion there is no sign of any late material. Thus, there is no reason not to consider it as an old one. See also above, in this section (VI.1), the dispute with the Christians.

[43] See H.S. Horovitz and I.A. Rabin (eds.), *Mechilta d'Rabbi Ismael* (Jerusalem: Bamberger & Wahrmann, 1960), p. 227 (Hebrew).

[44] See also the source cited in Mechilta de-Rabbi Ishmael (*Ki-Tissa, Parasha* 1; Horovitz – Rabin, *Mechilta d'Rabbi Ismael,* p. 343); and compare to the parallel source in Sifre Deuteronomy, *Reah, Piska* 76; H.S. Horovitz and L. Finkelstein (eds.), *Sifre on Deuteronomy* (Berlin: Gesellschaft zur Förderung der Wissenschaft des Judentums, 1889; reprinted, New York: The Jewish Theo-

Moreover, the echo of these Hadrianic persecutions occurs also in Midrash Psalms 13,3:[45]

> *How long shall I take counsel in my soul, having sorrow in my heart daily?* [Ps 13,3]: Although I am sorrowfully oppressed by the kingdoms, yet I continue with my whole heart to observe the Torah and the command-ments which You gave me on Sinai. I practice circumcision, I keep the Sabbath, ... In a different interpretation, *in my soul*: I risk my life on account of the decrees issued against me by the nations of the earth for the purpose of destroying Your Torah and commandments; for their sake I expose myself to death.

Against this historical background one may understand the rabbis' denunciation of uncircumcision as a "detestable" thing on the one hand, and glorification of circumcision as one of the most significant commandments on the other (Mechilta de-Rabbi Ishmael, *Jethro*, *Parasha* 1; Mishnah, *Nedarim* 3,11).[46]

Furthermore, earlier we saw that Antiochus IV Epiphanes preceded Hadrian by almost 300 years in his prohibition of circumcision and imposed the death penalty on those who, despite the decree, still practiced it. We showed that the author of Jubilees responds to Antiochus' ban and/or its results. He encourages those Jews who could not practice circumcision precisely according to the Biblical law, to resemble God's angels who were created circumcised. It is reasonable to assume that this was also the purpose of the above mentioned rabbinical sources later on in the time of Hadrian's ban.

The glorification of the practice of circumcision is understandable obviously also on the background of its denunciation and mockery by some Hellenistic writers, such as the influential anti-Semitic Graeco-Egyptian author of Alexandria, Apion (first half of the first century CE). Apion is cited by Josephus Flavius at the beginning of

logical Seminary of America, 1969), p. 141 (Hebrew); Leviticus Rabbah 32,1; M. Margulies (ed.), *Midrash Wayyikra Rabbah – A Critical Edition Based on Manuscripts and Genizah Fragments with Variants and Notes* (Jerusalem: Central Press, 1956), pp. 635-636 esp. 635 (Hebrew).

[45] See Buber, *Midrash Tehillim*, p. 110; for the English translation, cf. Braude, *The Midrash on Psalms*, vol. I, pp. 178-179.

[46] See Horovitz – Rabin, *Mechilta d'Rabbi Ismael*, pp. 191-192.

the second century CE, as denouncing the Jews (in his *Aegyptiaca*) "for sacrificing domestic animals and for not eating pork, and [as] derid[ing] the practice of circumcision" (*Contra Apionem* 2, 137).[47] Indeed, Josephus himself also argued sharply against Apion's negative views (*Contra Apionem* 2, 141-144).[48]

Therefore, possibly the list under discussion was composed originally at the time of the Bar-Kochba war or slightly thereafter.[49] The potential polemic with the Christians concerning the validity of circumcision, can indicate as well the early date of the source.

VII. Conclusion

According to the rabbinical concept to be born circumcised means to be without blemish. It is considered a preliminary sign of a forthcoming important personality.

The roots of the idea can be found in the Book of Jubilees, in a passage related to Antiochus IV Epiphanes who outlawed circumcision. Later on, in *Liber Antiquitatum Biblicarum*, Pseudo-Philo describes Moses as one who was born circumcised. The idea can be traced, probably, also to the Fourth Gospel, which makes an analogy between an ill man and an uncircumcised man. It was developed the most, however, in midrashim which listed several well-known Biblical figures, and claimed that they were born circumcised. One can better appreciate these homilies specifically against the historical background of the events in the Land of Israel in the second half

---

[47] See H.St.J. Thackeray, *Josephus in Nine Volumes* (The Loeb Classical Library; Cambridge, MA: Harvard University Press / London: William Heinemann, 1961), vol. I, p. 347; M. Stern, *Greek and Latin Authors on Jews and Judaism* (Jerusalem: The Israel Academy of Sciences and Humanities, 1974), vol. I, p. 415 no. 176. See, too, already Strabo of Amaseia (ca. 64 BCE to the twenties of the first century CE; *Geographica* XVI, 2:37) – Stern, *ibid.*, no. 115, p. 300.

[48] Thackeray, *Josephus in Nine Volumes*, vol. I, p. 349.

[49] Although Moshe is mentioned as one who was born circumcised already by Pseudo-Philo (*Liber Antiquitatum Biblicarum* 9,13; Harrington, "Pseudo-Philo", p. 316); in the second half of the first century CE. See also Babylonian Talmud, *Sotah* 12a; Exodus Rabbah 1,20 which expounded ותרא אתו כי טוב הוא "and when she saw him that he was a *goodly* child" (Ex 2,2): טוב = perfect = circumcised!

of the first and the first half of the second centuries CE, that is, the dispute with the Pauline Christianity concerning circumcision and the Hadrianic ban of circumcision.

4

Joseph's Slander of His Brethren

Perspectives on the Midrashic Interpretation in the Light of the Jewish – Christian Controversy

I. Joseph Slanderer of His Brothers: The Biblical, Pseudepigraphical and Rabbinical Sources

The Biblical story relates that Joseph brought an evil report of his brothers unto their father (Gen 37,2). The story, however, lacks specific detail about the slander itself, and whether or not he was punished for his misconduct. The Biblical author also does not impose his own position toward the slander, but rather reports it "objectively".

In *De Josepho*, Philo of Alexandria (ca. 20 BCE to ca. 50 CE) simply disregarded this information, apparently since it lowers the image of Joseph.[1] Other famous writers from the first century CE, Pseudo-Philo and Josephus Flavius, also ignored this issue, probably for the same reason (*Liber Antiquitatum Biblicarum* 8,9;[2] *Antiquitates Judaicae* 2,9-10). Contrarily, the author of *The Testament of Gad*

---

[1] See H.W. Hollander, "The Portrayal of Joseph in Hellenistic Jewish and Early Christian Literature", in M.E. Stone and T.A. Bergren (eds.), *Biblical Figures Outside the Bible* (Harrisburg, PA: Trinity Press International, 1998), pp. 237-263 esp. 245.

[2] For an English text, see Harrington, "Pseudo-Philo", in Charlesworth, *The Old Testament Pseudepigrapha*, vol. 2, p. 314. Noteworthy to stress, that all in all Pseudo-Philo dedicated very little space for Joseph – two verses only (8,9-10).

1,6-7,[3] does not worry about the declining of Joseph's figure, and fills in the gap of the Biblical text as follows:

> And Joseph said to our father: The sons of Zilpah and Bilhah are slaying the best animals (of the flock) and are eating them against the judgment of Judah and Reuben. For he had seen that I snatched a lamb out of the mouth of the bear and had put the bear to death, and slain the lamb concerning which I was grieved that it could not live, and that we had eaten it. And he said it to our father.[4]

The rabbis, however, paid closer attention to the point and filled in the gap of the text much differently. They raised assumptions in several directions while showing that Joseph's slander was worse than simply *"killing the best animals* and eating them", that is, far beyond the economic calculations related to the conduct. In Genesis Rabbah 84,7,[5] for example, is expounded:

> Rabbi Meir said [Joseph told Jacob]: Your sons are to be suspected of [eating] *limbs torn from a living animal.*[6] Rabbi Judah said [Joseph related Jacob]: They [= Leah's sons] insult the sons of the bondmaids [= Bilhah and Zilpah] and call them slaves. Rabbi Simeon said [Joseph informed Jacob]: They cast their eyes upon the Canaanites' daughters.

Moreover, unlike the *Testament of Gad*, the Sages conclude that Joseph's slander is a non-ethical deed, and express a clear-cut, ulti-mate, denunciation of it. They determine that Joseph was punished *within a short term* according to the juristic principle of "measure for

---

[3] The book existed, in the framework of *The Testaments of the Twelve Patriarchs*, already in the beginning of the second century CE, see M. de Jonge, "Patriarchs, The Testaments of the Twelve", *ABD*, vol 5, pp. 181-186 esp. 182.

[4] The translation is according to Hollander and de Jonge, *The Testaments of the Twelve Patriarchs − A Commentary*, p. 321, and see also their notes on pp. 322-323. For a different translation, see Kee, "Testaments of the Twelve Patriarchs", in Charlesworth, *The Old Testament Pseudepigrapha*, vol. 1, p. 814.

[5] Theodor - Albeck, *Bereschit Rabba*, p. 1009.

[6] Compare Pirke de-Rabbi Eliezer 38 (Friedlander, *Pirke de Rabbi Eliezer*, p. 291); Pseudo-Jonathan on Gen 37,2 (Clark, *Targum Pseudo-Jonathan*, p. 45). For the relation between the *Testament of Gad* and Genesis Rabbah, see also Kugel, *In Potiphar's House*, pp. 80-82.

measure", for these assumed slanders altogether. Midrash Tanchuma (Buber; *Parashat Wayyesheb*, 9) states that Joseph was imprisoned for *ten years*.[7] Exodus Rabbah 7,1 adds: "on account of slandering his *ten brothers*".

In contrast to these rabbinical sources, Midrash Psalms *Shocher-Tov* neither filled in the gap of the Biblical text nor discussed the *immediate* punishment, in this world, for the spoiled son who slandered. Here Joseph's slander of his brothers is in direct opposition with Benjamin's silence later on. Benjamin was aware that "Joseph was sold into slavery (by his brethren), and did not reveal it to his father" (Midrash Psalms 15,6). The midrash praises Benjamin's loyalty to his brothers, and the verse "That has no slander upon his tongue" (Ps 15,3) is associated with him. In this way, actually, the Midrash rebuked indirectly Joseph's disloyalty to his brothers. Furthermore, it stresses that in the *long-run* Joseph's misbehavior had negative consequences.

Although, without any doubt, the rabbis knew clearly that Aaron and his descendants were appointed priests (i.e., Ex 28,1; Num 16; 17,16-26), thus excluding all the tribes, they 'played' with the idea that prior to Aaron's appointment as High Priest, a long dialog should have taken place between the Almighty and Moses concerning the matter. So, according to Rabbi Judah, "when the Holy One, blessed be He, said to Moses: 'Appoint a High Priest for Me', Moses asked God: 'From what tribe shall I appoint him?'". The Midrash suggests the names of tribes, among them Joseph, which Moses offered to God, but He refused to accept:

> When Moses asked God: 'Shall I appoint a High Priest for You out of the tribe of Joseph?' God answered, 'No! *Who slandereth his neighbor in secret, him will I destroy* (Ps 101,5). For Joseph slandered his brothers, as is said *'Joseph brought evil report of them unto their father'* (Gen 37,2)... (Midrash Psalms 101,2).[8]

---

[7] According to Gen 37,2; 41,46 Joseph was seventeen years of age when he was enslaved, and thirty years old when he was released from prison, since he spent another two years in prison after he had discovered the meaning of the chief butler's dream (Gen 41,1), and served only twelve months in the house of Potiphar (see Genesis Rabbah 86,5; Theodor – Albeck, *Bereschit Rabba*, p. 1059). Therefore, according to the rabbis, in between he wasted ten years in jail.

[8] See Buber, *Midrash Tehillim*, pp. 427-428; for the English translation

According to the rabbis, descendants of Joseph could not be appointed High Priests for their forefather had slandered! They could not represent the Israelite tribes in God's house, bless them (Num 6,23-27), and ask forgiveness on Atonement Day (Lev 16), etc., because of Joseph's slander of his brethren in the Israelites' pre-historical period. From the theological viewpoint, this Midrash indicates the existence of not only זכות אבות "ancestral merits" (which is well known from rabbinic literature) but also חובת אבות, that means, the children pay for their ancestors' transgressions: "The fathers have eaten sour grapes, and the children's teeth are set on edge" (Jer 31,28).[9] This concept is totally contradictory to the well known reward-concept of the prophets, such as: "Every one shall die for his own iniquity; every man that eats the sour grapes, his teeth shall be set on edge" (Jer 31,29); "the soul that sinneth, it shall die" (Ezek 18,4).[10]

compare Braude, *The Midrash on Psalms*, vol. II, pp. 150-151. This Midrash does not appear in the earlier sources. However, it is cited later on in Yalkut Machiri on Ps 101,4 (see S. Buber, *Yalkut Machiri zu den 150 Psalmen* [Berdyczew: Verlag von J. Scheftel, 1899], p. 122), and in Yalkut Shimeoni, 855. In the latter collection, the paragraph concerning Joseph somehow disappeared. Noteworthy to mention that the literary structure of the midrash is known also from another source in rabbinic literature: For instance, from the legend concerning the Edomites, Ishmaelites, Moabites and Ammonites who found themselves unworthy of receiving the Torah, which only the Israelites received willingly, see, for example, Targum Pseudo-Jonathan and the Fragment-Targums on Deut 33,2 (Clark, *Targum Pseudo-Jonathan*, p. 252; Klein, *The Fragment-Targums*, pp. 230-231); Mechilta de-Rabbi Ishmael, *deBachodesh, Parasha* 5 (Horovitz – Rabin, *Mechilta d'Rabbi Ismael*, p. 221); Pirke de-Rabbi Eliezer, 41 (Friedlander, *Pirke de-Rabbi Eliezer*, pp. 318-320); Pesikta Rabbati, *Piska* 21 ("Ten Commandments"); M. Friedmann (ed.), *Pesikta Rabbati* (Wien: Selbstverlag des Herausgebers, 1880), pp. 99a-b (Hebrew; for the English translation see W.G. Braude, *Pesikta Rabbati* [YJS 18; New Haven & London: Yale University Press, 1968], vol. I, pp. 416-417). For a review of several versions of the legend, and its development, see Heinemann, *Aggadah and its Development*, pp. 156-162, 194-195.

[9] Cf. Ezek 18,3; Lam 5,7; and see as well Ex 20,5b // Deut 5,9b; 2 Kgs 5, 20-27 esp. 27.

[10] See also Deut 24,16 // 2 Kgs 14,6 // 2 Chr 25,4. This doctrine is utilized clearly and almost systematically in the Book of Chronicles, see, for instance, Wellhausen, *Prolegomena zur Geschichte Israels*, pp. 195-205 (= idem, *Prolegomena to the History of Ancient Israel*, pp. 203-210); R.B. Dillard, "Reward

In spite of the sharp contrast between their own theological concept as is revealed in the Midrash Psalms, and that of at least some Scriptures (which are a fundamental part of sacred Jewish literature),[11] the rabbis did not refrain from stating that Joseph's sons were punished.

II. The Presumably Historical Context of the Midrashim

Why do these homilies condemn one of the most admirable figures in Jewish literature, and father of Ephraim and Manasseh the core tribes of northern Israel? For what reason are the rabbis so strict with Joseph, the teenage slanderer, and even declare that his descendants were punished for his slander after many generations, although it is in contrast with some Biblical verses? The question emerges particularly against the Talmudic background of the attempt "to purify" several Biblical figures from horrible transgressions. For instance, though the Scripture accuses King David of adultery with Bath-Sheba (at a time when "all Israel" was struggling in the battlefield!), and the murder of her husband (2 Sam 11,1-12,14),[12] the rabbis said: "Whoever says that David sinned is surely in error..." (Babylonian Talmud, *Shabbath* 56a).[13]

It seems that the response may lie within the historical context of these homilies. Rabbi Judah, who is mentioned in Midrash Psalms 101,2 as well as in Genesis Rabbah 84,7, is identified with Rabbi

and Punishment in Chronicles: The Theology of Immediate Retribution", *WTJ* 46 (1984), pp. 164-172.

[11] However, these contradictory concepts both are included in the same corpus, the Hebrew Bible, canonized and authorized equally! On this problematic topic, see Knierim, *The Task of Old Testament Theology*, pp. 1-5, 8-9, 52; and below, chapter seven, pp. 140-144.

[12] See also 1 Kgs 15,5b. This phrase is omitted in the parallel text, 2 Chr 13, as well as in Septuagint to the verse in 1 Kgs, most probably in defense of David. As a matter of fact, David's actions with Bath-Sheba were opposite to Joseph's behavior with Potiphar's wife (Gen 39).

[13] Similarly, "Whoever says that *Reuben* sinned [Gen 35,22] is simply mistaken... Whoever maintains that *the sons of Eli* sinned [1 Sam 2,12-17.22-25] is merely making an error... Whoever maintains that *Samuel's sons* sinned [1 Sam 8,1-5] is merely erring... Whoever says that *Solomon* sinned is simply mistaken..." (Babylonian Talmud, *Shabbath* 55b-56b); see E. Margaliot, *Those Who are Blamed in Mikra but Blameless in the Talmud and Midrashim* (London: Ararat Press, 1949), pp. 60-67 (Hebrew).

Akiva's disciple, the *Tanna* Rabbi Judah bar Elai (fourth generation of the Tannaim).[14] He lived in Eretz-Israel during the second and third quarters of the second century CE. His contemporary colleagues, Rabbi Meir and Rabbi Simeon (who is no one other then Rabbi Simeon bar Yochai, also a disciple of Rabbi Akiva), are mentioned in Genesis Rabbah 84,7.[15] Thus, if we are allowed to conclude on the basis of this evidence – and there is little reason to doubt the reliablity of it, if at all – the historical context of these midrashim probably originated from the circumstances in Judaea around the Bar-Kochba war (132-135 CE) and the decades after. That era is distinguished as one of the most difficult – politically, economically, demographically and culturally – for Jews in their land.[16] Did these rabbis' criticism of Joseph's slander and their stress that he and his descendants were punished as a result reflect their intention to deliver a message (via expounding of Torah verse) against these sorts of non-ethical actions during those days of persecutions and uneasiness?

The question of slanderers and those who talked evil behind another's back was becoming more frequent at that time. These included, certainly, some corrupt individuals who spoke ill of others for whatever reason. Thus, in the Babylonian Talmud, *Shabbath* 33b-34a, is accounted that once, at the assembly of rabbis, which included Rabbi Judah bar Elai, Rabbi Jose ben Chalafta, Judah ben Gerim, and Rabbi Simeon bar Yochai (in the immediate generation follows Rabbi Akiva), Simeon made derogatory statements against the Roman government. Judah ben Gerim informed the statements to others, and thus they became known to the authorities who condemned Rabbi Simeon to death. He escaped however by hiding in a cave for thirteen years. Though the credibility of some details in this story are questionable, one thing seems clear: Rabbi Simeon, a colleague of Rabbi Judah bar Elai, was victimized by an ill-report to the Roman authorities. Furthermore, slander is a well-known

---

[14] See M. Margaliot (ed.), *The Encyclopedia of Talmudic and Gaonic Sages* (2nd edn.; Tel Aviv: Yavneh Publishing House, 1995), vol. II, pp. 160-163. Rabbi Akiva died ca. 135 CE.

[15] Cf. also Babylonian Talmud, *Erubin* 46b: "In a dispute between Rabbi Meir and Rabbi Judah the *halacha* is in agreement with Rabbi Judah..., In a dispute between Rabbi Judah and Rabbi Simeon the *halacha* is in agreement with Rabbi Judah".

[16] See above, chapter three, pp. 73-75.

social phenomena in any society at any time and place.[17] However, despite the fact we do not know for sure who were exactly all the informers, slanderers, etc. at the times around the Bar-Kochba war, there was probably a large number of them because of their ideological – theological diversity from the main part of the nation, particularly among the heretical Jewish sects, specifically the Judeo-Christians.[18] This sect came to be a bitter enemy of the mainstream of the nation and some of them brought slanderous reports about the Jews to the Romans.

The problem of the slanderers became acute at that time because of the Roman's prohibition of several Jewish religious rituals such as circumcision, keeping Shabbath, etc.[19] Since at least the dominant group of Christians argued against the validity of circumcision, for example (Acts 15,1-29; 16,1-3; Gal 2,3; 5,2.6; 6,11-17; Rom 2,25-29; 3,1; 4,9-12; Col 2,11-12),[20] some of them possibly betrayed the Jews by telling the Romans that the law of circumcision was still being practiced in spite of the order issued against it.

The Jewish-Christians were motivated to take revenge for their neglect and isolation by the mainstream.[21] They expressed impulsively

---

[17] It is illustrated, for example, by the mosaic inscription which is located near the main entrance of En Gedi Synagogue (5th to early 7th century CE) curses (in Aramaic): "Anyone causing a controversy between a man and his friend, or whoever slanders his friend before the Gentiles [= Christian Byzantine authorities?]..." (lines 10-16 esp. 10-11). For the inscription, see L.I. Levine, "The Inscription in the 'En Gedi Synagogue", in idem (ed.), *Ancient Synagogues Revealed* (Jerusalem: Israel Exploration Society, 1981), pp. 140-145 esp. 140-141.

[18] The relations between Jews and Christians, as pointed out by Barnard, the "antagonism was most marked where Christians were of Jewish decent", see Barnard, "Judaism in Egypt", pp. 41-55 esp. 52-53. See also below concerning the *birkath ha-minim*.

[19] See, for example, Mechilta de-Rabbi Ishmael, *Jethro, Parasha* 6 (Horovitz – Rabin, *Mechilta d'Rabbi Ismael*, p. 227); Midrash Psalms 13,3 (Buber, *Midrash Tehillim*, p. 110; for the English translation, cf. Braude, *The Midrash on Psalms*, vol. I, pp. 178-179). For more references, see above, chapter three, pp. 73-74 note 44.

[20] On this issue, see in detail, above, chapter three.

[21] For the isolation of the Jewish-Christians, see, for example, Babylonian Talmud, *Shabbath* 116a, concerning the burning books of the *Minim* that one is not allowed to save from fire at Shabbath, which applies to the usage of Christian Scriptures as well, and the *Birkath ha-Minim* (see below).

their radical religious fanaticism and abhorrence towards the believers
of the "old religion"; or, to cite Barnabas (ca. 130-132 CE), the
"former people" of God (The Epistles of Barnabas 5,7; 13,1; 14,4).[22]
Through these activities they desired to curry favor with the Roman
persecutors against the "common enemy". By doing so they
attempted also to break out from the isolation in which they were.
Thus, "the words דילטורין and מוסרים (informers) became
synonymous for Christians".[23] Just about a generation prior to the
time of Rabbi Judah bar Elai, in response to the threats made upon
the Jewish community by slanderers, evil informers, specifically from
the heretics / sectarians, Rabban Gamaliel II of Jabneh / Jamnia
(second-third generations of Tannaim; ca. 85 to sometime in the first
two decades of the second century CE) searched for a volunteer who
could compose the *Birkath ha-Minim* ("the heretics' / sectarians'
benediction", euphemism for "cursing of the heretics"). His request
was fulfilled by Samuel *haQatan* ("the Lesser"), and Rabban Gamaliel
who included the new "blessing" as the twelfth in the daily prayers
of the *Amida* ("the Eighteen Benedictions").[24] One of the early

[22] On the dating of the Epistles of Barnabas, see the references in chapter
three.

[23] See I. Elbogen, *Jewish Liturgy – A Comprehensive History* (Translated by
R.P. Scheindlin based on the original 1913 German edition, and the 1972
Hebrew edition; Philadelphia/New York/Jerusalem: The Jewish Publication
Society & The Jewish Theological Seminary of America, 1993), p. 32. On the
heretics acting as slanderers, see already Manuel Joel, *Blicke in die
Religionsgeschichte zu Anfang des zweiten christlichen Jahrhunderts* (Breslau: S.
Schottländer, 1880-83), 1:32-33; 2:49-50 (this item is cited here according to
Elbogen, *ibid.*, p. 395 note 19); J. Guttmann, "Über zwei dogmengeschichtliche
Mischnastellen", *MGWJ* 42 (1898), pp. 337-345 esp. 344; W. Bacher, "Ein
polemischer Ausspruch Jose b. Chalaftha's", *ibid.*, pp. 505-507 esp. 506.

[24] See Babylonian Talmud, *Berakot* 28b-29a; *Megillah* 17b; Midrash Tanchuma
(Buber), *Parashat Wayykra*, 3 (English translation, Townsend, *Midrash Tanḥuma*,
vol. II, pp. 187-188); Maimonides, *Mishneh Torah, Hilchoth Tefillah* 2,1. "The
Minim", i.e., all different heretic groups (in this case includes specifically the
early Christians), who challenged the rabbinic doctrines. For a detailed discussion on the benediction of the *Minim*, see Elbogen, *Jewish Liturgy*, pp. 31-33,
45-46; L.H. Schiffman, *Who was a Jew? – Rabbinic and Halachic Perspectives on
the Jewish Christian Schism* (Hoboken, NJ: Ktav Publishing House, 1985), pp.
53-61; C. Thoma, *Das Messiasprojekt: Theologie Jüdisch-christlicher Begegnung*
(Augsburg: Pattloch Verlag, 1994), pp. 345-350; W. Horbury, *Jews and Christians in Contact and Controversy* (Edinburgh: T&T Clark, 1998), pp. 67-110, and

versions contained the word נצרים "Christians" next to the word *Minim* "heretics" (*hendiadys*): "May the *Christians* and the *heretics* suddenly be laid low and not be inscribed with the righteous", as appears in the Oxford manuscript of Amram Gaon and in a manuscript from the Cairo Genizah. In other versions there is also a word מלשינים "slanderers", which is comparable to מוסרים "informers", that appears repeatedly in association with *Minim*.[25] Furthermore, in several rabbinic sources מוסרות (informers) are specified alongside the "*Minim*" and משומדים ("apostates"), all who opposed theologically the mainstream of Judaism.[26] In *Seder Olam* they are listed among those who are doomed to remain in Gehenna forever (distinguished from those who remain in Gehenna for twelve months).[27]

In some Sefardic Siddurim (which by contrast to the Ashkenasic Siddurim have not been censured by Christians) the *Birkath ha-Minim* also states:

וכל אויביך וכל שׂונאיך מהרה יכרתו
ומלכות הרשׁעה מהרה תעקר ותשבר
ותכלם ותכניעם במהרה בימינו

there review of the earlier literature. For a different view see, for instance, R. Kimelman, "*Birkat Ha-Minim* and the Lack of Evidence for an Anti-Christian Jewish Prayer in Late Antiquity", in E.P. Sanders, A.I. Baumgarten & A. Mendelson (eds.), *Jewish and Christian Self-Definition*, Volume II: *Aspects of Judaism in the Graeco-Roman Period* (London: SCM Press, 1981), pp. 226-244. Kimelman concludes that only *Jews*, whether Christian or heretic, are visualized in the "blessing". See also the references to the Christian sources and the literature which were mentioned by Townsend, *ibid.*, pp. 187-188 note 11.

[25] For this and other versions of the benediction, see Elbogen, *Jewish Liturgy*, pp. 45-46, 396; Schiffman, *Who was a Jew?*, pp. 53-61.

[26] See Tosefta, *Baba Mezia* 2,33 (Zuckermandel, *Tosephta*, p. 375); Babylonian Talmud, *Avoda Zara* 26b; Avot de-Rabbi Nathan, version A, chapter 16 (Schechter, *Avot de-Rabbi Nathan*, p. 64; English translation: Goldin, *The Fathers According to Rabbi Nathan*, p. 86); *Seder Olam*, the last part of chapter 3 (B. Ratner [ed.], *Midrash Seder Olam* [New York: The Talmudical Research Institute, 1966], pp. 16-17).

[27] For detailed discussion on this source, see Ch. Milikowsky, "Gehenna and 'Sinners of Israel' in the Light of *Seder Olam*", *Tarbiz* 55 (1986), pp. 311-343 (Hebrew).

"Let all Your (= God) enemies and haters be speedily cut off, and the
dominion of wickedness do You uproot and crush, cast down and
humble speedily in our days."

Without a doubt, God's "*enemies and haters*" are references to those
slanderers, *Minim* and apostates (just mentioned previously) that informed on observant Jews who kept the commandments of God and
his Torah (such as "the covenant" of the circumcision, Shabbath,
etc.), to "*the dominion of wickedness*", that is, the Roman government.
    Are these homilies originally a part of an urgent response to
specific circumstances? Could they be considered as partial attempts
to condemn all slanderers and evil informers (while stressing that they
and their descendants will be punished) particularly during those
horrible times? It is worth to notice, that although the rabbis "puri-
fied" David from adultery and murder as referred to above, they did
not hesitate to condemn him sharply for his attitude towards the
slander related by Ziba against Mephibosheth. David accepted Ziba's
evil information against his lord, the grandson of Saul, and accordingly granted the former half the possession of the latter (2 Sam
16,1-5; 19,25-30):

> Rab Judah said in the name of Rab [first half of the third century CE]:
> If David had not accepted a slanderous report [of Ziba], the kingdom of
> the House of David would not have been divided [1 Kgs 11,29-12,25],[28]
> ... and we would not have been exiled from our land (Babylonian
> Talmud, *Shabbath* 56b).

Indeed, the rabbis were very strict towards slanderers and informers,
as emerges from several other midrashic exegeses as well. So, for
instance, the verse "Then Moses was afraid, and he said, 'Hence
surely the thing is known' " (Ex 2,14), was expounded in Exodus
Rabbah 1,30 as follows: "Moses was meditating in his heart, 'Wherein have Israel sinned that they should be enslaved more than all the
nations?' When he heard these words, he said: 'Slanderers are rife
among them, and how can they be ripe for salvation?' *Hence surely
the thing is known* – now I know the cause of their bondage".[29]

[28] See also Babylonian Talmud, *Yoma* 22b.
[29] See A. Shinan (ed.), *Midrash Shemot Rabbah Chapters I-XIV* (Jerusalem &
Tel Aviv: Dvir Publishing House, 1984), pp. 91-92 esp. 92. For the English

From this viewpoint, the homilies had indeed a long life, much more beyond the specific historical period. The rabbis condemn this kind of action at any time and in any place; those who slander inside of the Jewish community and, of course, those who relate slander against Jews to foreign rulers.

III. Conclusion

The Biblical story lacks details of the slander that Joseph brought unto Jacob concerning his brethren, and whether or not he was penalized for his misbehavior. Because of these gaps, Philo of Alexandria, Pseudo-Philo and Josephus Flavius were not provided with information required by them. These gaps are clarified, however, in the *Testament of Gad*, and later on by the rabbis of the *aggadic* Midrashim. The latter paid much closer attention to this issue and raised assumptions in several directions while showing that Joseph's slander was an absolutely non-ethical act. They determine that Joseph was punished within a short term, "measure for measure", and was imprisoned for ten years on account of slandering his ten brothers. Midrash Psalms' introduction of Joseph's slander of his brothers is in direct opposition to Benjamin's silence later on. Furthermore, it stresses that also in the long-run Joseph's misbehavior had negative consequences. God prohibits Moses to appoint a High Priest from among his descendants. In spite of the sharp contrast between their own theological concept as revealed in the Midrash Psalms, and that of at least some Scriptures in Jeremiah and Ezekiel (which are a fundamental part of sacred Jewish literature), the rabbis did not refrain from stating that Joseph's sons were punished.

One can better appreciate these homilies specifically against the historical background of the events in the Land of Israel in the second half of the first and the first half of the second centuries CE. The strict attitude of the rabbis towards Joseph's slander are reasonable in light of the dispute with the (Judeo-) Christians, and the sharp struggle against slanderers and informers, although we do not know for sure who they were.

translation cf. H. Freedman and M. Simon, *The Midrash Rabbah – Volume Two: Exodus – Leviticus* (London / Jerusalem / New York: Soncino Press, 1977), pp. 38-39. See also Midrash Tanchuma (Jelamdenu), *Parashat Shemot*, 10; Midrash Tanchuma (Buber), *Parashat Waera*, 17 (Townsend, *Midrash Tanḥuma*, vol. II, pp. 45-46); Rashi's commentary on Ex 2,14.

5

Joseph Between Potiphar and His Wife

The Biblical Text in the Light of a Comparative Study on
Early Jewish Exegesis

I. Introduction

The episode concerning Joseph and Potiphar's wife (Gen 39)[1] comprises an essential place in some Pseudepigraphical writings. In *The
Testament of Joseph* (second century BCE), for example, it is almost
the only topic discussed.[2] The theme takes an important position also
on the midrashic books of the Torah such as Genesis Rabbah,
Midrash Tanchuma (Buber as well as Jelamdenu recensions).[3] The

---

[1] Like many other Biblical figures (female and male), the author did not
reveal her personal name(s), compare, i.e., "Lot's wife" (Gen 19,26); "Manoah's
wife" (Judg 13,3.6.9 etc.), "Pharaoh's daughter" (Ex 2,5.7.8.10); "Ethiopian
woman" (Num 12,1), "the wise woman of Tekoa" (2 Sam 14,2.4.8.9 etc.),
"a wise woman" of Abel Beith-Maacah (2 Sam 20,16.17.21.22), "one who had
escaped" (Gen 14,13; cf. 1 Sam 4,12-17), "a man who gathered sticks" (Num
15,32-36), "a man came from Saul's camp" (2 Sam 1,2). Even some
Pseudepigraphical writers, Josephus and the Talmudic Sages, who usually
invented names for anonymous Biblical figures (see Kalimi, *Zur Geschichtsschreibung des Chronisten*, pp. 70-72; idem, *The Book of Chronicles: Historical Writing
and Literary Devices*, pp. 77-80), did not invent a name for her (see, e.g., *AJ*
2,41ff.). Presumably, they were of the opinion that such a wicked woman (who
was described negatively, a just antitype to Tamar and Ruth, see Genesis
Rabbah 87,4), deserved to stay anonymous forever!

[2] See Kee, *The Testaments of the Twelve Patriarchs*, in Charlesworth, *The Old
Testament Pseudepigrapha*, vol. 1, pp. 819-825; Hollander and de Jonge, *The
Testaments of the Twelve Patriarchs – A Commentary*, pp. 372-402; cf. Kugel, *In
Potiphar's House*, pp. 23-24.

[3] For the main features of Joseph's figure in the Pseudepigraphical and

current chapter concentrates particularly on passages devoted to this issue in Midrash Psalms *Shocher-Tov* comparing them with the early Jewish exegesis. The purpose is to achieve better understanding of Biblical interpretation through the generations in post-Biblical and rabbinical sources concerning this and related episodes.

II.   Did Joseph Touch Potiphar's Wife?

The ambivalent verse in Gen 39,11: "One day, when he came into the house *to do his work*, and there was not a man of the household there inside", was omitted by Philo of Alexandria from his *De Josepho* (first century CE).[4] However, later on this verse was interpreted in the Babylonian Talmud, *Sotah* 36b as following:

> Rab and Samuel [first generation of the Babylonian Amoraim]: One said that it really means *to do his work*; but the other said that he went *to satisfy his desires*.[5]

According to the latter opinion (as usual in these cases it is hard to say who said what) Joseph actually went in to lie with Potiphar's wife, but at the last minute something happened there, something that prevented him from sinning (Gen 39,12). But what happened exactly?

In Genesis Rabbah 87,11, Rabbi Samuel bar Nachman (second and third generations of the Palestinian Amoraim) explained "*And there was not a man* – on examination he [= Joseph] did not find

midrashic texts, see, for example, H.W. Hollander, *Joseph as an Ethical Model in the Testaments of the Twelve Patriarche* (SVTP 6; Leiden: E.J. Brill, 1981); Kugel, *In Potiphar's House*, pp. 11-155; M. Niehoff, *The Figure of Joseph in Post-Biblical Jewish Literature* (Leiden / New York / Köln: E.J. Brill, 1992), pp. 111-141 (the figure of Joseph in Genesis Rabbah); see also pp. 146-164 on Joseph's figure in the Targumim (= idem, "The Figure of Joseph in Targums", *JJS* 39 [1988], pp. 234-250); Hollander, "The Portrayal of Joseph in Hellenistic Jewish and Early Christian Literature", in Stone and Bergren, *Biblical Figures Outside the Bible*, pp. 237-263 esp. 239-243.

[4] For detailed discussion on Joseph in Philo's writing, see Hollander, "The Portrayal of Joseph in Hellenistic Jewish and Early Christian Literature", pp. 245-248.

[5] Compare with the parallel version in Tanchuma (Jelamdenu), *Parashat Wayyesheb*, 9.

Figure 4 Potiphar's wife attempting to seduce Joseph (Vienna Genesis, Vienna, Öster-reichische Nationalbibliothek, cod. theol. gr. 31, p. 31, 6th century)

himself a man", that is, he found himself impotent, and could not perform the sexual act.[6] Rab Huna (fourth generation of the Palestinian Amoraim) in Rabbi Mattena's name, explained that – miraculously – "his *father's* image appeared in front of him, at which his blood cooled."[7] The parallel version of this view in Babylonian

---

[6] See also Jerusalem Talmud, *Horayoth* 2,5 (46d); Targum Pseudo-Jonathan on Gen 49,24 (Clark, *Targum Pseudo-Jonathan*, p. 63). There is also another opinion, stated by Rabbi Isaac: "His seed was scattered and issued through his finger-nails".

[7] See Theodor – Albeck, *Bereschit Rabba*, pp. 1071-1073. For the English translation cf. Freedman – Simon, *The Midrash Rabbah: Genesis*, pp. 811-812

Talmud, *Sotah* 36b stresses that "his *mother's* image appeared in front of him."[8] There is also a third version of the tradition in the Jerusalem Talmud, *Horayoth* 2,5 (46d) that states Joseph saw both, his *father's* and his *mother's* images.

One can define Rab Huna's explanation either as a kind of psychological interpretation for Joseph's last minute avoidance of sin, or as a peaceful divine interference that caused him to stay away from the married woman. However, among the rabbinic sources there is also another description, an aggressive and frightening divine intervention, which has been preserved in a late aggadic Midrash, called *Avkir*, which is cited in Yalkut Shimeoni 145:

> Rabbi [= Rabbi Judah, died 219 CE] said, he [= Joseph] wanted but...;
> At the second time the Holy One, blessed be He, took a huge rock and said: 'If you [= Joseph] will touch her I will throw the rock and destroy the whole world!'

According to this tradition, Joseph had actually no other choice but not to touch his master's wife. By the exceptional power of the Almighty he was forced to stay away from her. This rabbinic view disagrees greatly with the concept of "free choice" which explicitly gives everyone the right to act as he wishes, due to his own will and decision (Deut 30,15). Moreover, from first glance, the Biblical Joseph story could be considered as a typically 'secular' narrative. The story's beginning, middle and end, are each quite naturally a continuation of the other. Altogether they form a coherently unique piece of quality prose. There is no divine interference, no miracles, angels or demonic activity.[9] To cite Claus Westermann, "Es gibt wohl keinen Teil der Bibel, der so menschlich von Gott redet wie die Joseph-Erzählung. ...was hier in einem kleinen Menschenkreis geschieht, das ist uns alles vertraut. ...das meiste, was hier erzählt wird, könnte heute ebenso oder ähnlich geschehen."[10] Within the

---

(here it appears under section 87,**7**); and cf. Pirke de-Rabbi Eliezer 38 (Higger, "Pirke Rabbi Eliezer", *Horeb* 10 [1948], p. 215; English translation: Friedlander, *Pirke de-Rabbi Eliezer*, p. 305 – note, here it appears in chapter 39).

[8] Compare Tanchuma (Jelamdenu), *Parashat Wayyesheb*, 9; Yalkut Shimeoni, 146.

[9] In the entire story only once God appeared in a short night vision and encouraged Jacob, "Fear not to go down into Egypt..." (Gen 46,2-4).

[10] See C. Westermann, *Die Joseph-Erzählung* (Calwer Taschenbibliothek 1;

whole thirteen chapters of the story, even God's name(s) is (relatively) rarely mentioned.[11]

Not so in the Midrash. Whenever it seems necessary to support their own view, the rabbis invent also divine interference as an explanation for human activity or inactivity, as the case may be.[12] Nevertheless, these divine interferences in talmudic literature are only one significant step beyond the simple statement in the Pseudepigraphical work *The Testament of Joseph* which involves God, but without mentioning any specific miracles:

> And I struggled against a shameless woman, urging me to transgress with her, but the God of Israel my father guarded me from the burning flame (2,2).[13]

In contrast to *The Testament of Joseph* and the above-mentioned midrashic traditions, Midrash Psalms *Shocher-Tov* not only avoids any negative view of Joseph at this point, but also definitely emphasizes that Joseph did not ever touch Potiphar's wife and never had even any intention to do so. He chooses, by his own free will, not to sin,

---

Stuttgart: Calwer Verlag, 1990), p. 9. This does not mean, however, that one must consider the Joseph story as a Greek novel, as some scholars did.

[11] See especially in chapter 41 (Pharaoh's dreams), verses 16. 25 // 28. 32. 38-39. 51-52 (God / *Elohim*); but also Gen 39,3.5.23 (Lord); 43,14 (*El Shaddai*); 44,16; 46,2; 50,24-25 (God). The divine plan is specified only twice, both times in Joseph's speech to his brothers. One is in Gen 45,5-9; while the other is actually a parallel repetition of the first, when Joseph reaffirms his promises to them after Jacob's death (50,19-20). This feature of the Biblical narrative to furnish the reader with a short statement indicating that God's hidden hand directs all events and human acts is also known from elsewhere (Judg 14,4; 2 Sam 17,14; 1 Kgs 12,15 // 2 Chr 10,15). Later on the concept appears also in Matt 26,24: "The Son of man goes as it is written of him, but woe to that man by whom the Son of man is betrayed".

[12] Just for instance, it is worthy to refer to the rabbinic interpretation on Gen 37,15 "And *a man* found him (= Joseph) wandering in the fields". In Tanchuma (Buber), *Parashat Wayyesheb*, 2 the rabbis identified "a *man*" with an *angel* Gabriel, to show God's guidance of Joseph. See also Rashi's commentary on the verse, and compare with that of Rabbi Abraham Ibn Ezra.

[13] Compare *The Testament of Joseph* 9,5 (Hollander and de Jonge, *The Testaments of the Twelve Patriarchs – A Commentary*, pp. 366 [see also on p. 370 ad loc.], 387; cf. Kee, "Testaments of the Twelve Patriarchs", pp. 819, 821); Jubilees 39,6.

without any kind of divine interference at all, precisely like the Biblical narrative itself:

> And... his master's wife cast her eyes upon Joseph, and said, 'Lie with me'. But *he refused...* And although she spoke to Joseph day after day, *he would not listen to her*, to lie with her or to be with her. But one day... she caught him by his garment, saying, 'lie with me'. But *he left his garment in her hand, and fled* and got out of the house (Gen 39, 7-12).

Accordingly, due to Joseph's excellent character there was no need for a metaphysical power to keep him away from the married woman. Indeed, in Midrash Psalms 81,7 it is related:[14]

> In the verse *He appointed it* (שׂמו / samo) *in* Jehoseph *for a testimony* (Ps 81,6), *al-tiqre samo, ella šemo* (שׁמו; read not 'he appointed it' but 'his name'). Jeh [which is part of Jehoseph], that is the name of the Holy One, blessed be He, testified that Joseph had not touched Potiphar's wife.[15]

In fact, while the short form of the theophoric name *Joseph* appears 206 times in the Hebrew Bible, the full one *Jehoseph* occurs only in

---

[14] See Buber, *Midrash Tehillim*, p. 368; for the English translation compare Braude, *The Midrash on Psalms*, vol. II, p. 57. For another explanation of the name *Jehoseph,* see for example, Babylonian Talmud, *Sotah* 10b.

[15] Another example, according to the Babylonian Talmud, *Sotah* 36b, "At the moment when Pharaoh said to Joseph, *And without you shall no man lift up his hand,...* (Gen 41,44) Pharaoh's *astrologers* exclaimed, 'Will you set in power over us a slave whom his master bought for twenty pieces of silver?" He replied to them, 'I discern in him royal characteristics'. They said to him, 'In that case he must be acquainted with the seventy languages'. Gabriel came and taught [Joseph] the seventy languages...", in order to prepare him to be a qualified governor of Egypt (cf. Pirke de-Rabbi Eliezar 38; Higger, "Pirke Rabbi Eliezer", *Horeb* 10 [1948], p. 215; English translation: Friedlander, *Pirke de-Rabbi Eliezer*, p. 306 – note, here it appears in chapter 39). Once again, in Midrash Psalms the rabbis refrain from introducing elements of divine interference, and prefer to interpret without miraculous elements when possible: "When Pharaoh sought to make Joseph governor, all his *legislators* protested: 'Should a slave be a ruler?' As soon as Joseph began to govern, he had the senators seized and bound and then bided his time. When his brothers came and made it known that he was of good stock, Joseph had the senators dragged about with ropes" (Midrash Psalms 105,7; Buber, *Midrash Tehillim*, p. 451; for the English translation compare Braude, *The Midrash on Psalms*, vol. II, p. 183; and cf. Babylonian Talmud, *Sotah* 13b).

Ps 81,6. Therefore, the rabbis interpreted the unusual spelling of the name, by utilizing the formula *al-tiqre … ella*, a well known rabbinic exegetical device.[16] By applying a minor change in the vocalization of the consonants שמו, the rabbis reveal a completely different interpretation, far from the simple meaning (פשׁם) of the original text.[17] This interpretation, however, is not suggested as an alternative to the simple meaning, rather as an addition to it, which generally supported some rabbis' view. What is their intention in this case?

The incident with his master's wife takes precedence in importance over all of Joseph's positive and responsible actions: wisdom in elucidating dreams, his official responsibilities as an Egyptian ruler, and the salvation of the entire population of the Land of the Nile and his own family from starvation. God himself testifies that Joseph overcame his sexual desires and refused Potiphar's wife's proposal to lie together. Already in the first century CE this merit of Joseph was used in 4 Maccabees 2,1-6 as a model for overcoming sexual passions.[18] Of course, the rabbis, as usual, attempted also to derive some moral and ethical virtues from the story. However, why does Midrash Psalms stress specifically this virtue in Joseph's biography? It is reasonable to assume that by emphasizing this point, the rabbis tried to address those who inquired concerning the reliability of the story in the Book of Genesis. Although there is no allusion to this sort of inquiry in Midrash Psalms, it occurs in another rabbinic work:

---

[16] On the use of this device in rabbinic literature, see C. McCarthy, *The Tiqqune Sopherim* (OBO 36; Freiburg/Schweiz: Universitätsverlag and Göttingen: Vandenhoeck & Ruprecht, 1981), pp. 139-166.

[17] It is the most usual sort of *al-tiqre* in the Babylonian Talmud and the midrashim. For similar examples, see McCarthy, *The Tiqqune Sopherim*, p. 141 (the example under discussion is not mentioned there). Noteworthy to mention, that in the Babylonian Talmud, *Sotah* 36b, the unusual spelling of Joseph's name is related to an aggadic interpretation: "Gabriel came and taught [Joseph] the seventy languages, but he could not learn them. Thereupon [Gabriel] added to his name a letter from the Name of the Holy One, blessed be He, and he learned [the languages] as it is said, *He appointed it in Jehoseph for a testimony* [Ps 81,6]…".

[18] It is very difficult to date precisely the composition of the 4 Maccabees. Presumably the book is, as Anderson considered, "roughly contemporaneous with the mission and letters of the Apostle Paul", see H. Anderson, "Maccabees, Books of – Fourth Maccabees", *ABD*, vol. 4, pp. 452-454 esp. 453.

Figure 5   Zulaycha (=Potiphar's wife) watching Yusuf (=Joseph) with her maidens. By 'Abd Sayyid Shams al-Din Yusuf u Zulaycha *by Jami (Sultanate India, Bengal?, 1508).*

A matron asked Rabbi Jose:[19] 'Is it possible that Joseph, at seventeen years of age, with all the hot blood of youth, could act thus?' Thereupon he produced the Book of Genesis and read the stories of Reuben [with Bilhah, Gen 35,22] and Judah [with Tamar, Gen 38]. If Scripture did not suppress aught in the case of these, who were older and in their father's home, how much more in the case of Joseph, who was younger and his own master [Had he really been guilty, Scripture would certainly not have concealed it] (Genesis Rabbah 87,10).[20]

Let us not forget that we are dealing not just with a young man, seventeen years old, with "all the hot blood of youth" and passion, but also with someone who has lived alone, far away from home, family (specifically his father), land and cultural roots. He was under intense pressure, "day after day" (Gen 39,10), with a powerful woman, a minister's wife (*ibid.*, 37,36; 39,1), who begged him repeatedly "lie with me" (*ibid.*, 39,7), and once even caught him intimately in order to impose her sexual lusts upon him (*ibid.*, 39,11-12). Thus, there is no wonder that although the rabbis did not doubt the reliability of the Holy Scripture's story, they did state that Joseph was actually saved from the transgression at the last minute, miraculously. However, there were others who questioned the credibility of the Biblical story. Presumably, against such a background Midrash Psalms states clearly, without any hesitation, that no one less than God himself testifies that Joseph without any outside interference, in spite of all the unusual circumstances, did not touch Potiphar's wife!

In the light of this statement in *Shocher-Tov*, it is quite surprising that Joseph was never called in this Midrash הצדיק, "the righteous one" (which was probably based on the uncommon conduct with his master's wife),[21] as in many other sources.[22] However, in another

---

[19] He could be identified, probably, with Rabbi Jose ben Chalaphta, the fourth generation of Tannaim (ca. mid-second century CE). There are many stories about his disputes with "a matron", see also, for instance, Tanchuma (Buber), *Parashat Mikketz*, 9.

[20] Theodor – Albeck, *Bereschit Rabba*, pp. 1070-1071; and compare to the parallel version of the story in Yalkut Shimeoni, 145. For the English translation cf. Freedman – Simon, *Midrash Rabbah: Genesis*, p. 811 (here it appears under section 87,6).

[21] See Ginzberg, *Legends of the Jews*, vol. V, p. 325; *Kugel, In Potiphar's House*, p. 25. However, in Midrash Tanchuma (Buber), *Parashat Noah*, 5,

place Midrash Psalms glorifies the extraordinary virtue of Joseph, particularly relating to his behavior in this incident.

III. Joseph's Righteousness

On his death-bed, Joseph adjured his brethren that his bones be carried up out of Egypt unto the land of Canaan (Gen 50,24-25). The Biblical story relates that Joseph's corpse was placed "in a coffin in Egypt" (Gen 50,26),[23] and later on Moses complied with the request (Ex 13,19).[24] Indeed, Midrash Psalms 15,6 praises Moses who "despised Egypt's plunder... for while all Israel were busy taking spoil, Moses was busy taking up the bones of Joseph".[25] This eulogy is based, probably, on one of the earlier rabbinic sources, such as the

another reason is given for this: "So also Joseph: Inasmuch as he fed the creatures for seven years, he was called righteous, as stated (in Amos 2,6): *because they sell a righteous one for silver.* Thus, because he fed the creatures for seven years, he was therefore called righteous". For the English translation cf. Townsend, *Midrash Tanḥuma*, vol. I, p. 35.

[22] See, for instance, in some manuscripts of Avot de-Rabbi Nathan, version B, chapter 16 (Schechter, *Avot de-Rabbi Nathan*, p. 36 note 8); Babylonian Talmud, *Kethuboth* 111a; Genesis Rabbah 93,7; Numbers Rabbah 14,6; Midrash Hagadol on Genesis 47,22; Pesikta Rabbati, at the end of *Piska* 3 (Friedmann, *Pesikta Rabbati*, p. 12). This title has been given to Joseph according to the verse "they have sold for silver a righteous man" (Amos 2,6), which was expounded by rabbis about him, see Tanchuma (Buber), *Parashat Noah*, 5 (above, note 20); Tanchuma (Jelamdenu), *Parashat Wayyesheb*, 2; Pseudo-Jonathan on Gen 37,28 (Clark, *Targum Pseudo-Jonathan*, p. 46).

[23] The author does not indicate in *which kind of coffin, where in Egypt* the corpse was put, and *why* specifically there and not elsewhere. The rabbinic Midrashim filled in these gaps. Concerning the bones of Joseph, three main types of legend survived in a variety of aggadic sources (some of them are listed above). The first type is set against an Egyptian mythological background. For the comparative analysis of this material, see Heinemann, *Aggadah and its Development*, pp. 49-56. However, Heinemann does not refer to the traditions in Midrash Psalms.

[24] This action is also alluded to in Ben-Sira 49,15. According to Josh 24,32 the Israelites buried the bones of Joseph in Shechem. The rabbis explained this as a closure of a circle: "My brothers, you have stolen me from Shechem while I was alive, I pray you, return my bones to Shechem" (Exodus Rabbah 20,19; cf. Mechilta de-Rabbi Ishmael, *Beshalach*, *Parasha* 1; Horovitz – Rabin, *Mechilta d'Rabbi Ismael*, p. 80; Babylonian Talmud, *Sotah* 13b).

[25] Buber, *Midrash Tehillim*, p. 118; Braude, *The Midrash on Psalms*, vol. I, 193.

halachic midrash, Mechilta de-Rabbi Ishmael (*Beshalach, Parasha* 1),[26] Tosefta, *Sotah* 4,7.[27] Nonetheless, in addition, *Shocher-Tov* points out that the righteousness of Joseph was the reason for the division of the Red Sea:

> *The sea saw it, and fled* (Ps 114,3)... Another explanation: The sea beheld Joseph's coffin coming down into the water. The Holy One, blessed be He, said: Let the sea flee from him who fled from transgression, he of whom it is said, *He... fled forth* (Gen 39,13). And so the sea fled from before Joseph, as is said: *The sea saw it, and fled* (Midrash Psalms 114,9).[28]

Glorified here by the rabbis the unusual righteousness of Joseph, shows that it contained an extraordinary potential, which could cause even change in nature's order, a great miracle. This specific aggadic feature of the midrash is well known also from other rabbinic sources, for instance Targum Ruth 1,6; 3,7.8.[29]

IV. Mete out Evil unto Wickedness: Potiphar's Punishment

As soon as Joseph's master heard his wife saying, "after this manner did your servant to me", his wrath was kindled (Gen 39,19-20). He believed without hesitation her false allegations that Joseph had tried to rape her.[30] Potiphar did not bother even to hear the version of

---

[26] See Horovitz − Rabin, *Mechilta d'Rabbi Ismael*, pp. 78-79.

[27] See Zuckermandel, *Tosephta*, pp. 299-300; S. Lieberman, *Tosefta Ki-Feshutah − A Comprehensive Commentary on the Tosefta* (New York: The Jewish Theological Seminary of America, 1973), Part VIII, pp. 647-651. See as well their parallels in later collections like Babylonian Talmud, *Sotah* 13a; Exodus Rabbah 20,19.

[28] Buber, *Midrash Tehillim*, p. 475; Braude, *The Midrash on Psalms*, vol. II, pp. 221-222 esp. 221.

[29] On this source, see Y. Komlosh, *The Bible in the Light of the Aramaic Translations* (Tel Aviv: Bar Ilan University Press & Dvir, 1973), p. 84 and the earlier bibliography which was cited there in note 74 (Hebrew). For the English translation of the Targum, see D.R.G. Beattie, *The Targum of Ruth* (The Aramaic Bible 19; Edinburgh: T&T Clark, 1994), pp. 18, 26-27.

[30] On this point, see especially Genesis Rabbah 87,19: "*And it came to pass, when his master heard, etc.* Rabbi Abbahu said: This happened during cohabitation" (Theodor − Albeck, *Bereschit Rabba*, p. 1074; Freedman − Simon, *The Midrash Rabbah: Genesis*, p. 812). Cf. the Rashi's commentary on Gen 39,19:

his loyal slave, nor attempt to investigate the accusations, and handle them in a judicial manner. He immediately punished the unprotected servant by sending him to prison.[31] Because of Potiphar's irresponsible behavior, the innocent Joseph was jailed several years. By contrast to the Egyptian story of the Two Brothers which recounts that Anpu's wife was punished, there is no allusion in the Hebrew Bible if, when, and how Potiphar was penalized for this.

The Sages could not tolerate this injustice in the world of a just God. Accordingly, they attempted to 'correct' the story as much as possible. Some of them claimed that Potiphar actually did not believe his wife's accusations, for if he really did, he would have certainly executed Joseph.[32] They state that Potiphar clarified to Joseph:

> I know that you are innocent, but I have to do this lest a stigma fall upon my children (as the children of a prostitute, if I do not pretend to believe her) (Genesis Rabbah 87,9).[33]

"She said this when he was alone with her, caressing her. This is what she meant by '*things like these did your servant do to me*' – caresses such as these." See, however, Nachmanides' critical view on these opinions, in his commentary on the same verse.

[31] From a literary-topological viewpoint only, it is noteworthy to compare this phenomenon with that in the Egyptian folktale of the Two Brothers, "Anpu and Bata" (ca. 14th century BCE), see J.A. Wilson, in J.B. Pritchard (ed.), *Ancient Near East Texts Related to the Old Testament* (= *ANET*; 3rd edn.; Princeton: Princeton University Press, 1969), pp. 23-25; Y.M. Grintz, *From the Ancient Egyptian Literature* (Jerusalem: Bialik Institute, 1975), pp. 59-63 (Hebrew); M. Lichtheim, *Ancient Egyptian Literature – A Book of Readings,* Vol. II: *The New Kingdom* (Berkeley / Los Angeles / London: University of California Press, 1976), pp. 203-211. For occurrence of the essential lines of the story in world literature, see J.D. Yohannan (ed.), *Joseph and Potiphar's Wife in World Literature* (New York: A New Directions Book, 1968). Yohannan is concerned more with similarities and differences among the tales than with their possibly historical association. Indeed, it is reasonable to say, that "some stories resemble each other *because* they were diffused from a common source, and others *despite* the fact that they were independently created" (*ibid.*, p. 2).

[32] According to Pseudo-Jonathan on Gen 39,20 (Clark, *Targum Pseudo-Jonathan,* p. 49), Potiphar even investigated some of the accusations against Joseph and found them false, and that's why he avoided killing him. Compare, however, the same Targum on Gen 47,22 (Clark, *ibid.*, p. 60) which reveals an opposite opinion.

[33] Theodor – Albeck, *Bereschit Rabba,* pp. 1074-1075; for the English

Presumably, Potiphar's justification was unacceptable to the rabbis of Midrash Psalms 105,7. They interpreted Ps 105,22: "*To bind his minister(s)* – to bind Potiphar, as Rabbi Meir[34] taught: This verse proves that Pharaoh kept Potiphar bound up in chains all his life; though it is written שָׂרוֹ "*his minister*", it is pronounced שָׂרָיו "*his ministers*".[35]

V.   How Long was Joseph Imprisoned?

The great hate of the brethren towards Joseph caused him to be moved from the safety of his home to being enslaved in a foreign land. Here, the great "love" of Potiphar's wife towards him, and his refusal to satisfy her desire and passion led him to jail. He was falsely accused by her, and was imprisoned by his master (Gen 39,6b-20). The Biblical narrative does not account for the number of years that he was forced to waste in jail. Midrash Tanchuma (Buber; *Parashat Wayyesheb*, 9) expresses that Joseph should have been imprisoned for *ten* years.[36] Exodus Rabbah (7,1) appends: "on account of slandering his *ten* brothers". Obviously, the rabbis attempted here to justify, theologically, and explain why the innocent Joseph should spend such a long time in prison, instead of being rewarded for his refusal to sin.

Several rabbinic sources (Genesis Rabbah 89,3,[37] Exodus Rabbah 7,1, Pseudo-Jonathan, the Fragment-Targums on Gen 40,23, and Midrash Psalms) stress that Joseph's term of imprisonment was extended two years from that originally planned by the Almighty. The explanation for this is that he placed his hope and trust, to be released from prison, in a mortal (the Pharaoh's chief butler) rather than in God:

---

translation cf. Freedman – Simon, *Midrash Rabbah: Genesis,* p. 812. Theodor – Albeck (*ibid.*, p. 1075 on the notes apparatus) quote another version as well: "If I will not believe her, there will be a quarrel between us".

[34] He was from the fourth generation of the Tannaim (ca. mid-second century CE). However, in manuscript no. 6 of the Midrash appears the name: "R. Iddi", which was the name of several *Amoraim.*

[35] See Buber, *Midrash Tehillim*, p. 451; Braude, *The Midrash on Psalms*, vol. II, p. 183. Compare Rashi's commentary on Ps 105,22.

[36] For the rabbinical calculation of Joseph's term of slavery, see above, chapter four, p. 79 note 7.

[37] See Theodor – Albeck, *Bereschit Rabba*, pp. 1088-1089.

For after Joseph said to the chief of the butlers: *Have me in your remembrance when it shall be well with you... and make mention of me unto Pharaoh*
(Gen 40,14), the Holy One, blessed be He, said to Joseph: For having
spoken thus, as you live, you will spend two years longer in prison, as
is said *And it came to pass at the end of two full years* (Gen 41,1). Hence
Until the time that his word came to pass (Midrash Psalms 105,6).[38]

As alluded to in the Fragment-Targums, the core of this explanation
was based, probably, on the concept stated in Jer 17,5-8: "Cursed
is the man that trusts in man, and makes flesh his arm... Blessed is
the man who trusts in the Lord, and whose trust the Lord is...".[39]
However, it seems that the rabbis could provide another interpretation for the span of two years in which Joseph had been totally
forgotten by the chief butler, and remained in jail. They could
interpret it as a part of God's comprehensive plan: If Joseph was
mentioned earlier and released from prison before the Pharaoh's
parallel dreams, he may have gone (or been re-sold by Potiphar)
elsewhere, and would not have been available to elucidate the royal
dreams, and thus would never have been appointed governor![40]
Presumably, the rabbis chose to interpret it as they did, because it
corresponds to their actualization of the Holy Scripture. Through
their interpretation of the ancient text, they attempted also to relay
a theological message to a contemporary audience, who lived in
problematic circumstances under foreign rulers: Do not put your trust
and hopes in princes and kings but in God himself only, then the
redemption will come on time.[41] Consequently, they tried to avoid
many disappointments in exile.

The punishment was appropriate, once again, "measure for measure": Through his trust in a mortal man, Joseph used *twice* the root
זכ"ר (זכרתני... והזכרתני) "have me in your remembrance... and

---

[38] See Buber, *Midrash Tehillim*, p. 451; Braude, *The Midrash on Psalms*, vol.
II, pp. 182-183; see also Clark, *Targum Pseudo-Jonathan*, p. 50; Klein, *The
Fragment-Targums*, p. 62.

[39] Cf. this concept with that in 2 Chr 16,12 (an 'addition' to 1 Kgs 15,23).

[40] For such an explanation, compare A.B. Ehrlich, *Mikrâ ki-Pheschutô*, vol.
I: *Divre Tora* (Berlin: M. Poppelauer's Buchhandlung, 1899; reprinted: Library
of Biblical Studies; New York: Ktav Publishing House, 1969), p. 110 (Hebrew).

[41] For such a plausible actualization, cf. J. Bowker, *The Targums and Rabbinic
Literature* (Cambridge: Cambridge University Press, 1969), p. 251.

make mention of me"), accordingly he was punished for *two* more years in prison. By the utilization of this judicial principle, the rabbis tried repeatedly to demonstrate the integrity and accuracy of heavenly judgment.

VI. When was Joseph Liberated From Jail?

The Biblical narrative accounts that Joseph was released from prison at the end of two full years (Gen 41,1ff.), but does not furnish us with any information concerning the precise date on which Joseph was freed. Once more, the rabbis filled in this gap:

> The end of the verse, *When he went out through the land of Egypt* (Ps 81,6b), implies, so our masters taught, that on *Rosh-Hashanah* (= New Year's Day), Joseph left his prison, for the next verse (*ibid.*, 7) reads: *I removed his shoulder from under the burden* (Midrash Psalms 81,7).[42]

Indeed, one can include this midrash as an example of the rabbis' custom to ascribe several 'historical events' to a known Jewish Holiday/Feast.[43] As a matter of fact, this admission appears among other 'events' which were enumerated by the *beraita* which is cited in the Babylonian Talmud, *Rosh-Hashanah* 10b-11a:

> It has been taught: R. Eliezer[44] says: In Tishri the world was created; in Tishri Patriarchs were born; in Tishri the Patriarchs died; on Passover Isaac was born; on New Year Sarah, Rachel and Hannah were visited (נפקדו); on New Year Joseph went forth from prison; on New Year bondage of our ancestors in Egypt ceased; ....[45]

The date of Joseph's release from prison on the New Year, has dual importance. It shows not only the notability of the holiday on which such a personality was released; but also the significance of the figure

---

[42] Buber, *Midrash Tehillim*, p. 368; Braude, *The Midrash on Psalms*, vol. II, p. 57.

[43] See I. Heinemann, *The Methods of the Aggadah* (2nd edn.; Jerusalem: Magnes Press & Massadah, 1974), pp. 31-32 (Hebrew).

[44] Probably, he was Eliezer ben Horkenos, from the second generation of the Tannaim, about the second half of the first century.

[45] The *Gemara* continues and cites also R. Joshua's opinion on this issue, who states, *inter alia*, that "on New Year Joseph went forth from prison".

itself: Joseph's freedom was regained on one of the major Jewish high-holidays. Symbolically, he opened a new page in his life precisely at the beginning of the New Year.

VII. Conclusion

Midrash Psalms *Shocher-Tov* avoids any negative view towards Joseph in the episode of Potiphar's wife. It rejects possible doubts about the reliability of the Biblical story, and emphasizes that God himself testifies that Joseph did not touch her. He was loyal to his master all the way. Due to Joseph's fine moral character there was no need for interference of divine forces to keep him away from Potiphar's wife. The midrash has derived some ethical virtues from glorification of the uncommon righteousness of Joseph in this incident, and points it out as the reason for the division of the Red Sea. By contrast, Joseph was imprisoned ten years for slandering his brethren, and his term of imprisonment was extended two years from that originally planned by the Almighty, because he placed his hope and trust to be released from prison, in a mortal rather than in God. Joseph was released from prison on New Year's day, a sign of his notability. The Sages of Midrash Psalms presented Joseph as a perfect man physically,[46] morally, socially and religiously; as a model for one of the finest personalities of all generations. However, they did not refrain from criticizing some of Joseph's behavior. They considered him like many other Biblical figures, that is, after all he was a human being, and as such was not excluded from the framework of the concept: "Surely there is not a righteous man on earth who does good and never sins" (Eccl 7,20).[47]

---

[46] See above, chapter three, pp. 61-65.
[47] Similarly in the prayer of Solomon, 1 Kgs 8,46b // 2 Chr 6,36b.

III

Biblical Theology, Judaism and Christianity

6

History of Israelite Religion or Hebrew Bible / Old Testament Theology? Jewish Interest in Biblical Theology

I. History of Israelite Religion or Hebrew Bible / Old Testament Theology?

The presentation of the subject under discussion, as indicated by a question mark[1] suggests the option of choosing one subject over another. Choosing one subject automatically rejects the other. It is misleading to assume that there is a choice. These are two different aspects of the same literary corpus – Hebrew Bible / Old Testament. In other words, the "History of Israelite Religion" and the "Hebrew Bible / Old Testament Theology" are incompatible. It is not a case of choosing between them. They are two different and independent branches of Biblical studies. Each one has a unique function and accordingly has independent, legitimate merit:

The one deals with the history of the Israelite religion on many levels and through many changes during the passage of generations in the Biblical era. Such research is similar to any historical research of any other religion in the ancient period. Research in this field is diachronic and is done with philological and historical critical tools, in comparison with other religions in general, and with those of the ancient Near East in particular. According to its nature this research should strive to reach as much objectivity as possible.

The other, "Hebrew Bible / Old Testament Theology", is a close study of the different religious messages in their entirety. It unfolds before us the meaningful, social and human values of the Bible, by

---

[1] So the subject has been offered, at the special symposium of the SBL International Conference, Leuven, August 8, 1994.

applying the achievements of textual, linguistic, literary and exegetical methods in addition to various findings from other disciplines. In essence, "Hebrew Bible / Old Testament Theology" is synchronic, ahistorical and from time to time even subjective. So the differences between one theologian and another, certainly between Christian Biblical theologians and Jewish Biblical theologians, are more pronounced than the differences among historians.

At different times and in different places scholars have supported the distinction between these two areas of research. Already in the first quarter of the twentieth century, Otto Eißfeldt attempted to separate the two. He stated the case as follows:

> Zwei Auffassungen stehen sich da gegenüber. Die eine, die historische oder religionswissenschaftliche, fordert, dass die Religion des AT mit denselben Mitteln erforscht werde, mit denen sonst die Geschichtswissenschaft arbeitet: sprachliche und historisch-kritische Durchdringung der Quellen und Darstellung ihres Inhalts auf Grund persönlich-nacherlebenden Sich-Einfühlens in ihn. Die Wertung der Religion des AT aber und vollends die Frage nach ihrer Wahrheit erklärt diese Auffassung als Sache der persönlichen Überzeugung, vor der die Wissenschaft halt mache. Die andere Auffassung, die theologische (im engeren Sinne des Wortes) oder kirchliche, behauptet demgegenüber, dass die Erkenntnis des eigentlichen Wesens der Religion des AT bei blosser Anwendung der sonst üblichen historischen Forschungsmethoden unmöglich sei. Es erschliesse sich vielmehr nur dem Glauben, und der sei etwas anderes als nacherlebendes Sich-Einfühlen, nämlich ein Überwältigt- und Gebeugt-Werden und innerer Gehorsam gegen das, was einen ergriffen habe.[2]

An additional attempt to distinguish between these two areas of research was made by Moshe H. Goshen-Gottstein some years ago:[3]

---

[2] See O. Eißfeldt, "Israelitisch-jüdische Religionsgeschichte und alttestamentliche Theologie", *ZAW* 41 (1926), pp. 1-12 esp. 1-2 (= idem, *Kleine Schriften*, herausgegeben von R. Sellheim und F. Maass, vol. I, Tübingen: J.C.B. Mohr [Paul Siebeck], 1962, 105-114 esp. 105-106).

[3] See M.H. Goshen-Gottstein, "Jewish Biblical Theology and the Study of Biblical Religion", *Tarbiz* 50 (1980/81), pp. 37-52 (Hebrew). This is the main paper of Goshen-Gottstein on the subject; for a shortened version of it, see "Tanakh Theology: The Religion of the Old Testament and the Place of Jewish Biblical Theology", in P.D. Miller, Jr., P.D. Hanson, and S.D. McBride

חוקר דת מחוייב כלפי נושאו באותה מידה של אובייקטיביות המקובלת
בתחום המקצועות ההיסטוריים הפילוסופיים... אמות מידותיו שלו אל לחן
להיות מושפעות... אין לבוא אל מי שתחום התמחותו דת התנ"ך אלא
בדרישות מקצועיות של מידע ומיומנות... אולם כל זה רחוק מאמונה
מהזדהות מהודיה בערכיות או משמעותיות זו או זו מנקיטת עמדה אישית
בהווה היונקת ממש מאותו מעיין שממנו נבעו תורות העבר...

> A scholar who deals with religion is obliged to treat his subject in the same 'objective way' that is applied in historical-philosophical fields... his criteria should not be affected [by any bias]. ...we cannot demand from a TaNaK religious scholar anything less than knowledge and expertise... however, all this is far from belief, from identification and from admission of value and meaning of this or that; from taking up a personal stand in the present, which was absorbed from the same fountain that flowed the teachings of the past...[4]

It is worth noting that Eißfeldt's essay[5] on the one hand, and Goshen-Gottstein's essay on the other, were written in different research situations: Eißfeldt wrote at a time when "Hebrew Bible / Old Testament Theology" research actually lost its identity and aimed in favor of the "History of Israelite Religion". Only one year before Eißfeldt's essay was published, Carl Steuernagel stressed this point clearly: "Wenn es damals notwendig war, die biblische Theologie aus den Fesseln der Dogmatik zu befreien, so gilt es heute, wie mir scheint, die alttestamentliche Theologie von den Fesseln der alttestamentlichen Religionsgeschichte zu befreien, in denen sie völlig zu verkümmern Gefahr läuft".[6]

Goshen-Gottstein's essay was written at a time when little attention was directed towards 'Hebrew Bible Theology', instead attention was focused on the 'History of Israelite Religion' among Jewish-Israeli Biblical scholars.

(eds.), *Ancient Israelite Religion - Essays in Honor of Frank Moore Cross* (Philadelphia: Fortress, 1987), pp. 617-644.

[4] Goshen-Gottstein, "Jewish Biblical Theology", p. 45.

[5] See also, C. Steuernagel, "Alttestamentliche Theologie und alttestamentliche Religionsgeschichte", in K. Budde (ed.), *Vom Alten Testament – Festschrift Karl Marti* (BZAW 41; Gießen: Verlag Alfred Töpelmann, 1925), pp. 266-273 esp. 266.

[6] Steuernagel, "Alttestamentliche Theologie", p. 266.

All in all, it is apparent that both branches have equal merit. Both are essential in themselves. The choice of the researcher to deal with the "History of Israelite Religion" or "Hebrew Bible / Old Testament Theology" is legitimate and dependent on personal preference.

II. Biblical Theological Study

Some scholars tend to reject Biblical theological study absolutely.[7] They are incorrect. In the following paragraphs I will attempt to clarify my position, while distinguishing three types of theology:

1. The Theology of the Biblical Authors and Editors

(1) There is a consensus in Biblical scholarship that the Torah is composed of a number of sources (e.g., J,E,D,P). The author / editor of each of these sources is guided most probably by his own theological principles. The author/editor of one of the sources, for instance, excluded ספר מלחמת יהוה "the book of the wars of JHWH" (Num 21,14).[8] However, the sources of the Torah came from different times of the Biblical period. It is reasonable to assume that the final editor of the Torah assembled and included only certain sources and excluded others.[9] This final editor certainly based his work along some theological lines.

---

[7] See, for example, R. Albertz, "Religionsgeschichte Israels statt Theologie des Alten Testaments!", *JBTh* 10 (1995), pp. 3-24 (paper delivered at the SBL International Conference, Münster, July 28, 1993); cf. also his book, *Religionsgeschichte Israels in alttestamentlicher Zeit* (ATDER 8,1; Göttingen: Vandenhoeck & Ruprecht, 1992), vol. I, pp. 37-38 (English version, idem, *A History of Israelite Religion in the Old Testament Period, Volume I: From the Beginning to the End of the Monarchy* [OTL; Louisville, KY: Westminster / John Knox, 1994] pp. 16-17); P.R. Davies, Review of H.D. Preuss [sic!], *Theologie des Alten Testaments. I. JHWHs erwählendes und verpflichtendes Handeln* (Stuttgart / Berlin / Köln: W. Kohlhammer, 1991), *JSOT* 59 (1993), p. 122: "But whose is this 'Old Testament Theology' anyway? No human has ever actually expressed or believed it... so what is it for?"; J.J. Collins, "Historical Criticism and the State of Biblical Theology", *Christian Century* (July 28 – August 4, 1993), pp. 743-747.

[8] Cf. also ספר הישר which is mentioned in Josh 10,13; 2 Sam 1,18, and in the Greek version of 1 Kgs 8,13.

[9] Although ספר מלחמת יהוה is not a source like J,E,D,P etc., it may support my viewpoint.

(2) The Book of Psalms is a collection of poems composed by a variety of poets in different eras. The final composition included only 150 psalms and excluded others. For example, an extra Psalm is found in the Septuagint and in the Scroll of Qumran Cave 11 (11QPs[a]). In addition, the Scroll of Qumran contains six other poetical compositions not found in the Psalter.[10] Certainly the editor(s) of the Book of Psalms acted according to theological guidelines. Since the Biblical writers/editors themselves used theological criteria, it can not be invalid for the modern researcher to investigate sections of the Bible for the purpose of uncovering theological principles.

2. The Theology of the Canonists

The Biblical corpus is an anthology of ancient Israelite literature written and formed during hundreds of years. Books included in the canon were chosen strictly from a larger selection. The selection was probably formulated according to certain criteria, certainly including proper theological views. Conflicting opinions on the composition of the Hebrew Canon are reflected in many sources in Rabbinic Literature. They testify the difficulties that the canonists encountered in deciding what to include in the Holy Scriptures and what to exclude. The decisions were probably made on the basis of strict theological lines. For example, the story on Hananiah son of Hezekiah, bears witness to the fact of these struggles:

אמר רב יהודה אמר רב ברם זכור אותו האיש לטוב וחנניה בן
חזקיה שמו שאלמלא הוא נגנז ספר יחזקאל שהיו דבריו סותרין דברי
תורה. מה עשה העלו לו שלש מאות גרבי שמן וישב בעלייה ודרשן

> Rab Judah said in Rab's name: In truth, that man, Hananiah son of Hezekiah by name, is to be remembered for blessing (lit. 'for good'): but for him, the Book of Ezekiel would have been hidden (the technical term for exclusion from the Canon), for its words contradicted the Torah.[11] What did he do? Three hundred barrels of oil were taken up

---

[10] They appear neither in the Hebrew Bible nor in the Septuagint; see J.A. Sanders, *The Psalms Scroll of Qumran Cave 11* (ASOR, Discoveries in the Judaean Desert of Jordan, IV; Oxford: Clarendon, 1965), pp. 53-93.

[11] Compare, for example, Ezek 18,20 with Lev 26,39-40; Ezek 44,22 with Lev 21,7; Ezek 44,31 with Lev 11,23-25.39-40.

to him and he sat in an upper chamber and reconciled (lit. 'expounded')
them.[12]

Also books like Proverbs, Qoheleth and the Song of Songs were in
question.[13] The theological-canonical criteria for including and for
excluding various books were sharply drawn. This sharpness can be
seen in the theological principles of the Mishnah, *Sanhedrin* 10,1:

ואלו שאין להם חלק לעולם הבא
האומר אין תחיית המתים מן התורה[14] ואין תורה מן השמים ואפיקורוס
רבי עקיבא אומר אף הקורא בספרים החיצוניים

And these are they that have no share in the world to come: he that says
that there is no resurrection of the dead prescribed in the Torah, and [he
that says] that the Torah is not from Heaven, and an Epicurean. Rabbi

---

[12] See Babylonian Talmud, *Shabbath* 13b; For English translation, see H.
Freedman, *Shabbath – Translated into English with Notes, Glossary and Indices*
(London: Soncino Press, 1938), vol. I, p. 55. See also *Menahoth* 45a. For
another story regarding the book of Ezekiel, see Babylonian Talmud, *Hagigah*
13a. Unfortunately, the reconciliation of Hananiah son of Hezekiah has been
lost.

[13] See Babylonian Talmud, *Shabbath* 30b: "Rab Judah son of Rabbi Samuel
ben Shilath said in Rab's name: The Sages wished to hide the Book of
Ecclesiastes, because its words are self-contradictory; yet why did they not hide
it? Because its beginning is religious teaching (literally: 'words of the Torah')
and its end is religious teaching". The same source tells also that the Sages
wanted to hide the Book of Proverbs "because its statements are self-contradictory". Also, in Avot de-Rabbi Nathan, version A, chapter 1: "Abba Saul says:
It does not mean that they took their time, but that they interpreted. Originally, it is said, (literally: 'originally they used to say'), Proverbs, the Song of
Songs, and Ecclesiastes were suppressed; for since they were held to be mere
parables and not part of the Holy Writings, (the religious authorities) arose and
suppressed them; (and so they remained) until the men of Hezekiah came and
interpreted them" (see Schechter, *Avot de-Rabbi Nathan*, p. 2; for the English
translation, cf. Goldin, *The Fathers According to Rabbi Nathan*, p. 5, for the
erroneous version, "Men of the Great Assembly" instead of "men of Hezekiah", see p. 176 note 22).

[14] Some manuscripts do not have the words מן תורה "prescribed in the
Torah", cf. Danby, *The Mishnah*, p. 397 note 3; Ch. Albeck, *The Mishnah, Vol.
IV – Seder Nezikin* (Jerusalem: Bialik Institute / Tel Aviv: Dvir, 1953), p. 102
(Hebrew).

Akiva says: Also he that reads the external books (i.e. books excluded from the canon of Hebrew Bible – Apocrypha).[15]

Moreover, there are differences within the scope of the book lists between the Hebrew Canon and the Greek Canon.[16] It seems that they both exemplify the theological differences and emphasize the standards the canonists applied in choosing the books. Therefore, it is essential to discover the theological lines which guided the canonists.

3. Biblical Theology

There is nothing wrong in dealing with Biblical theological research. On the contrary, it is necessary to know what the theological lines are that control the Biblical corpus. It is essential to read the Bible for its religious messages and for the moral promotion of humanity. It is important to discover the values of the Scriptures for our generation, since each generation has its own unique values, interpretations and theologies. By no means can research on 'History of Israelite Religion' replace 'Biblical Theology' research, nor can the latter replace the former.

Here I would like to point out that the theologian is not allowed to impose a single idea, concept or thought on the whole Bible. In contrast to the New Testament, except for the idea of monotheism, the Hebrew Bible does not have one unique theme – "die Mitte". As an anthology which was composed over hundreds of years, in different eras and places, under a variety of circumstances, by a variety of authors and schools, in numerous literary genres, it seems that the Hebrew Bible contains several theologies, and, therefore, also several different themes. Other than the concept of monotheism, there is nothing in common, for instance, between the Book of Leviticus and the Book of Proverbs. Thus, it is impossible to do what some Christian theologians try to do when they are looking for – or imposing – one single thought, concept or idea on the entire Bible, for example, "covenant" or "covenant formula", "Is-

---

[15] For the English edition, see Danby, *The Mishnah*, p. 397. It is also worth mentioning the Midrash on Ecclesiastes 12,12: "The more than 24 books, the more turmoil is brought into ones own house" (Qoheleth Rabbah 12, 12-13).

[16] In addition to the 24 Hebrew Bible books, the Septuagint also contains books that are not included in the Hebrew Canon, such as Baruch, Epistle of Jeremiah, Prayer of Manasseh, Wisdom of Solomon, Tobit, Judith, the additions to the Book of Daniel, and others.

rael", "Promise", "the idea of the holiness of God", "that God is
the Lord who commands", "God is the Lord who imposes his will",
the "Kingdom of God," etc.,[17] or even a single Biblical book, such
as "Das Deuteronomium".[18] The existence of so many proposals
suggestive in Biblical theological scholarship for such a central theme,
and the weakness of each, strengthen my viewpoint.

III.   Biblical Theology, Judaism and Christianity

Biblical theological research is at home with a variety of religions.
It may be a form either of Judaism or of Christianity.[19] As a branch
of university learning, however, it is not obligatory and certainly
does not have to be so. It can and must deal − as objectively as
possible − with secular, academic-intellectual viewpoints. Then the
synagogue as well as the church can apply the results of such research as they see fit. The object of such research is theology or
several forms of theology, but the research itself is not theological
in nature; in other words, it is not religious or denominational.
From all sides, there are two things that are not allowed − or even
forbidden − in theological research:

1. There is nothing vague in the difference between "Old Testament theology" and the "History of Israelite Religion". These are
two distinct legitimate demarcations. Deep differences exist between
them, differences that can never overlap. To confuse the demarcation

[17] For a survey and full references on these and other suggestions, see H.G.
Reventlow, *Problems of Old Testament Theology in the Twentieth Century* (Philadelphia: Fortress, 1985), pp. 125-133.
[18] See S. Herrmann, "Das konstruktive Restauration − Das Deuteronomium
als Mitte biblischer Theologie", *Gesammelte Studien zur Geschichte und Theologie
des Alten Testaments* (München: Chr. Kaiser, 1986), pp. 163-178.
[19] See for example, the studies done by Childs and Levenson: B.S. Childs,
*Biblical Theology of the Old and New Testament: Theological Reflection on the
Christian Bible* (Minneapolis, MN: Fortress, 1993); J.D. Levenson, *Sinai & Zion
− An Entry into the Jewish Bible* (San Francisco: Harper & Row, 1985); idem,
*The Hebrew Bible, The Old Testament and Historical Criticism: Jews and Christians
in Biblical Studies* (Louisville, KY: Westminster / John Knox, 1993). The latter
study by Levenson is actually not a methodical theology but a collection of
articles. The theological principles that he outlines result somewhat from his
polemic with other scholars.

is like mixing different views that require different disciplinary methods.[20]

2. Christian theologians concentrate generally on the "Old Testament" from the Christian-Christological view. They are combining both testaments, and moving from the "Old" to the "New" and back from the "New" to the "Old". To cite Otto Procksch "Alle Theologie ist Christologie"![21] They have, as Brevard S. Childs stated, the "fundamental goal to understand the various voices within the whole Christian Bible, New and Old Testament alike, as a witness to the one Lord Jesus Christ, the selfsame divine reality".[22] In another place Childs states that "Jesus Christ, God's true man, who is testified to in both testaments, is the ultimate criterion of truth for both testaments".[23] It seems, however, that each of these corpora – Hebrew Bible / Old Testament as well as New Testament – should be studied and researched first and foremost independently, each for its own merits and values.[24] Moreover, it goes without saying, in this way that the Christian theologian does not leave room for joint work with his Jewish colleague (contrary to the study of "History of Israelite Religion", where there is ample space for joint production). In any case, even if there is a combination of the two testaments, it should be understood that the Christian theologians may not introduce anti-Semitic and anti-Jewish theology; the defining of Christianity through the negation of Judaism; portraying the Jewish people in an unfavorable light to show the superiority of the Christian faith, as has been done many times.[25] Christian theologians must

---

[20] On the perils of confusing the demarcations, see Steuernagel, "Alttestamentliche Theologie", pp. 266-273; Eißfeldt, "Religionsgeschichte," pp. 1-12 (= idem, *Kleine Schriften*, vol. I, pp. 105-114); Goshen-Gottstein, "Jewish Biblical Theology", pp. 39-45.

[21] See O. Procksch, *Theologie des Alten Testaments* (Gütersloh: C. Bertelsmann Verlag, 1950), p. 1.

[22] See Childs, *Biblical Theology of the Old and New Testament*, p. 85, see also p. 452, and compare already Procksch, *Theologie des Alten Testaments,* p. 7.

[23] See Childs, *Biblical Theology of the Old and New Testament*, p. 591.

[24] On this issue see in detail, below, chapter seven, pp. 144-149.

[25] On the anti-Semitism in Christian theology, see G.F. Moore, "Christian Writers on Judaism," *HTR* 14 (1921) 191-254; M. Schmaus, *Der Glaube der Kirche* (München: Max Hueber Verlag, 1969) vol. I, pp. 508-509; Ch. Klein, *Theologie und Anti-Judaismus* (München: Chr. Kaiser, 1975); English version with "A Short Survey of Anglo-American Authors": idem, *Anti-Judaism in Christian*

try to neutralize all the anti-Jewish statements and all the negative images and stereotypes that are associated with Judaism and the Jewish people, particularly in the New Testament (e.g. Matt 27,12-23.25.28-31.38-41; John 8,37-50; 19,6.12-16; Act 2,36; 3,13-15; 1 Thess 2,14-16),[26] and in Christian theological literature in general.[27]

Theology (London: SPCK / Philadelphia: Fortress, 1978); R.R. Ruether, *Faith and Fratricide: The Theological Roots of Anti-Semitism* (New York: Seabury, 1974), pp. 64-261, 267-285; R. Rendtorff, "Die Hebräische Bibel als Grundlage christlisch-theologischer Aussagen über das Judentum", in M. Stöhr (ed.), *Jüdische Existenz und die Erneuerung der christlichen Theologie* (München: Chr. Kaiser, 1981), pp. 33-47; J.G. Gager, *The Origins of Anti-Semitism: Attitudes Toward Judaism in Pagan and Christian Antiquity* (New York & Oxford: Oxford University, 1983), pp. 117-133, 160-264; J. Blenkinsopp, "Old Testament Theology and the Jewish-Christian Connection", *JSOT* 28 (1984), pp. 3-15; L. Siegele-Wenschkewitz, "Antijudaismus", in E. Grossmann, E. Moltmann-Wendel et al. (eds.), *Wörterbuch der Feministischen Theologie* (Gütersloh: Güters-loher Verlags-Haus Mohn, 1991), pp. 22-24; J. Kohn-Roelin, "Antijudaismus – die Kehrseite jeder Christologie?", in D. Strahm und R. Strobel (eds.), *Vom Verlangen nach Heilwerden: Christologie in feministisch-theologischer Sicht* (Freiburg / Luzern: Exodus, 1991), pp. 65-80; C.M. Williamson, *Has God Rejected His People? – Anti-Judaism in the Christian Church* (Nashville, TN: Abingdon Press, 1982); idem, *A Guest in the House of Israel – Post-Holocaust Church Theology* (Louisville, KT: Wesmister / John Knox Press, 1993), pp. 1-3, 174-188; E. Schüssler Fiorenza, "Christlicher Antijudaismus aus feministischer Perspektive", in C. Hurth and P. Schmid (eds.), *Das christlich-jüdische Gespräch* (Judentum und Christentum, 3; Stuttgart: W. Kohlhammer, 2000), pp. 56-75.

[26] See Gager, *Origins of Anti-Semitism*, pp. 134-159; J.T. Townsend, "The New Testament, the Early Church, and Anti-Semitism", in J. Neusner, E. S. Frerichs and N.M. Sarna (eds.), *From Ancient Israel to Modern Judaism* (BJS 159; Atlanta, GA: Scholars Press, 1989), pp. 171-186; idem, "Anti-Judaism in the New Testament", *Mercer Dictionary of the Bible* (Macon, GA: Mercer University Press, 1990), pp. 33-34; C.A. Evans and D.A. Hagner (eds.), *Anti-Semitism and Early Christianity: Issues of Faith and Polemic* (Minneapolis, MN: Fortress, 1993); R.E. Brown, *The Death of the Messiah* (ABRL; New York / London / To-ronto / Sydney & Auckland: Doubleday, 1994), pp. 384, 386-391; L.C. Freudmann, *Anti-Semitism in the New Testament* (Lenham, MD / New York / London: University Press of America, 1994).

[27] For an example of anti-Jewish theology that is drawn from the New Testa-ment, see G.B. Caird and L.D. Hurst, *New Testament Theology* (Oxford: Claren-don Press, 1994), p. 55: "Matthew... gives the impression that the destruction of Jerusalem was Israel's final forfeiture of her calling to be God's people... 'The Kingdom of God will be taken away from you and given to a nation that yields

Such negative teachings and theological feuds have resulted, tragically, in the most horrible persecutions and abuse of Jews by Christians. Of late – maybe too late – a few Christian scholars have become aware of this terrible history. For example, amongst the Protestant scholars, Friedrich-Wilhelm Marquardt from Berlin writes:

> Die Judenmorde unseres Jahrhunderts und ihre von Theologie und Kirche zu verantwortenden Voraussetzungen und Folgen sind die Zeichen unserer Zeit, die jede Theologie in bisher unbekannter Weise radikal fraglich machen.[28]

And amongst Catholic scholars, Erich Zenger from Münster has stated: "Nach Auschwitz muss die Kirche das 'Alte Testament' anders lesen".[29]

However, it is worthwhile noting that recently several Christian scholars have provided some imperative methodological guidelines for dealing with some of the anti-Jewish passages in the New Testament, within their socio-historical contexts.[30]

---

the proper fruit' (Matt 21,43). We might therefore draw the inference that he regarded the Church as a substitute for Israel rather than a continuation of it, a new structure built upon a new rock (16,18)". On pages 56-57, they write: "There can be no doubt that the author of Revelation thought of himself and his churches as heirs to all the riches of the Old Testament, or that he regarded the Church as Israel. Among the enemies of the churches are 'those who claim to be Jews but are not' (2,9; 3,9). *True* Jews are in the Church. The Holy City is now the Church (11,2), and Jerusalem, along with Sodom and Egypt, has become a symbol for the great city, by which the Church is persecuted... A true child of Israel is one who recognizes Jesus as King of Israel." A different example, in the *International Herald Tribune* (No. 34,874; Thursday, April 13, 1995, p. 2), reported that the Christian Community Bible, which has sold 20 million copies, both in Spanish and English editions, and 60,000 copies in France since a French translation appeared last year, "contains at least two passages that 'could revive anti-Semitism' the court in Paris ruled... The court ruled as anti-Semitic a commentary saying the Jews killed Jesus because 'they were unable to control their fanaticism', and another describing Jewish rites and customs as 'folkloric duties involving circumcision and wearing hats' ".

[28] F.-W. Marquardt, *Von Elend und Heimsuchung der Theologie* (München: Chr. Kaiser, 1988), p. 74.

[29] E. Zenger, *Das Erste Testament: Die jüdische Bibel und die Christen* (4th edn.; Düsseldorf: Patmos Verlag, 1994), pp. 12-27. This view stated already by F. Mußner in 1979, see Zenger, *ibid.*, 12 note 1.

[30] See Townsend, "New Testament"; Brown, *Messiah*; R. Kysar, "Anti-

To sum up, there is a place and a need for research in both branches, for the "History of Israelite Religion in Biblical times" and for the "Hebrew Bible / Old Testament Theology". The research in each area must be separate and follow differently defined methods, so as to avoid confusion. Nevertheless, "Hebrew Bible / Old Testament Theology" can profit from some of the results of the research on the "History of Israelite Religion". The Hebrew Bible / Old Testament and New Testament must be investigated above all separately. Christian theologians should not introduce any sort of anti-Semitic and anti-Jewish theology.

IV. Is There Really No Jewish Interest in Biblical Theology?

In 1987 Jon D. Levenson published an article entitled "Why Jews are Not Interested in Biblical Theology".[31] The intention of the article can already be determined from its title. The assumption exists, so to speak, that Jews are not interested in Biblical theology, and all that is permitted is to deal out the suitable arguments. It is, however, inaccurate to say that the Jews are not interested in Biblical theology.

They are not interested in Christian Biblical theology. This view is understandable, and requires no further explanation. Why should Jews – as a religious-national collective – be interested in Christian theology?

Semitism and the Gospel of John", in Evans and Hagner (eds.), *Faith and Polemic*, pp. 113-127; idem, "John's Anti-Jewish Polemic", *Bible Review* IX (1993), pp. 26-27; K. Stendahl, "Anti-Semitism and the New Testament", *Explorations – Rethinking Relationships Among Jews and Christians* vol. 7, number 2 (1993), p. 7. Charlesworth suggested a new translation of these texts "on the literary contexts and the social milieu of the passage", see J.H. Charlesworth, "Is the New Testament anti-Semitic or anti-Jewish?", *ibid.*, pp. 2-3 esp. 3. See also Freudmann's discussion "Necessary Steps to re-antisemitize the New Testament", in idem, *Anti-Semitism*, pp. 303-311; J.G. Gager, *Reinventing Paul* (Oxford & New York: Oxford University Press, 2000).

[31] The article was published in J. Neusner, B.A. Levine, and E.S. Frerichs (eds.), *Judaic Perspectives on Ancient Israel* (Philadelphia: Fortress, 1987) pp. 281-307. The author republished it in his collection of essays: *The Hebrew Bible, the Old Testament, and Historical Criticism – Jews and Christians in Biblical Studies*, pp. 33-61.

Figure 6 Ecclesia et Synagoga: *The Church Triumphant and the Synagogue blindfold (Strasbourg Chathedral, ca. 1230)*

In Biblical scholarship there is an opinion that defines the Chronicler as an "Old Testament theologian". For example, Peter R. Ackroyd describes the Book of Chronicles "as the first 'theology of the Old Testament'". He writes: "We may... see the Chronicler's presentation and endeavour to unify, to draw together the diverse strands of Israel's thought into a more coherent whole. We may be even more precise in our delineation of him as a theologian, and see him as one who aimed at presenting a unifying concept of the nature of the Jewish religious community and hence of its theology and the meaning of its rich and varied tradition."[32] Most recently, William Johnstone states also in this direction: "C [= Chronicles] is a theological work: it is concerned with the universal relationship between God and humanity, and the vocation of Israel within that relationship."[33] According to these opinions the Jewish Biblical theology started already in Hebrew Bible itself. Nevertheless, in whatever way we define the Chronicler and his work,[34] there is no doubt that the Jewish Midrashim and commentaries for generations absorbed the theological views and values of the Bible. They concentrated highly on the different aspects of God as they are reflected in the Bible, on the relations between God and humanity, the election of Israel, the relations between the people of God and the Nations, the Land of Israel as a religious value, the special association between the Land and the nation of Israel, Creation, Revelation, Covenant, Holiness, Sin, and other theological issues. It is true that the theology that is found in the Jewish commentaries does not unite the theology of the Bible into one book. But this fact does not lessen the importance of theology in Jewish commentaries. Moreover, are not expressions of Jewish Biblical theology present in such magna opera as Book of Beliefs and Opinions of Saadia Gaon (882-942);[35] the *Kitab al-Hazari*

---

[32] See P.R. Ackroyd, "The Theology of the Chronicler", *The Chronicler in His Age* (JSOT Suppl. 101; Sheffield: Sheffield Academic Press, 1991), p. 280.

[33] W. Johnstone, *1 and 2 Chronicles: Volume 1: 1 Chronicles 1 – 2 Chronicles 9: Israel's Place Among the Nations* (JSOT Suppl. 253; Sheffield: Sheffield Academic Press, 1998), pp. 9-10, 23 (the citation is from p. 10).

[34] For a critical review of these and other opinions, see I. Kalimi, "Was the Chronicler a Historian?", in M.P. Graham, K.G. Hoglund and S.L. McKenzie (eds.), *The Chronicler as Historian*, (JSOT Suppl. 238; Sheffield: Sheffield Academic Press, 1997), pp. 73-89.

[35] See S. Rosenblatt, *Saadia Gaon, The Book of Beliefs and Opinions – Translated from the Arabic and the Hebrew* (New Haven: Yale University Press / London: Geoffrey Cumberlege / Oxford: Oxford University Press, 1948). Indeed, Saadia Gaon's book could be considered as Jewish Biblical theology. The book contains the following ten main treatises: (1) the creation of the world; (2) God's unity and other divine attributes; (3) the divine commandments and the means of their revelation; (4) man's freedom either to obey or to disobey God; (5) virtue and vice; (6) man's soul and its immortality; (7) the doctrine of resurrection; (8) the age of the Messiah and redemption; (9) reward

(*Kuzari* in Hebrew), that is, *The Book of Argument and Proof in Defence of the Despised Faith*, of Rabbi Jehuda Halevi (ca. 1085-1141);[36] *The Guide for the Perplexed* (*Moreh Nevuchim* in Hebrew) of Moses Maimonides (Rambam, 1135-1204)?[37] In the modern era of Jewish Biblical research there is, first of all, the important pioneer Biblical-theological composition by David Neumark, *The Philosophy of the Bible*.[38] The author defined its subject as: "the presentation of the spiritual development of Judaism in biblical times in its theoretical principles as well as in the expressions these principles found in the cultural manifestations of life".[39] There is also the chapter entitled "The Basic Ideas of Biblical Religion" in *The Philosophy of Judaism* by Julius (Yitzchak) Guttmann (1880-1950).[40] Somewhat later are the

and punishment in the hereafter; and (10) the golden mean. Rosenblatt pointed out that "he drives home his points by means of apt quotations from the Bible, which he cites no less than 1,300 times. Even though as a Gaon who was the authority in his day on the Talmud he made comparatively sparing use of this source of Jewish tradition", see Rosenblatt, *ibid.*, pp. XXV, XXVI. Moreover, a brief glance at the index of the sources which were cited by Saadia Gaon in his book (see Rosenblatt, *ibid.*, pp. 476-494), shows that while the Biblical passages are 17 pages in length, the Rabbinic sources take up less than two pages!

[36] See H. Hirschfeld, *Book of Kuzari by Judah Hallevi — Translated from the Arabic, with Introduction, Notes and Appendix* (New York: Pardes Publishing House, 1946) = idem, *An Argument for the Faith of Israel — The Kuzari* (New York: Schocken, 1971).

[37] See S. Pines, *Moses Maimonides, The Guide of the Perplexed — Translated with an Introduction and Notes* (Chicago & London: Chicago University Press, 1963). Here also, a brief look at the index of the sources which were cited by Maimonides in this book (see Pines, *ibid.*, pp. 645-656), shows that while the Biblical passages appearing in the text are 10 pages in length, the Rabbinic passages comprise no more than one page and a half! The book contains the following main theses: (1) Biblical terms applied to God, (2) demonstration of the existence, unity and incorporeity of God, (3) prophecy, (4) the account of the chariots, (5) Providence, (6) the actions commanded by God and done by God, (7) man's perfection and God's Providence. In his introduction, Shlomo Pines writes as follows: "The Guide is devoted to the Torah or more precisely to the true science of the Torah... Its first purpose is to explain Biblical terms and its second purpose is to explain Biblical similes" (p. XIV).

[38] Cincinnati: Ark Publishing Company, 1918.

[39] Neumark, *Philosophy*, p. XIII.

[40] New York / Chicago / San Francisco: Holt, Rinehart and Winston, 1964, pp. 3-17, 413. The book was first published in German: *Die Philosophie*

writings of Martin Buber (1878-1965); including *The Prophetic Faith*;[41] *The Kingship of God*;[42] the studies of Abraham Joshua Heschel (1907-1972), such as *The Prophets*;[43] and *A Jewish Theology* by Louis Jacob.[44] Today, all who read Moshe Greenberg's *On the Bible and on Judaism*,[45] will find many examples of the theology of the Bible. The work includes articles like "The Biblical Grounding of Human Values";[46] "The Question of the Freedom of the Worshipper of God in the Bible";[47] "The Connection between the Nation and the Land in the Bible";[48] "The Festival in the Bible and the Holy Time";[49] "The Reflections on Job's Theology".[50] Such articles certainly come under the category of the theology of the Bible. In a paradoxical way, the same Levenson, who tries to explain why Jews are not interested in Biblical theology, has himself published works which, in principle, are theological.[51] It is also necessary to mention the theological compositions on separate books of the Bible. Examples include the treatise of S. Japhet, *The Ideology of the Book of Chronicles and Its Place in Biblical Thought*;[52] also articles like: M. Weinfeld's "Theological Trends in Torah Literature";[53] "God the Creator in

---

des Judentums (München: Verlag Ernst Reinhardt, 1933), pp. 12-25.

[41] New York: Macmillan, 1949. German original: *Der Glaube der Propheten* (Zürich: Manesse Verlag, Conzett & Huber, 1950).

[42] New York: Harper & Row, 1967; German original: *Königtum Gottes* (3rd edn.; Heidelberg: Verlag Lambert Schneider, 1956).

[43] New York: Harper, 1962; German original: *Die Prophetie* (Cracow: Polish Academy of Sciences, 1936). It is also worth mentioning Heschel's essay "Depth Theology", *The Insecurity of Freedom* (New York: Farrar, Straus & Giroux, 1966), pp. 115-126 (see also idem, *God in Search of Man* [New York: Farrar, Straus & Giroux, 1955], pp. 7-8); and his articles collected in J. Neusner (ed.), *Understanding Jewish Theology* (New York: Ktav Publishing House, 1973), pp. 14-22, 24-31.

[44] L. Jacob, *A Jewish Theology* (London: Darton, Longman and Todd, 1973).

[45] Edited by A. Shapiro (Tel Aviv: Am Oved, 1984; Hebrew).

[46] Greenberg, *On the Bible and on Judaism*, pp. 13-23.

[47] Greenberg, *On the Bible and on Judaism*, pp. 85-97.

[48] Greenberg, *On the Bible and on Judaism*, pp. 110-124.

[49] Greenberg, *On the Bible and on Judaism*, pp. 161-167.

[50] Greenberg, *On the Bible and on Judaism*, pp. 235-243.

[51] For example, Levenson, *Sinai & Zion*; see above, note 19.

[52] Translated by A. Barber from the Hebrew edition of 1977, BEATAJ 9; Frankfurt am Main / Bern / New York / Paris: Peter Lang, 1989.

[53] *Beit Mikra* 16 (1971), pp. 10-22 (Hebrew).

Genesis 1 and in Deutero-Isaiah";[54] S.E. Loewenstamm's "God's Property";[55] M. Weiss' "Psalm 23: The Psalmist on God's Care";[56] Y. Hoffman, "The Creativity of Theodicy."[57] Recently M.A. Sweeney has published several studies that address the question of Jewish Biblical theology directly.[58] Are these not sufficient examples to ascertain that the Jews are interested in the theology of the Hebrew Bible and in Biblical theology?

Levenson claims there is no "Jewish equivalent" to Walter Eichrodt's *Theology of the Old Testament* or Gerhard von Rad's *Old Testament Theology*.[59] The claim is inaccurate. One can ask, for instance, which scholarly Jewish commentary series on the Bible is equivalent to the series of scholarly commentaries that were developed in the Christian cultural world (principally Protestant), like: The International Critical Commentary (= ICC); Kurzer Hand-Commentar zum Alten Testament (= KHCAT); Die Heilige Schrift des Alten Testamentes (=HSAT); Handbuch zum Alten Testament (= HAT); Die Neue Echter Bibel (= NEB); The New Century Bible Commentary (= NCBC); Word Biblical Commentary (= WBC); The New International Commentary on the Old Testament (= NICOT),

---

[54] *Tarbiz* 37 (1968), pp. 105-132 (Hebrew).

[55] In *Festschrift S. Deim* (Jerusalem: Kiryat-Sepher, 1958), pp. 120-125 (Hebrew).

[56] In M. Fishbane and E. Tov (eds.), *Sha'arei Talmon — Studies in the Bible, Qumran, and the Ancient Near East Presented to Shemaryahu Talmon* (Winona Lake, IN: Eisenbrauns, 1992), pp. 31*-41*.

[57] In H.G. Reventlow and Y. Hoffman (eds.), *Justice and Righteousness — Biblical Themes and Their Influence* (JSOT Suppl. 137; Sheffield: JSOT Press, 1992), pp. 117-130.

[58] M.A. Sweeney, "Tanak versus Old Testament: Concerning the Foundation for a Jewish Theology of the Bible", in H.T.C. Sun and K.L. Eades (eds.), *Problems in Biblical Theology — Essays in Honor of Rolf Knierim* (Grand Rapids, MI / Cambridge: W.B. Eerdmans, 1997), pp. 353-372; idem, "Why Jews Should be Interested in Biblical Theology", *CCAR Journal* 46 (1997), pp. 67-75; idem, "Reconceiving the Paradigms of Old Testament Theology in the Post-*Shoah* Period", *BI* 6 (1998), pp. 142-161; idem, "The Emerging Field of Jewish Biblical Theology", in Z. Garber (ed.), *Academic Approaches to Teaching Jewish Studies* (Lanham, MD / New York / Oxford: University Press of America, 2000), pp. 83-105; idem, "Isaiah and Theodicy after the *Shoah*", in T. Linafelt (ed.), *Strange Fire — Reading the Bible after the Holocaust* (Sheffield: Sheffield Academic Press, 2000), pp. 208-219.

[59] Levenson, "Biblical Theology", p. 281.

and etc. The list is quite long.[60] There is evidence that as of today there is no comprehensive Jewish scholarly commentary on the Hebrew Bible.[61] Only several years ago Moshe Greenberg and Shmuel Aḥituv initiated a modern Jewish commentary to the Bible: *Mikra leYisra'el*, and so far commentaries on Joshua, Judges, Samuel, Ruth, Esther, the Song of Songs, Jonah and Obadiah, Amos and Joel have appeared. Indeed, noteworthy also is the JPS Torah Commentary.[62] In the light of this situation is it possible to say that Jews are not interested in critical Biblical commentary? Of course they are interested! What Jewish equivalent is there to the 50 books of 'Introduction to the Bible' that were published by Christian researchers?[63] The picture is not very different from other branches of the field.[64] The situation is clarified by the youthfulness of Jewish-scholarly Biblical research.[65] The interest of modern Jewish scholars in Biblical theology and in theology of the Hebrew Bible are not very different from their interest in other Biblical areas. In other words Jews are interested in theology of the Bible and in Biblical theology, but until now did not produce very much either in this field or in others. Nevertheless, how can one explain the absence of many Jewish publications in the area of Biblical theology in comparison to their publications in Biblical history? Levenson explained that Jews simply are not interested in Biblical theology. He lets the matter be

---

[60] For samples of scientific series of commentaries on the Hebrew Bible, see I. Kalimi, *The Books of Chronicles – A Classified Bibliography* (SBB 1; Jerusalem: Simor, 1990), pp. 45-52, item nos. 112-162.

[61] The religious Biblical commentary, which is being published by Mossad haRav Kook, is not scholarly and is tied by religious-traditional bonds, and from all sides it is still incomplete. Abraham Kahana's series of commentaries is incomplete and out of date.

[62] See N.M. Sarna, *Genesis* (Philadelphia / New York / Jerusalem: The Jewish Publication Society, 1989); idem, *Exodus* (1991); B.A. Levine, *Leviticus* (1989); J. Milgrom, *Numbers* (1990); J.H. Tigay, *Deuteronomy* (1996). Recently, the same Society published also commentaries on *Jonah* by U. Simon (1998); and *Esther* by A. Berlin (2000).

[63] For the list of introductions see Kalimi, *A Classified Bibliography*, pp. 34-38, item nos. 11-61; the recently published introduction: E. Zenger u.a., *Einleitung in das Alte Testament* (SBT 1,1; 3rd edn.; Stuttgart / Berlin / Köln: W. Kohlhammer, 1998) to be added there.

[64] And again, if one looks in Kalimi, *A Classified Bibliography*, as a sample – he will get a clear enough picture on the subject.

[65] On this subject see appendix, below.

determined by two characteristics of Biblical theology written by Christian researchers:

1. The theology written by the Christians on the "Old Testament" is not self-contained because it is connected to the theology of the "New Testament". The "Old Testament" has been viewed as a preparation for the "New Testament", and so the "New Testament" is seen only as a fulfilment of the "Old Testament".[66]
2. Anti-Semitism exists in many classic works of Christian theologians, and this fact discourages Jewish Biblical scholars from engaging in this area.

These points in themselves may explain why Jewish scholars do not engage in Christian theology, but they do not explain why Jews do not have an alternate Jewish Biblical theology, dependent exclusively on the TaNaK and, of course, without anti-Semitism. In other words, the Christians wrote and still write Biblical theologies for themselves and their needs. These points do not explain why Jews do not form a comprehensive theology of their own, different from the Christians in content, in approach and even in method. Moreover, it should not be a surprise that Christians look at the 'New Testament' as a continuation of the 'Old Testament'. In fact, they bind the two corpora to each other in their written theology, just as they believe and profess. Furthermore, anti-Semitism is evident also among Christian historians and particularly in the writings of a number of Germans, for example, Eduard Meyer,[67] Julius Wellhausen,[68] and even after the Shoah – Martin Noth.[69] This anti-Semitism

---

[66] Levenson, "Biblical Theology", p. 286. He cites R. C. Dentan, but this point emerges repeatedly in the works of many Christian theologians, e.g. Eißfeldt, "Religionsgeschichte", p. 2; Childs, *Biblical Theology of the Old and New Testament*, p. 452: "The old covenant is a preparation for the new"; Caird – Hurst, *New Testament Theology*, pp. 57-62.

[67] See C. Hoffmann, *Juden und Judentum im Werk Deutscher Althistoriker des 19. und 20. Jahrhunderts* (Leiden / New York / Kopenhagen / Köln: E.J. Brill, 1988), pp. 133-189.

[68] See Wellhausen, *Prolegomena zur Geschichte Israels*, pp. 237, 400-401, 417-424 (= idem, *Prolegomena to the History of Ancient Israel*, pp. 227, 400, 419-425). So, for instance, "Thus arose that artificial product, the sacred constitution of Judaism... The Mosaic theocracy appears to show an immense retrogression... If the Priestly Code makes the cultus the principal thing, that appears to amount to a systematic decline into the heathenism" (German version, pp. 420,

does not deter Jews from investigating the history of the Biblical era. On the contrary, in this field there is a fruitful production of Jewish-Israeli research. Furthermore, the fact that anti-Jewish expressions also exists in the Christian writings on "History of Israelite Religion",[70] did not deter Jewish scholars from dealing with it.[71]

It seems that the explanation of the limited interest of Jews in theological research is inherent in: (1) the focus of Jewish-Israeli interest in Biblical research; (2) the formation of higher educational institutions in Israel (as well as some Jewish institutions in America). Let us now turn to these issues in some detail.

1. The Focus of Jewish-Israeli Interest in Biblical Research

Modern Jewish Bible research centers are, first and foremost, found in the Israeli universities and research institutes. Here, a quick examination shows that the most important place is taken up by a historical approach of the Bible, on its variety and different branches: political history, military history, economic history, historical geography, Biblical historiography, Biblical archaeology, and the history of Israelite religion. All these professional branches are in reference to languages and literatures, to religions and cultures of the other ancient Near Eastern nations and their histories, also in reference to archaeological excavations in the Land of Israel and its neighbors.

The Bible considers that Israel holds a title deed to its historical homeland, and has an inalienable right to nationhood. Israel has been and continues to be an integral part of the Near East.[72] However,

---

421; English Translation: pp. 421, 422, 423). See also my critical view of Wellhausen's anti-Jewish remarks, Kalimi, "Was the Chronicler a Historian", pp. 74-77.

[69] M. Noth, *Geschichte Israels* (3rd edn.; Göttingen: Vandenhoeck & Ruprecht, 1956), pp. 383-386, 406 (= idem, *The History of Israel*, pp. 428-432, 454).

[70] For example, W.M.L. de Wette, in L. Perlitt, *Vatke und Wellhausen* (BZAW 94; Berlin: Verlag Alfred Töpelmann, 1965), p. 92 (for detailed reference of the work of de Wette, see pp. 248-249); G. Fohrer, *Geschichte der israelitischen Religion* (Berlin: Walter de Gruyter, 1968), p. 369; English version: idem, *History of Israelite Religion* (Nashville, TN & New York: Abingdon Press, 1972), p. 359. Fohrer published this study before his conversion to Judaism.

[71] See below, excursus.

[72] It is not a political usage of the Bible but the stating of points that exist in it.

in modern times this is a new experience. We are trying to find the renewed Jewish-Israeli nationality based precisely on the Bible and not on Rabbinical Literature, that characterized the Diaspora's bitter experience for hundreds of years. The decision to call the new state by the name "Israel" and not "Jehudah" or "Jewish State" (*Der Judenstaat*, as Theodor [Benjamin Ze'ev] Herzl suggested in 1896) points in this direction.

The massive concentration on historical viewpoints of the Bible, to a certain extent the product of the social-political situation of the nation of Israel of recent generations, does not leave much space for delving into Biblical theology. It is reasonable to assume that with the passage of time and circumstances, the interest in scholarly theological viewpoints of the Bible will be strengthened. Indeed, Moshe H. Goshen-Gottstein drafted a book directed to this end: Prolegomena to Jewish Biblical Theology.[73] But, unfortunately, his work was stifled by his death in 1993.

2.   Excursus: The History of Israelite Religion in Jewish Biblical Scholarship

Of the two branches, the Jewish researchers engaged in the "History of Israelite Religion" more than in "Hebrew Bible Theology" and "Theology of the Bible". Here should be mentioned first and fore-most the magnum opus of Yehezkel Kaufmann (1889-1963), *History of Israelite Religion – From the Ancient Times to the End of the Second Temple*.[74] This is the most comprehensive work ever written by an Israeli, in Hebrew, on the history of Israelite religion. Researchers preceding him wrote on specific subjects, such as Menachem Haran, Kaufmann's student, who wrote: *Temples and Temple-Service in Ancient Israel – An Inquiry into Biblical Cult Phenomena and the Historical Setting of the Priestly School*.[75] This book deals, generally, as Haran himself defined it: "with the activities of the temple's inner sphere and

---

[73] Goshen-Gottstein, "Jewish Biblical Theology", p. 37 at note.

[74] Eight books in four volumes (6th print; Jerusalem: Bialik Institute / Tel Aviv: Dvir, 1972; Hebrew). For abridgement and English translation of volumes. I-III by M. Greenberg, see Y. Kaufmann, *The Religion of Israel: From Its Beginning to the Babylonian Exile* (Chicago: Chicago University Press, 1960); vol. IV, *The Babylonian Captivity and Deutero-Isaiah*, translated by C.W. Efroymson (New York: Union of American Hebrew Congregations, 1970).

[75] Originally published in Oxford: Clarendon Press, 1978. Reprinted with corrections by Eisenbrauns, Winona Lake, IN 1985.

belonging to the priestly circle".[76] Also, it is worthwhile mentioning other works by Haran, like: "The Graded Taboos of Holiness";[77] "The Priestly Image of the Tabernacle";[78] "Shiloh and Jerusalem";[79] and "The Religion of the Patriarch: Beliefs and Practices".[80]

There are also several studies on Israelite cult, like the studies of Baruch A. Levine, *In the Presence of the Lord – A Study of Cult and Some Cultic Terms in Ancient Israel*;[81] and Jacob Milgrom, *Cult and Conscience*;[82] *Studies in Cultic Theology and Terminology*.[83] Important studies were published also on different issues of ancient Israelite religon, for example by Mordechai Cogan, *Imperialism and Religion: Assyria, Judah and Israel in the Eighth and Seventh Centuries BCE*;[84] Benjamin Uffenheimer, *Early Prophecy in Israel*;[85] Yair Hoffman, *Exodus in the Bible Belief*,[86] and Alexander Rofé, *The Belief in Angels in the First Temple Period According to Biblical Traditions*.[87] Also there are other articles worth mentioning, for example: "The Origin of the 'Day of the Lord' – Reconsidered", by Meir Weiss;[88] "Religion: Stability and Ferment" by Moshe Greenberg;[89] Moshe Weinfeld's

---

[76] See Haran, *Temples and Temple-Services*, p. V.

[77] In *Festschrift M.Z. Segal* (Jerusalem: Kiryat-Sepher, 1965), pp. 33-41 (Hebrew).

[78] In *HUCA* 36 (1965), pp. 191-226.

[79] In *JBL* 81 (1962), pp. 14-24.

[80] In B. Mazar (ed.), *The World History of the Jewish People, Volume II: Patriarchs* (Jewish History Publication; Givatayim: Peli & Rutgers University Press, 1970), pp. 219-245, 285-288. See also some articles in M. Haran, *Ages and Institutions in the Bible* (Tel Aviv: Am Oved, 1972; Hebrew).

[81] Leiden: E.J. Brill, 1974.

[82] Leiden: E.J. Brill, 1976.

[83] Leiden: E.J. Brill, 1983.

[84] SBLMS 19; Missoula, MT: Scholars Press, 1974.

[85] Jerusalem: Magnes Press, 1973 (Hebrew); the English version published in 1999 by the same publisher.

[86] Tel Aviv: Am Oved, 1983 (Hebrew).

[87] Unpublished dissertation; Jerusalem: The Hebrew University, 1969.

[88] In *HUCA* 37 (1966), pp. 29-60.

[89] In A. Malamat (ed.), *The World History of the Jewish People: The Age of the Monarchies – Culture and Society* (Jewish History Publication; Jerusalem: Massadah Press, 1979), pp. 79-123, 296-303.

"The Work of the Israeli Molech and his Background",[90] and his studies on the covenant and other issues.[91]

3. The Formation of Higher Educational Institutions in Israel

The Christian theological faculties – both Catholic and Protestant – in Europe, as well as the Schools of Theology, Theological Seminaries and Divinity Schools (as distinct from Departments of Religion) in America are, first and foremost, preparing ministers, priests, Christian teachers and educators who will serve ecclesiastical, pedagogical and philanthropic purposes. In some of these institutions attention is given to research in many various branches of theological studies. Accordingly, the study of the Christian Bible in these institutions takes up a small part of the theological programs. And within the Christian Biblical studies, the emphasis is placed, in principle, on the studies of the "New Testament", with a focus on religious-theological viewpoints. In these institutions there are here and there those who are interested in the history of ancient Israel and sometimes even in the Land of (Eretz) Israel, but such subjects generally are not the central theme of religious teaching and research. The "search for roots" does not play any part here. In truth, why should it be important to a priest serving in the Church, or to a teacher of Christian religion, to know in what exact place the eastern border of Canaan was, and where a particular Biblical site can be located, or what the historical course of a certain battle was or the political results, the militarism, etc. of the so-and-so connection that connected the kingdom of Israel or Judah with the kingdoms of the ancient Near East?

By contrast, Biblical studies in Israeli universities are located in independent departments and in affiliated divisions in related departments. For example, the history of the Biblical period is studied within the framework of the history of the Jewish people; Biblical Hebrew and Aramaic lay within the framework of the Hebrew language; Biblical thought within the framework of the Jewish

---

[90] In *Proceedings of the Ninth World Congress of Jewish Studies* (The World Union of Jewish Studies; Jerusalem: Magnes Press, 1969) pp. 37-61, 152 (Hebrew).

[91] For detailed references see M. Weinfeld, *Deuteronomy 1-11* (AB 5; New York / London / Toronto / Sydney / Auckland: Doubleday, 1991), pp. 116-120.

thought; Biblical archaeology is within the larger framework of the institute of archaeology. All departments connected to Bible studies are part of the framework of humanities. It should be pointed out that in all these departments the reference is to 24 books, namely TaNaK. The "New Testament" is studied in the department of Religious Studies. The university, like any secular academic institution, employs professional teachers and researchers. It does not prepare rabbis and others who deal with religion and synagogues. The Rabbinate has no authority to interfere with academic policy. Consequently, theological and religious viewpoints receive less attention.

The Jew living in the Land of Israel, is closely acquainted therefore, with its cities, ruins, limits, etc. He drinks from the same wells that his ancient ancestors drank from, and walks on the same pathways, mounts and hills. He is tied deeply with its landscapes, flora and fauna. All these things are close to him and affect him. The political and military strokes that determined the fate of his nation, land and culture are important for him. Indeed, a Christian bases some of his religious lines also on the historical realities of ancient Israel as expressed in the Bible, and he is therefore obligated to come to terms with the national dimensions of Judaism as well as the religious. But can it really be comparable to how a Jew relates to his homeland, history and cultural-religious roots?

The education of rabbis, pious scholars and teachers of religion (including teachers of the Bible for religious educational institutions), is done at Yeshivot (excluding the conservative Jews studying in The Jewish Theological Seminary of America, and the Reform Jews studying in the Hebrew Union College). Here they deal rather with theological viewpoints, significant values and in principle with the Halacha, of Israel's ancient heritage and, in general, the Bible from a Rabbinical standpoint. Therefore, it seems that these are the main reasons for the limited interest of Jewish scholars in Biblical theology.

V. Conclusion

Both branches – the "History of the Israelite Religion" and "Hebrew Bible / Old Testament Theology" – are significant and have equal merit. There are also distinct demarcations and deep differences between them. Thus, the research of each one must be separate and follow clearly defined unique methods so as to avoid confusion. It is interesting to discover the theological guidelines of the Biblical

Figure 7   A dispute between Christians and Jews. An illustration on the Manuscript of the Bible (French, mid 13th century. The Bodleian Library, Oxford University, Ms. Bodley 270b fol. 43v.).

authors, editors and canonist(s). There is also a necessity to be aware of the theological guidelines controlling the Biblical corpora; to read the Bible for religious messages and moral values which may be derived from it. Nevertheless, it is impractical to look for or to impose one sole idea on the whole Bible. To Christian theologians we say: "theology without anti-Judaism and anti-Semitism, please! After all your human sensitivity should act not only towards the believers but especially towards those who are thinking and believing otherwise. Your tolerance is testified first and foremost by your attitude towards those who are dissimilar in belief and religion. Your ethics should apply not only when you are writing on Christianity and Christians, but particularly when you are doing so towards those whose beliefs are different from yours – Jewish people (and Judaism)"[92]

---

[92] There is no nation that has been treated so cruelly and paid such a high price for keeping its religious and cultural heritage as did the Jewish people. Paradoxically, this treatment was carried out mostly by the people to whom "love" – even of an enemy (see, for example, Matt 5,43-48; Rom 12,14.20)! – is one of the important theological principles of their own religion! and towards the nation of the founders (like Jesus and his Apostles) of their religion! Most likely, this treatment of the Jewish people is contrary to the original will of Jesus himself and of at least some of his adherents.

Jews are interested in the theology of the Hebrew Bible and in Biblical theology. The main reasons for the limited interest of Jewish scholars in Biblical theology is inherent in the youthfulness of scholarly Jewish Biblical research; the focus of Jewish-Israeli interest on Biblical research in the last generations; and in the formation of higher educational institutions in Israel as well as in some Jewish institutions in America.[93]

VI. Appendix: "My People are Afraid to Approach this Mission" – Study of the Bible Among Jewish People

The study of the Bible among Jewish people in the antiquity and Medieval ages, I discussed in other essays.[94] Here I would like to stress that the *Baraita* cited in the Babylonian Talmud, *Baba Mezia* 33a is used even today as a guiding methodological principle in various religious institutions – especially orthodox ones – in Israel and the Diaspora.

In the introduction to his commentary on the Bible, Arnold B. Ehrlich (1848-1919) wrote at the beginning of the 20th century, that the Jews "are fearful" to explore and write a modern critical commentary on the Bible: "My people are afraid to approach this mission. For who will search the work of earlier [Biblical] authors when he [the modern scholar] has been taught that if they [the Biblical authors] were as angels we are mere men, and if they were men we

---

[93] This subject was treated recently by James Barr, and he came to similar conclusions. Barr stresses: "There is... in fact, a very rich and substantial tradition of theology within Judaism", and concludes: "It is uncertain whether Jewish scholars will ever write works called 'Biblical Theology' or 'Theology of the Hebrew Bible'. But they are already integrated within many of the same set of operations which are essential to [...] biblical theology". Moreover, Barr adds: "...My latest impressions at the time of writing, however, are that interest in Jewish biblical theology has been stimulated, rather than dampened, by the recent discussions", see J. Barr, *The Concept of Biblical Theology – An Old Testament Perspective* (London: SCM Press, 1999), pp. 286-311, 671-674 esp. 287, 311.

[94] See I. Kalimi, "Die Bibel und die klassisch-jüdische Bibelauslegung – Eine Interpretations- und Religionsgeschichtliche Studie", *ZAW* 114/₂ (2002), forthcoming; idem, "Die Auseinandersetzung mit den internen und äußeren Opponenten in mittelalterlicher-jüdischer Schriftauslegung", *ZAW* 114/₃ (2002), forthcoming.

are as donkeys?"[95] And he attacks in the sharpest manner the Jewish scholars who have no interest in modern Biblical research:

חכמי ישראל אשר אלה ארבע אמות של הלכה תחומם, ולהם ביצה
שנלדה ביום טוב ראויה לדרישה וחקירה מכל הנולדות שבעולם,
ואלה מבלים ימיהם במשא ומתן על דבר פיוטים ופייטנים שאין
לדבריהם חן ולא תועלת, ולא לשתי הכתות הכתוב כתבי הקודש ענין לענות בו.
הלא יבושו העושים כן ומניחים נחלת ספר שהנחילום אבותיהם
לחכמי הגוים לעבדה ולשמרה ולאכול פריה

> Jewish scholars, whose field is four square cubits of halacha, and for whom an egg laid on a holy day is more worthwhile to be studied and researched than anything being born in the world; and those who waste their time discussing liturgical hymns and hymnologists, whose phrases have neither beauty nor benefit; both groups find no interest in the study of the Holy Scriptures. Those who are doing so and leaving the literary heritage of their forefathers to gentile scholars to fertilize, guard and enjoy its fruits, are the ones who should be ashamed.[96]

The Jewish scholars did not overcome the 'fear' of dealing with research of the Bible in the subsequent generation. In his inauguration lecture at the opening of the Institute for Jewish Studies in The Hebrew University of Jerusalem, P. Perles says:

> Still there are many that hesitate to deal with Biblical scholarship and not only this, but they also fight a total battle against it, in thinking that this science is liable to ruin the religious structure. And so I am obligated to show that this science does not come to destroy but rather to build, and the purpose of my work is to return the crown that was removed.[97]

In continuation, Perles indicates that:

> The number of Jewish scholars that work in this field [that is, in Biblical research] is still very small. I see in this a big disgrace and a big loss to

---

[95] Ehrlich, *Mikrâ ki-Pheschutô*, vol. I: *Divre Tora*, p. XXXVI (Hebrew).

[96] Ehrlich, *Mikrâ ki-Pheschutô*, vol. I: *Divre Tora*, p. XXXVII.

[97] See P. Perles, "What is Biblical Scholarship for Us?", An Inaugural Lecture at the Institute for Jewish Studies, The Hebrew University of Jerusalem (Jerusalem: Association for the Hebrew University, 1926), pp. 5-21 esp. 6 (Hebrew).

Israel... and almost all the important books which were written on the Bible in the last century were the work of Christian scholars.[98]

Nevertheless, it is apparent that the interest of Jewish scholars in academic Biblical studies is also influenced by the socio-economic reality: then and today a Jewish Biblical scholar *generally* is not accepted as a regular academic professor in *Biblical* Studies in most Christian theological faculties, seminaries, divinity schools and schools of theology.[99] Indeed, Jewish Biblical scholarship advanced since the opening of a Biblical department at Hebrew Union College in Cincinnati and, especially, at The Hebrew University of Jerusalem, about 77 years ago. The study of the Bible as a completely independent professional area in modern Jewish research is, however, young when compared with the Protestant tradition. Accordingly, it must be remembered that even today the number of Jewish Biblical researchers is not large, in comparison with the number of Christian Biblical scholars. Therefore, the discussion of Jewish Biblical research in the "History of Israelite religion" and in "Hebrew Bible theology" should take into consideration the limited background of Jews dealing with modern Biblical research.

[98] Perles, "Biblical Scholarship", pp. 9-12.

[99] Though in the last decade there are some exceptions in America: some Jewish scholars are accepted by Christian institutions, mostly for teaching Jewish studies, others Hebrew Bible or even New Testament. It is indeed a good development. As of today, however, all of them, total, are not more than half a dozen.

7

The Task of Hebrew Bible / Old Testament Theology –
Between Judaism and Christianity

A Response to Rolf P. Knierim's *Task of Old Testament Theology*[*]

I. Structure and Content

As a former student of the renowned Heidelberg theologian Gerhard von Rad (1901-1971), it is not surprising that from the very early stages of his life Rolf Paul Knierim (born 1928) pursued Biblical thinking. Already in the beginning of his career, about forty-five years ago, he published a popular article called "Biblisches Denken" in the monthly newsletter of his German Lutheran congregation (1955).[1]

The book under discussion here, *The Task of Old Testament Theology: Substance, Method and Cases,* is not one more typical (Biblical) theology of the Old Testament. It is a collection of articles that were originally published in several languages (English, German and Portuguese) and in various periodicals and *Festschriften*. They were written over a span of approximately three decades, in different places as well as under different circumstances. In *The Task of Old Testament Theology* Knierim combined them into one volume, which represents his

---

[*] R.P. Knierim, *The Task of Old Testament Theology: Substance, Method and Cases* (Grand Rapids, MI: Eerdmans, 1995).
[1] See Knierim, *Task of Old Testament Theology,* p. xii.

complete and updated opinion on the issue in contemporary *lingua franca*, that is, English.

The book deals mainly with Biblical theology and with the theology of the Hebrew Bible and its fundamental task according to the author. Although it was not originally designed so, it is comprised of two major sections:

The first, and more significant, section is a methodological program for Hebrew Bible theology as a field of study, as indicated by the opening chapter, "The Task of Old Testament Theology". It is followed by three critical responses from other scholars (see below), and concludes with Knierim's answer to them. The extensive chapter "The Interpretation of the Old Testament" concentrates on general topics, such as Biblical exegesis; theology and hermeneutics; the method of Old Testament theology; justice in Old Testament theology; and the Old Testament, the New Testament, and Jesus Christ. Here, the author furnishes important knowledge about basic issues in the discipline and guides readers toward a better understanding of his own terminology, methods, and distinctions.

The second section includes several detailed case studies of Old Testament theology. Most of these essays treat a comprehensive Biblical subject, such as "Revelation in the Old Testament", "Cosmos and History in Israel's Theology", "Food, Land and Justice" (the first, to the best of my knowledge, treats extensively the theology of food in the Bible), "Hope in the Old Testament", "The Spirituality of the Old Testament", "The Old Testament – The Letter and the Spirit", "Israel and the Nations in the Land of Palestine in the Old Testament", "The Composition of the Pentateuch", "The Book of Numbers", "Science in the Bible" (which fills in a gap in the study of Old Testament theology), "On the Contours of Old Testament and the Biblical Hamartiology [= sin, I.K.]". Some essays, such as "Conceptual Aspects in Exodus 25,1-9" and "On the Theology of Psalm 19", concentrate on specific Biblical texts. The essay "A Posteriori Exploration" completes this section.

The book concludes with an extensive chapter (appendix?), "On Gabler". Right now this chapter represents the most fundamental and detailed research on the famous 1787 inaugural lecture of Johann Philipp Gabler (1753-1826) at the University of Altdorf (Bavaria, Germany), in which Gabler distinguished Biblical theology as an independent discipline separate from dogmatic theology.[2] The book also contains a bibliography and several useful indexes.

Despite Knierim's statement that "other essays already published or on file which do not exemplify the task of Old Testament theology, or exemplify it less, were excluded from the collection",[3] it seems that not all the essays are good cases of Old Testament theology. In fact, some of them have little to do with it, at least directly. For instance, the essay "The Composition of the Pentateuch" (in which the author attempts to identify the Torah as *Vita Mosis* – a biography of Moses – including the book of Genesis!) is stimulating for its own sake (even if one does not agree with the author on every point), but is not a good illustration of Knierim's writings on Old Testament theology.[4] The same can be said of the interesting and meticulous essay "The Book of Numbers", which does not contribute much to the main subject of the volume.

Although six of the book's essays (and part of a seventh) are published for the first time,[5] nearly two-thirds of them have appeared previously in diverse contexts. Therefore, it is unfortunate that the author did not designate their sources. For example, the first three chapters are derived from Knierim's lecture at the annual meeting of the Society of Biblical Literature in 1983, which was followed by responses from other scholars, namely, Walter Harrelson, W. Sibley Towner, and Ronald E. Murphy, along with Knierim's reply to

---

[2] See also recently M. Sæbo, "Johann Philipp Gabler at the End of Eighteenth Century: History and Theology", *On the Way to Canon: Creative Tradition History in the Old Testament* (JSOT Suppl. 191; Sheffield: Sheffield Academic Press, 1998), pp. 310-326; L.T. Stuckenbruck, "Johann Philipp Gabler and the Delineation of Biblical Theology", *SJT* 52 (1999), pp. 139-157.

[3] Knierim, *Task of Old Testament Theology*, p. xiii.

[4] The centrality of the Sinai pericope in the Pentateuch (around 42 percent, almost half of the Pentateuch text) has, of course, important theological consequences. Note the saying of the Sages: "the whole world and the fullness were not created but for the sake of the Torah" (Genesis Rabbah 1,4). Unfortunately, Knierim's article was not developed in this direction.

[5] The unpublished essays include "Food, Land and Justice", "Hope in the Old Testament", "The Spirituality of the Old Testament", "On the Contours of Old Testament and Biblical Hamartiology", "A Posteriori Explorations", "On Gabler", and the first part of "On the Theology of Psalm 19".

them. All these were published in *Horizons in Biblical Theology* 6 (1984), pp. 25-80, 91-128 and are republished in the book. The reader who is unaware of this background wonders why responses of these scholars, specifically Americans, were included in Knierim's book, and not those of well-known European theologians. Notes like those on the chapters "The Interpretation of the Old Testament" and "Israel and the Nations in the Land of Palestine in the Old Testament", which clarify why these chapters have the style of oral presentation,[6] contribute to a better understanding of the pieces. In short, it would benefit readers to know the background of all the essays, that is, to whom they were addressed, and how, when, and where.

A previous reviewer, Richard J. Coggins, remarked that "the book has much to say about 'Method' and discusses many 'Cases'; there is not the substance of an Old Testament theology here."[7] Accordingly, the absence of the word "substance" from the subtitle of the book's cover is considered to be a Freudian slip. And indeed, if we take the word "substance" to mean "concreteness", "actuality", "worthiness", "usefulness", "significance", and so forth, there is some justification for Coggins' remark. Nevertheless, one cannot ignore the possibility that Knierim uses "substance" as an equivalent for the well-known German term *Sachkritik* or *Inhaltskritik*, that is, subject, content, or thematic criticism of the Hebrew Bible. From this viewpoint there is clearly much of "substance" in the book under review.

II.　Some Critical Methodological and Theological Viewpoints

In the following pages I present a number of critical perspectives on several methodological as well as theological aspects of Knierim's book. Some of the perspectives have to do with the nature of

---

[6] See Knierim, *Task of Old Testament Theology*, p. 57 note 1 (this essay is based on the lectures that Knierim gave at the United Methodist Seminary in São Paulo, Brazil, in 1989); p. 309 note 1 (this article is based on the lecture that Knierim delivered at the Lutheran Theological Seminary in Gettysburg, Pennsylvania, in 1978).

[7] See R. [J.] Coggins, "Old Testament Theology – How?", *ExpTim* 107 (1996), p. 309.

Biblical scholarship in general and Biblical theology as a self-defined discipline in particular, while others specifically concern Jewish – Christian relationship.

First and foremost, I share Knierim's comprehensive methodological outlook, that is, to view a defined subject within a comprehensive issue; to see a limited picture (the micro) within the entire framework (the macro); to understand the bound Biblical text, topic or thought not only within the close context – namely, paragraph, literary unit, book, composition of the school, or literary genre – but also within the whole broad Biblical perspective.[8] Moreover, at least concerning the theologies of the Biblical authors and editors, I believe that we must greatly broaden our perspective. This means that we should observe them not only from the perspective of the all-inclusive Biblical horizon, but also be aware of their own historical time, their ancient Near Eastern and Mediterranean background and cultural context, as much as possible. Obviously, the Biblical authors and editors, like any other creative writers, are conditioned by their own time, place, and specific historical circumstances and religio-cultural norms and atmosphere. No one can ignore these. Only from this wide perspective, and not in isolation, will we be able to grasp the uniqueness of the Biblical thoughts and be able to evaluate properly their special contribution. Only from these wide perspectives of the entire Biblical horizon within its Oriental context (and not from the Western secular philosophical viewpoints or any of the religious / confessional points of view and biases, either Jewish or Christian), can we deepen our understanding of the theologies of Hebrew Bible writers and editors.

Knierim did not refrain from placing at least some of his theological discussions in the ancient Oriental spectrum. For instance, in his essay, "Revelation in the Old Testament" he states that "what has been said must be viewed within the broader horizon of ancient Near Eastern ontology and epistemology, to which the Old Testament belonged". Accordingly, he dedicates a special detailed subdivision to that issue.[9] And in the article "The Book of Numbers" he discusses the narrative genre of the cultic campaign in the book. He refers to other ancient cultures and notes that this genre is unique neither to the Priestly writers nor to Israel: "Egyptian sources report

---

[8] See, for instance, Knierim, *Task of Old Testament Theology*, p. 469.

[9] Knierim, *Task of Old Testament Theology*, pp. 145-148.

about both the planning stage in Pharaoh's court and the execution of the plan".[10] In this case, however, Knierim refers neither to a specific example nor to any bibliography, as the subject demands.

Knierim focuses essentially on the final form (*den Endtext*) of the Hebrew Bible, that is, the Scripture as it is in front of us, the form that has been canonized and authorized. Usually, he does not deal with the earlier stages of the Biblical beliefs, thoughts, ideas, etc., which might be revealed by historical-critical methods. In other words, Knierim researched the Hebrew Bible theologies primarily from the *synchronic* viewpoint. It appears that in his research and writing he distinguishes between the nature and methods of the scholarly investigation of the history of the Israelite religion in the Biblical period on the one hand, and Old Testament theology(/ies) on the other. These are two different aspects of the same literary corpus, and they are incompatible.[11] Unlike some Biblical scholars, Knierim avoids confusion between the two independent concepts.[12]

Over generations many Christian theologians attempted to uncover and define (sometimes even impose) one central unifying theological idea of the whole Hebrew Bible. Concepts such as "covenant", "salvation history", "God is the Lord who imposes his will", the "Kingdom of God" are among the many suggestions offered in

---

[10] See Knierim, *Task of Old Testament Theology*, p. 387.

[11] For detailed discussion on this issue see above, chapter six, pp. 107-110.

[12] In reaction to my essay "Religionsgeschichte Israels oder Theologie des Alten Testaments? Das Jüdische Interesse an der Biblischen Theologie", *JBTh* 10 (1995), pp. 45-68, Professor Knierim wrote to me in his letter of July 25, 1996: "Lassen Sie mich nur sagen, daß Ihre Bestimmung des *Unterschiedes* der beiden und der eigenständigen Berechtigung (ich würde sagen: der eigenständigen *Notwendigkeit* für...) jeder der beiden vollkommen klar und unwiderleglich ist. Daß dies in USA fast kaum diskutiert, in England ([here a British scholar is named] et al.) nicht verstanden, und auch in Deutschland vermasselt ist, ist eigentlich ein bedauerliches Zeichen intellektueller Unfähigkeit der Gilde, die Probleme klar zu analysieren und zu rekonstruieren. Ich selbst bin seit meinem Artikel für die 1971 von Rad *Festschrift* (nun in Englisch in meinem Buch, dessen *Programm*, auch in der Komposition der Artikel, ja kaum von jemand verstanden wird), also: seit 1971 bin ich in einem anderen Lager bezüglich des Programmes für AT Theologie als dem von Rad'schen" (the publication of the letter's paragraph is with kind permission of Professor Knierim).

Biblical theological scholarship for this central theme.[13] Just recently Horst Dietrich Preuß (1927-1993) has suggested that the unifying theological center of the Old Testament is "JHWH's historical activity of electing Israel for community with his world and the obedient activity required of this people (and the peoples)".[14] But how does the Biblical Wisdom Literature (Proverbs, Job and Ecclesiastes, for example) correlate with this central theology? The reader is offered no reply. Knierim accurately emphasizes[15] that the Hebrew Bible does not contain a single central theology but several different theologies.[16] This plurality of theologies coexists in the Hebrew Bible and demands the interpretation of their relationship, that is, how they are related to one another in the same corpus. Some of them complement each other. There are also, however, some parallels as well as clear contradictions between theologies in the Hebrew Bible, the contradictions occasionally occurring even within the very same book.[17] How could this diversity of parallel and contradictory theologies coexist in the same book, literary complex, or corpus?

Indeed, contrary to the New Testament, in which almost everything is centered on Jesus Christ,[18] there is no distinct prominent center point – *die Mitte* – that the entire Hebrew Bible / Old

---

[13] For a survey of different suggestions and references, see above, chapter six, pp. 113-114.

[14] See H.D. Preuß, *Old Testament Theology* (Edinburgh: T&T Clark, 1995), vol. I, p. 25. In the original German version: "So soll 'JHWHs erwählendes Geschichtshandeln an Israel zur Gemeinschaft mit seiner Welt', das zugleich ein dieses Volk (und die Völker) verpflichtendes Handeln ist, als Mitte des AT, damit als Grundstruktur atl. Glaubens... bestimmt werden" (see idem, *Theologie des Alten Testaments*, Band 1: *JHWHs erwählendes und verpflichtendes Handeln* [Stuttgart, Berlin & Köln: Verlag W. Kohlhammer, 1991], p. 29). Obviously, this idea is reflected already in the subtitle of the book.

[15] See, for example, Knierim, *Task of Old Testament Theology*, pp. 1-4.

[16] Compare above, chapter six, p. 113.

[17] Compare, for example, Gen 6,6-7: "And *the Lord repented* that he had made man...", and Ex 32,14: "*And the Lord repented* of the evil which he thought to do to his people" (see also 2 Sam 24,16 // 1 Chr 21,15; Jer 26,19; Jon 3,10) with Num 23,19 as well as with 1 Sam 15,29: "And also *Israel's Everlasting One [that is, the Lord] does not deceive and does not repent*; for he is not a man that he should repent"! Similarly, cf. 1 Sam 15,11: "*I [the Lord] repent that I have made Saul king*" with verse 29 of the same chapter!

[18] Although the Epistle of James does not specifically mention Jesus.

Testament surrounds.[19] If all parts of the Hebrew Bible share any common issue, it is monotheism.[20] After all, this corpus is an anthology of a variety of literary genres written and edited over hundreds of years, during different eras (i.e., kingdom era, exilic and Second Temple periods), under many circumstances, and in many places (i.e., Israel, Judah, Babylon), by numerous authors, editors and schools (Deuteronomic, Priestly, Holiness, etc.). This leaves no space for any sort of homogeneity of a single, central thought in the Hebrew Bible. It is natural, therefore, that this heterogeneous literary complex contains a variety of theologies, which together in a single corpus reflects somehow a chaotic, and, from time to time, complicated conglomerate. This heterogeneity of thoughts and theologies is not at all surprising. On the contrary, it would be surprising if the Hebrew Bible did not contain an anthology of diverse lines of thoughts and theologies. Nonetheless, generally, Biblical scholars and theologians have not emphasized or described these crucial problems. Knierim, on the other hand, justifiably attempts to put this issue at the top of the Hebrew Bible / Old Testament theological agenda as a fundamental and central problem. He calls for a theological criterion to interpret and understand this problem, and to examine "the relationship or correspondence of the individual theologies within this theological pluralism".[21] "In order to determine the

---

[19] On this issue see in detail Reventlow, *Problems of Old Testament Theology,* and above, chapter six, pp. 113-114.

[20] Note that the Book of Esther does not mention the name of God at all. Perhaps only Esth 4,14, "For if you keep silence at such a time as this, relief and deliverance will rise for the Jews from another quarter", can be read as alluding to God (see Septuagint and Targumim ad loc.; Josephus, *Antiquitates Judaicae* 11,227; Esther Rabbah 8,6). Nonetheless, all these could be considered as late theological commentary on the Biblical verse. Indeed, *Vetus Latina,* the Vulgate and the Syraic version of the verse are not leading to this direction (see also Rabbi Abraham Ibn Ezra's commentary on Esth 4,14). Similarly, the Song of Songs does not contain the name of God.

[21] Knierim, *Task of Old Testament Theology,* p. 5. For other central problems of Biblical theology see, for example, B.S. Childs, *Biblical Theology in Crisis* (Philadelphia: Westminster, 1970); H.-J. Kraus, *Die Biblische Theologie: Ihre Geschichte und Problematik* (Neukirchen-Vluyn: Neukirchener Verlag, 1977); Reventlow, *Problems of Old Testament Theology*; G. Hasel, *Old Testament Theology: Basic Issues in the Current Debate* (Grand Rapids, MI: Eerdmans, 1991); L.G. Perdue, *The Collapse of History – Reconstructing Old Testament Theology* (Minneapolis, MN: Fortress Press, 1994).

Figure 8   A dispute between Jews and Christians (Germany, a wood-cutting, 16th century)

relationship among the Old Testament's theologies", says Knierim, "we must be able to discern theologically legitimate priorities. We must ask which theology or theological aspect or notion governs others, and which is relative to, dependent on, or governed by others. Ultimately, we must ask whether there is one aspect that dominates all others, is therefore fundamental, and must be understood as the criterion for the validity of all others".[22] Knierim emphasizes, however, that he neither envisions nor proposes harmonizing the Old Testament, "at least not in the sense that the plurality of theological notion is replaced by one notion; that one notion is expected to be found everywhere; that it is imposed on others without the recognition of their own place and validity; that all notions mean the same; and that contradictions are excluded and differences overlooked".[23]

[22] Knierim, *Task of Old Testament Theology,* pp. 8-9.
[23] Knierim, *Task of Old Testament Theology,* p. 52.

Of course, there is nothing wrong with diverse portraits of God in the Hebrew Bible. It is, however, necessary to be aware of these theological features – all canonized and authorized – to compare them for better understanding of the uniqueness of each individual theology, and to look for the possibility of their potential correlation with other Biblical theology(ies).

Generally, Christian Biblical theologians consider what they call the 'Old Testament' as a prehistory (*Vorgeschichte*), a preparation to the New Testament, and thus the latter as a fulfillment of the former (*Verheißung – Erfüllung*).[24] They are combining both Testaments, and alternating back and forth between them. They read the Old Testament in the light of the New Testament, and utilize the Christian dogmas which are stated in the New Testament as the only criteria for evaluation of the Old Testament. We mentioned already the expression "Alle Theologie ist Christologie" of Procksch.[25] Later on he stresses: "Ist Christus der Mittelpunkt der Theologie, so scheint das Alte Testament außerhalb einer geschichtstheologischen Betrachtung zu liegen. Denn in Geschichte und Glauben Israels liegt eine vorchristliche Geisteswelt vor, die höchstens in Jesus Christus ihren Schlusspunkt findet. Der Neue Bund tritt dem Alten gegenüber und hebt ihn auf".[26] So the Christian Biblical theologians ignore the distinctive characters and principles of the Hebrew corpus. They select some parts of it which are found appropriate to impose the Christian doctrines on, and they neglect the others.

This attitude has been expressed in almost all Christian theological legacy from the earliest times until the present. In the modern era it is reflected not only in the writings of theologians such as Johann Philipp Gabler over two hundred years ago,[27] and Otto Procksch just

---

[24] This appears already in Luke 24,27: "And beginning with Moses and all the prophets, he interpreted to them in all the scriptures the things concerning himself". It emerges repeatedly, however, in the works of many Christian theologians, for example, Childs, *Biblical Theology of the Old and New Testament*, p. 452; Caird – Hurst, *New Testament Theology*, pp. 57-62. See also, above, chapter six, pp. 115, 125.

[25] See Procksch, *Theologie des Alten Testaments*, p. 1; see above, chapter six, p. 115.

[26] Procksch, *Theologie des Alten Testaments,* p. 7.

[27] Although Gabler distinguished between Biblical theology and those of dogmatics, he maintained that the New Testament must be the exclusive

fifty years ago,[28] but also in those of some contemporary Christian scholars. Antonius H.J. Gunneweg (1922-1990), for instance, was of the opinion that from a Christian theological viewpoint the New Testament is the exclusive measure for the legitimacy and under-standing of the Old Testament: "Das Neue Testament war und ist für die Rezeption des Alten Testaments als Buch der christlichen Kirche das Kriterium, und nicht etwa umgekehrt".[29] As a matter of fact, in his monograph *Biblische Theologie des Alten Testaments* Gunne-weg treated the Old Testament's issues in the light of the New Testament.[30] A similar view is stated by Brevard S. Childs. Childs, too, is of the opinion that Christian scholars and theologians have the "fundamental goal to understand the various voices within the whole Christian Bible, New and Old Testament alike, as a witness to the one Lord Jesus Christ, the self-same divine reality".[31] Childs expresses the view that "Jesus Christ... who is testified to in *both testaments*, is *the ultimate criterion of truth* for both testaments".[32]

This view of Biblical theologies obviously represents the needs of at least some Christian communities, if not all. They bind the two corpora in their written theology, just as they profess and believe.[33] Nonetheless, this attitude of Christian theologians toward the Hebrew

---

criterion for study of the Old Testament by Christians. See Knierim, "On Gabler", *The Task of Old Testament Theology,* pp. 554-556.

[28] See Procksch, *Theologie des Alten Testaments,* pp. 1,7.

[29] A.H.J. Gunneweg, *Biblische Theologie des Alten Testaments: Eine Religionsgeschichte Israels in biblisch-theologischer Sicht* (Stuttgart, Berlin & Köln: W. Kohlhammer, 1993), p. 36; compare Gunneweg's *Vom Verstehen des Alten Testaments: Eine Hermeneutik* (Grundrisse zum Alten Testament – ATDER 5; Göttingen: Vandenhoeck & Ruprecht, 1977), pp. 183-187 ("Das Neue Testa-ment als Kriterium der kanonischen Geltung des Alten").

[30] See, for instance, his discussion on covenant (*Bund*) on pp. 68-75, and compare R. Rendtorff, "Recent German Old Testament Theologies", *JR* 76 (1996), pp. 328-337 esp. 334. Gunneweg was also of the opinion that the Christians understand the Hebrew Bible better than Jews: "Der christliche Glaube wagt es, die Textworte besser zu verstehen, als sie sich selbst verstehen – besser auch, als die Juden sie verstanden und immer noch verstehen" (*Bibli-sche Theologie,* p. 52).

[31] See Childs, *Biblical Theology of the Old and New Testament,* p. 85 and compare p. 452.

[32] Childs, *Biblical Theology of the Old and New Testament,* p. 591 (italics added).

[33] Compare above, chapter six, pp. 115-116.

Bible as a non self-contained corpus, as an incomplete production without the New Testament, giving central place to the New Testament in Old Testament interpretation and theology, is unacceptable not only from the Jewish viewpoint but also from a scholarly one.

From the Jewish viewpoint this sort of theology contains anti-Jewish features. The παλαιᾶς διαθήκης of Paul in Second Corinthians 3,14, for example, which is usually translated as the "old testament" or the "old covenant", is invalid and replaced by the "new covenant" commonly called the "new testament".[34] To cite J.P. Gabler, for instance, the New Testament is "newer and better".[35] Only the "new / true Israel" (that is, the Church), carries on the spirit of ancient, original "Biblical Israel", not the so-called "Talmudic Jews".[36] In the same chapter (2 Cor 3,6) Paul introduces himself as minister of "the new testament, not of the letter, but of

---

[34] See also 2 Corinthians 3,6; 5,17. Noteworthy, too, the words of a Christian ("a certain philosopher") who said to Rabban Gamliel: "Since the day you people were exiled from your land, the Law of Moses has been taken away (i.e., superseded), and another book given in its place [in Codex Oxford, the reading is: and the law of the Evangelium has been given], wherein it is written..." (Babylonian Talmud, *Shabbath* 116a-b).

[35] For this point see Knierim, "On Gabler", *The Task of Old Testament Theology*, p. 537.

[36] The concept that Christianity is a continuation of "Biblical Israel" – or even a substitute for Israel – is deeply rooted in Christian theology. See, for example, Matt 2,9; 3,9; 8,11-12; 16,18; 21,43; Luke 13,24-30; Acts 15,14-17; 28,28; cf. R.R. Ruether, *Faith and Fratricide: The Theological Roots of Anti-Semitism* (New York: Seabury, 1974), pp. 84-86; Caird-Hurst, *New Testament Theology*, pp. 55-57; R. Rendtorff, "Das 'Ende' der Geschichte Israels", *Gesammelte Studien zum Alten Testament* (TB 57; München: Chr. Kaiser, 1975), pp. 267-276. It should be mentioned that in the last decades there are also different voices heard among Christians. For example, in 1980 the Synod of the Evangelical Church of the Rhineland (Germany) declared: "We believe the permanent election of the Jewish people as the people of God and realize that through Jesus Christ the church is taken into the covenant of God with his people" (see A. Brockway, P. von Buren, R. Rendtorff and S. Schoon, *The Theology of the Churches and the Jewish People: Statements by the World Council of Churches and its Member Churches – A Commentary* [Geneva: World Council of Churches, 1988], p. 93, §4). Some German theologians protested against this declaration, and Gunneweg (*Biblische Theologie*, p. 73) defined it as "eklatante Häresie" (clear heresy). Cf. Rendtorff, "Recent German Old Testament Theologies", p. 335, and there his sharp criticism of Gunneweg's statement.

the spirit, for the letter kills, but the spirit gives life". It means in Christianity that "the Old Testament has been considered to be the document of a false religion, a religion of laws and the letter, whereas the New Testament represents the true religion – a religion of the gospel and the spirit".[37] This attitude, the negation of Judaism and the Jewish people, has motivated the well-known terrible persecutions and discrimination against Jews by Christians over generations, and it leaves no room for cooperation between Jewish and Christian Biblical scholars and theologians.[38]

From a scholarly viewpoint New Testament supersessionist theology is unacceptable as well, first and foremost because it lacks any scientific objectivity. The methods of such theologians have an a priori one-sided confessional bias. Moreover, the New Testament is not a continuation of the Hebrew Bible. There is no real organic connection between the two corpora, either literally and historically, or linguistically (Hebrew and Aramaic versus Greek)[39] and philosophically (Oriental-Semitic thought versus Greco-Roman). They are somehow connected theologically to each other presumably sometime in the early stage of Christianity, when the Jewish-Christians accepted the new religious direction but simultaneously associated it with their original religious heritage. Apparently, they would have liked also to base their new religious ideas on the well-known and widely accepted ancient Hebrew traditions of the Prophets and Psalms, for example.[40]

---

[37] See Knierim, *Task of Old Testament Theology,* p. 298.

[38] On this issue see above, chapter six, pp. 115-118.

[39] For the possibility, however, that Matthew's Gospel was originally written in Aramaic, see W.F. Albright and C.S. Mann, *Matthew* (AB 26; Garden City, NY: Doubleday, 1971), p. vii. For the presumed Semitic background of several passages in the New Testament, see, for example, M. Black, *An Aramaic Approach to the Gospels and Acts* (3rd edn.; Oxford: Clarendon, 1967); J.A. Fitzmyer, *Essays on the Semitic Background of the New Testament* (London: Geoffrey Chapman, 1971); M. Casey, *Aramaic Sources of Mark's Gospel* (Cambridge / New York / Oakleigh: Cambridge University Press, 1998). The author of the last study, for instance, reviews four Marcan paragraphs only (Mark 9,11-13; 2,23-3,6; 10,35-45; 14,12-26). For each he offers the presumed Aramaic source "which would cause the translator to produce the sentences which we find in the Gospel" (p. 241).

[40] Since Jesus and at least some of his adherents (e.g., the apostles) were Jews – raised and educated on Judaism – it is very hard, if not impossible, to understand the New Testament without knowledge of and background from the Hebrew Bible / Old Testament and early Judaism.

Nonetheless, only the New Testament reflects the unique Christian religion. As of today the relationship between the two "Testaments" – the "New" (*novum*) and the "Old" (*vetus*) – is an unsolved question even in Christianity itself. An essay such as "Zur Frage der Notwendigkeit des Alten Testaments" (in the Christian canon, of course),[41] or "Warum gehört die Hebräische Bibel in den christlichen Kanon?" published in *Berliner Theologische Zeitschrift* just several years ago,[42] verifies this claim. Furthermore, in his 1993 monograph Gunneweg defined the historical and theological relationship between the two "Testaments" as the most difficult problem of Christian theology: "Er sieht sich mit dem wohl schwierigsten Problem der christlichen Theologie konfrontiert, nämlich mit der Frage nach der historisch und theologisch angemessenen Verhältnisbestimmung von Altem und Neuem Testament".[43] One can only agree with Preuß's conclusion in the last section of the second volume of his *Old Testament Theology*. In that section Preuß discusses the "openness of the Old Testament", stressing that such openness "does not necessarily imply or even mean an openness to the New Testament. Only a Christian theologian is able to speak of the Old Testament's openness to the New Testament. Such a theologian comes to the Old Testament by way of the New Testament using it as the basis to approach the Old Testament critically and questioningly".[44]

[41] H.G. Geyer, "Zur Frage der Notwendigkeit des Alten Testaments", *EvT* 25 (1965), pp. 207-237.

[42] M. Heymel, "Warum gehört die Hebräische Bibel in den christlichen Kanon?", *BTZ* 7 (1990), pp. 2-20. For further discussion on this issue see also H. von Campenhausen, "Das Alte Testament als Bibel der Kirche", *Aus der Frühzeit des Christentums: Studien zur Kirchengeschichte des ersten und zweiten Jahrhunderts* (Tübingen: J.C.B. Mohr [Paul Siebeck], 1963), pp. 152-196 esp. 154; J. Schreiner, "Das Verhältnis des Alten Testaments zum Neuen Testament", *Segen für die Völker – Gesamelte Schriften zur Entstehung und Theologie des Alten Testament* (Würzburg: Echter Verlag, 1987), pp. 392-407; W.H. Schmidt, "Das Problem des Alten Testaments in der christlichen Theologie", in *Festschrift H. Donner* (Wiesbaden: Otto Harrassowitz, 1995), pp. 243-251; F. Watson, "The Old Testament as Christian Scripture", *SJT* 52 (1999), pp. 227-232.

[43] Gunneweg, *Biblische Theologie*, p. 52; see also idem, *Vom Verstehen des Alten Testaments*, pp. 37-41, where Gunneweg writes (p. 41): "[D]as hermeneutische Problem des Verhältnisses der beiden Kanonteile und der christlichen Geltung des Alten Testaments bleibt eine jetzt erst recht unerledigte".

[44] H.D. Preuß, *Old Testament Theology* (Edinburgh: T&T Clark, 1995), vol.

Contrary to all those Christian theologians who relate the Old
Testament to the New Testament, Knierim focuses on the Old
Testament "in its own right".[45] He wants "to give back to the Old
Testament the right of its own voice".[46] He clarifies for Christians
that an interpretation of their Old Testament "must be mindful of
that dissensus [i.e., distinction] and, therefore, rest on the Old Testament itself and not on their New Testament or on an a priori
combination of both".[47] He stresses that the "Old Testament theology must systematize the theological traditions of the Old Testament".[48] Although according to Knierim "a united Biblical theology
should not be assumed to be ultimately elusive", he emphasizes that
"a separate focus on the theology of each testament is required so
that, before any Biblical theology is proposed, each testament receives
the right to its own case without interference from the other".[49] To
be sure, Knierim makes clear the necessity of dealing with the Old
Testament by Christians: "Because the Old Testament is part of our
canon, one way or another we must come to grips with it".[50] But
how do these statements by Knierim coordinate with what he says
in other places? Two examples follow:

1. "With regard to the question of the validity of the theology of
   Ex 3,7-8 ..., either this theology must be *replaced* by a theology
   of God's universal justice found elsewhere, partly in the Old
   Testament and partly in the New Testament, or its own paradigm
   must be *reconceptualized*... A reconceptualization is legitimate precisely because of the claim, found in both the Old and the New

---

II, p. 306. In the original German version: " 'Offenheit des AT' meint damit
nicht sofort oder gar nur dessen Offenheit hin zum NT. Von letzterer kann
nur ein christlicher Theologe sprechen, der bereits vom NT herkommt und
von ihm her an das AT forschend und fragend herantritt" (idem, *Theologie des
Alten Testaments*, Band 2: *Israels Weg mit JHWH* [Stuttgart, Berlin & Köln: W.
Kohlhammer, 1992], p. 326).

[45] See Knierim, *Task of Old Testament Theology*, pp. 1 note 1; 9 note 6.

[46] Knierim, *Task of Old Testament Theology*, p. 299. Knierim (p. 310) also
says: "I prefer to give the Old Testament its own say... I prefer this route to
the other in which the New Testament speaks for the Old Testament, thereby
depriving it of its own voice and authenticity".

[47] Knierim, *Task of Old Testament Theology*, p. 1 note 1.

[48] Knierim, *Task of Old Testament Theology*, p. 9 note 6.

[49] Knierim, *Task of Old Testament Theology*, p. 73.

[50] Knierim, *Task of Old Testament Theology*, p. 309.

Testaments, that all humanity is elected into the blessing of God's universal justice and salvation.... Inasmuch as Jesus Christ is proclaimed to be the ultimate revelation of the reign of God, *he, too, will have to be understood as representing this criterion*".[51] In this case, obviously, Knierim is not that far, for instance, from the previously cited statements of Childs.

2. "It seems that the Old and the New Testaments complement each other in that each helps rectify the deficiency of the other and in that each is partly in need of reconceptualization in light of the legitimate emphasis of the other".[52]

The Biblical concept regarding the election of Israel as the people of God from among all the nations is well known, especially from Deuteronomistic literature and Deutero-Isaiah.[53] Knierim knows and acknowledges this concept: "*Israel's election is valid*". "But", he continues, "the entire Old Testament overwhelmingly testifies to the fact that the elect community was at no time in its history without sin and guilt. *It never was what it was called to be*". Knierim then affirms equitably, "Nor has Christianity ever been what it was called to be. In light of the central claim of Christianity, this is an even *more serious deficiency*".[54]

It is an entirely different attitude than that of traditional church fathers and many Christian theologians over generations. They used Israel's prophets' rebukes and confrontations with guilt and sin (often greatly exaggerated) against Israel, and considered Jews as a stubborn

---

[51] Knierim, *Task of Old Testament Theology*, p. 135 (italics added in the last sentence).

[52] Knierim, *Task of Old Testament Theology*, p. 137. See also below, at the end, paragraph 6, in this essay.

[53] See, for example, Deut 4,19-20; 7,6-8 // 14,2; 10,14-15; 26,17-19; 32,8-9 (in verse 8 read: בני אל, with LXX and 4QDeut^q (in 4QDeut^j: בני אלהים), instead of MT בני ישראל, cf. Deut 4,19-20); 1 Kgs 3,8a; Isa 41,8-9; 44,1-2.8-10; see also Ex 19,5-6; Ezek 20,5; Ps 33,12; 105,43; 135,4. The concept is unique to the Israelites and unknown among other ancient Near Eastern religions. For scholarly literature on the issue, see Preuß, *Theologie des Alten Testaments*, vol. 2, p. 305 note 1, as well as his own discussion on pp. 305-327; F.W. Golka, "Universalism and the Election of the Jews", *Theology* 90 (1987), pp. 273-280 (for the German version of the article, see idem., "Die Geschöpflichkeit des Menschen und die Erwählung Israels", *Jona* [CBK; Stuttgart: Calwer Verlag, 1991], pp. 25-33).

[54] Knierim, *Task of Old Testament Theology*, p. 440 (italics added).

people and children of those who killed God's messengers and prophets (e.g., Matt 5,12; 23,30-37; Luke 11,47-51; 13,34; 16,31). To cite Acts 7,50-51: "You stiff-necked and uncircumcised in heart and ears, you do always resist the Holy Spirit. As your fathers did, so do you".

As a Biblical researcher and exegete, Knierim points out that "the prophetic texts contain the record of Israel's failure to live up to and maintain the conditions of its election history. Israel failed specifically with regard to internal societal [should be: "social", I.K.] justice and exclusive loyalty to its savior God, Yahweh, and the purity of Yahweh's cult".[55] Therefore he sees, correctly, a serious "tension between Israel's election and failure". Is there anything wrong with confronting this problematic theme as it appears in the Hebrew corpus? Should we not at least admit it as it is without any bias and apology? If one ignores or attempts to cover it, will it disappear from the Bible? Nonetheless, Knierim views this as a paradigm for humanity: "Israel would thus be the symbol not for a new but for the old, imperfect humanity through the toleration of the tension at the crossroads of election and failure".[56]

Knierim emphasizes that in the Torah and the Deuteronomistic history, Israel's election "is both the purpose and aim of creation and the condition wherein the nations can be blessed or cursed. The status of the nations depends on whether they bless or curse Israel" (Gen 12,1-3; cf. 27,29b; Num 24,9b).[57] Accordingly, says Knierim: "it is nowhere said, except for the attempt in Numbers 22-24, that the Canaanites cursed Israel. Hence, in the light of their experience vis-à-vis the conquest, why are they cursed when they do no more than fail to bless Israel and become Yahweh worshippers?"[58] But Biblical statements such as "Not because of your [Israelites'] righteousness... are you going in to possess their [Canaanites'] land; but *because of the wickedness of these nations* the Lord your God is driving them out from before you..." (Deut 9,5; cf. 9,4; 18,12; Lev 18,24-28.30; 20,23-24), clarify that the occupation of the Canaanites' land was not because "they do no more than fail to bless Israel and become Yahweh worshippers", but because of their own long-term,

---

[55] Knierim, *Task of Old Testament Theology*, p. 450.
[56] Knierim, *Task of Old Testament Theology*, p. 450.
[57] Knierim, *Task of Old Testament Theology*, p. 451.
[58] Knierim, *Task of Old Testament Theology*, p. 451, compare pp. 134-135, 317.

accumulative heavy transgression and guilt.[59] Knierim does not mention these verses here, but he discusses them in another place and defines them as "traditio-historically, and especially substantively, a secondary, derivative rationalization".[60] He states, "In the book of Genesis (from Gen 12,1.7 on), the sins of the Canaanites play no role as a reason for that promise [i.e., Yahweh's promise to give the land to the patriarchs decendants', I.K.]".[61] But what about Gen 15,16: "And they [the Israelites] shall come back here [to Canaan] in the fourth generation; for *the iniquity of the Amorites* [i.e., Canaan-ites][62] *is not yet complete*"? Knierim's statement "If they did, it would not make no [better: any, I.K.] sense anyway" is unconvincing. Moreover, it seems that in this case, at least, there is no controversy between the election theology and the Biblical "claim to Yahweh's universal justice". According to the theology of Gen 15,16 and Deut 9,5 etc., the conquest of Canaan absolutely does not negate the affirmation "that Israel's God, Yahweh, does not violate justice".[63] This theology does not confirm the rest of Knierim's conclusion: "[B]y subjecting the theology of creation to the theology of exclusionary election, it discredits the claim that Yahweh is truly and justifiably the universal deity".[64] From the Biblical-theological view-point the Canaanites were conquered and dispossessed because of their wickedness, just as in the earlier time the whole generation of the Flood (except for the Noahic remnant) was destroyed because

---

[59] It is also worth noting that the attempt in Numbers 22-24 to curse the Israelites was made by the Moabites and Midianites with the help of Balaam the son of Beor the Aramean (Num 22,5; Deut 23,4-5). The Moabites, Midianites and the Arameans are not included among the six / seven / ten nations that inhabited the promised land / Canaan (Gen 15,19-21; Ex 3,8; 23,23; 34,11; Deut 7,1; Josh 3,10). Indeed, according to Deut 2,9 the Lord ordered "Do not harass Moab or contend with them in battle, for I will not give you any of their land for a possession, because I have given Ar to the sons of Lot for a possession". Moreover, Num 22-24 together with Deut 2,9 are opposed to the idea of Gen 12,3: the Moabites that cursed Israel not only were not cursed by God, but received His protection.

[60] See Knierim, *Task of Old Testament Theology*, pp. 96-100 esp. 98.

[61] Knierim, *Task of Old Testament Theology*, p. 98.

[62] The name Amorites in the Hebrew Bible is occasionally parallel to the name Canaanites, and thus the "Land of Amori" to the "Land of Canaan". See, for example Josh 10,6.12; 24,8; Am 2,9-10.

[63] Knierim, *Task of Old Testament Theology*, p. 452; see also 318.

[64] Knierim, *Task of Old Testament Theology*, p. 452.

of its corruption and wickedness (Gen 6,1-8,19). This viewpoint is reflected later on by the punishment of the Israelites themselves. The kingdoms of Israel and Judah were conquered and destroyed, their inhabitants exiled, and the land inherited by others because of their social sins as well as disloyalty to God (2 Kgs 17,4-23; 24,18-25,21; 2 Chr 36,11-20).

If, however, one observes the Biblical material otherwise, that is, not from the theological viewpoint of Knierim but rather from that of history, as has been done, for instance, by Friedemann W. Golka,[65] one comes to a different conclusion. Golka surveys the theology of the election of Israel versus the theology of creation of the world and humanity in the Hebrew Bible. On the basis of the Israelites' connections with the other nations in the ancient Near East during the Biblical period, he concludes that at least "in post-exilic literature the priority of creation [that is, *all humans* are God's creatures and hence participate in his blessing] over the election of Israel has been fully recognized".[66]

Knierim points out that the Hebrew Bible is not, throughout, "particularly concerned with Israel's election". The question of "where this concern reflects a particularistic paradigm for the exclusivity of Israel's election at the expense of the election equally of all, and where it reflects a universalistic paradigm of Israel's election as a sign of the equal election of all"[67] is still unanswered. But the clarification of this question affects the Hebrew Bible's claim of the universality of God of the whole world (monotheism) as a God of universal justice and righteousness.

Knierim uses within one small paragraph the words "the election equally of all" and once again in chiastic order the words "the equal election of all". Is he of the opinion that each religious group (including Christians, naturally) has its own equal process of election? Is he attempting to say that the Christian community, as well as Israel, is elected by God? In another section of the book, Knierim expresses what is probably the New Testament's perspective: "Inasmuch as Israel's election is recognized and not replaced by the equally problematic Christian community, it is recognized as a servant in God's plan of universal salvation, *together with and alongside*

---

[65] See Golka, "Universalism and the Election of the Jews", pp. 273-280.
[66] Golka, "Universalism and the Election of the Jews", p. 280.
[67] Knierim, *Task of Old Testament Theology*, p. 549.

the Christian community".[68] Does he hint here at this "equal election"? In any event, at least from a scholarly viewpoint, this "equal election" is not confirmed in the Jewish Scriptures.

Does the intensive focus of Knierim on universalism and God's universal justice represent, in fact, the ideals of both Protestant Christianity, the Enlightenment, and German idealism? It seems that his commitment to the ideal of abstract truth from time to time clouds his perceptions of the Biblical – historical realities / contexts in which truth is expressed. Knierim's concept of universal justice, which somehow questions Jewish chosenness in an era following the Holocaust (and does not seriously engage Christian chosenness) is an example of this issue.

Being a Protestant theologian (who was also trained as a pastor in the Evangelisch-theologische Fakultät of Ruprecht-Karls Universität Heidelberg for many years) *generally* does not affect Knierim's academic objectivity (as much as that is possible). But let us not forget that after all every person is connected, consciously or unconsciously, to his own original religious roots, and it is not easy to be released from them completely. Furthermore, contrary to the history of Israelite religion(s), the nature of theology of Hebrew Bible / Old Testament is generally ahistorical, and occasionally subjective or even confessional.[69] Thus, it is not entirely surprising that Knierim's book, which includes in its title the words "Old Testament Theology", reflects occasionally the individual religious views of its author and / or "the Christian voice".[70] In fact, Knierim declares, "I prefer to give the Old Testament its own say in the hope that it may tell something which is in the spirit of Christ".[71] Later on the same page he inquires, "Where in these events is Jesus Christ whom we confess to be Lord?" On another occasion he discusses Paul's statement in 2 Cor 3,6[72] and confesses frankly, "I do not want to belittle the importance of this Christology, even as it affects the understanding of the Old Testament".[73]

---

[68] Knierim, *Task of Old Testament Theology*, p. 135 (italics added).

[69] Compare above, chapter six, pp. 107–110.

[70] Knierim, *Task of Old Testament Theology*, p. 309.

[71] Knierim, *Task of Old Testament Theology*, p. 310; other examples are on pp. 135, 137, 309, 311, 317, 321, 549.

[72] See the discussion on this verse, above.

[73] Knierim, *Task of Old Testament Theology*, p. 298.

But should Hebrew Bible theology, as a branch of university study, necessarily be related to the New Testament? Must it always be confessional? As I have stated elsewhere, the learning of Hebrew Bible theology at university level can and must proceed objectively – as much as that is achievable – from academic, intellectual viewpoints. Then the synagogue and the church can apply the results of such research as they see fit.[74]

Unfortunately, Knierim sometimes is imprecise in his accounts of specific Biblical or historical data. Three examples follow.

1. In the chapter "Israel and the Nations in the Land of Palestine in the Old Testament" he writes: "What was important for the Jews was their return to their land after more than twenty-five hundred years of exile, and their claim of independence in that land after twenty-five hundred years of dependence on foreign empires".[75] Knierim refers here to the epoch from the destruction of Jerusalem and the Babylonian exile in 586 BCE to the establishment of the state of Israel in 1948 CE. But he overlooks some important historical events:

The first event, almost fifty years after the Babylonian exile, when at least a portion of the Jews returned to Zion (Cyrus' decree of 538 BCE; Ez 1-2; Neh 7; 2 Chr 36,21-23), was the rebuilding of the Temple, resettlement of Judah, and achievement of a religio-cultural autonomy which existed for a long time.

The second event, from the time of the high priest Simon the Hasmonaean (ca. 142 BCE; 1 Macc 13,41-42) until the invasion of Judaea by the Roman commander Pompey to (63 BCE), almost eighty years later, the Jews controlled their own destiny in an independent Kingdom in the Land of Israel.

The third event, after the capture of Jerusalem by Pompey, was when the Jewish people lost their political and military independence, even though their entity in Judaea existed – in one form or another

---

[74] See above, chapter six, p. 114.

[75] Knierim, *Task of Old Testament Theology*, p. 310. Knierim (p. 314) also says: "In 722 BCE and in 586 BCE, respectively, that control [of the land] was lost; it remained so until 1948 and 1967. For 2,500 years, the land was a province under foreign powers (the Babylonians, the Persians, the Greeks, the Romans, Constantinople [=Byzantine Empire – I.K.], the Arabs, [and what about the 'Kingdom of Jerusalem', which was established by Crusades? – I.K.], the Turks, and the British Mandate)".

– until the destruction of Jerusalem and its Temple by Titus (70 CE).

The fourth event, one is not allowed to forget Bar Kochba's restoration, as short as it was (132-135 CE), which was put down by a European power – Hadrianus, the Caesar of Rome.

2. Later on Knierim states: "That was the time from 1200 to 900 BCE... the time from Joshua through David and Solomon. It was the time of conquest, settlement, and integration of the land".[76] But the particular time span of this period as designated by the author is inexact. On the one hand, Israel is mentioned in the stela from the fifth year of Pharaoh Merneptah (ca. 1220 BCE) as a people which was defeated by him in his campaign to Canaan.[77] That is, Israel as an entity already existed in the land of Canaan at the beginning of the last quarter of the thirteenth century BCE. Obviously, this evidence cannot be ignored by anyone who speaks about the time of conquest. On the other hand, King Solomon died probably circa 928 BCE. Thus, the era that Knierim refers to is actually from 1225 to 928 BCE, not 1200 to 900.

3. At the end of the same chapter Knierim writes: "Lot (Edom!) is offered the choice of land by Abraham (Genesis 13 [,1-12, I.K.])".[78] But Lot is considered in the Bible as eponymous of the Ammonites and Moabites (Gen 19,37-38), not the Edomites, who were related to Esau (Gen 25,30; 36,1).

Accordingly, one must conclude that some of Kinierim's arguments / theological positions are based, unfortunately, on inaccurate historical facts.

The task of Hebrew Bible / Old Testament Theology is to present the full viewpoint of the Scriptures – not only the "light sides" of God, the nice and the friendly sides, but also God's "dark sides", such as vengefulness, excommunication, wrath, perverseness, which are associated with God in a variety of Biblical texts (i.e., Gen 21,9-13; 22,1-19; Ex 4,21 and 7,3; 4,24-25; Lev 10,1-2; Num 22,20-22; 1 Sam 15,2-3 among many others). How are these contradictory theological views of God correlated in the same single corpus – the

---

[76] Knierim, *Task of Old Testament Theology*, p. 314.

[77] See Pritchard, *Ancient Near Eastern Texts Related to the Old Testament*, pp. 376-378 esp. 378.

[78] Knierim, *Task of Old Testament Theology*, p. 320.

Hebrew Bible / Old Testament – sometimes even within the same book? Moreover, how should we – Jews and Christians, rabbis, priests and ministers, theologians, Biblical scholars and intellectual laymen, teachers and educators – deal with these difficult theological points, that is, God's "dark sides"? Are we allowed just to ignore them totally? One would expect some of Knierim's chapters or at least cases to deal particularly with these issues as well.[79]

Finally, like many other Christian theologians and Biblical scholars, Knierim employs the common Christian term "Old Testament". In Christian theology this term originally had negative and anti-Jewish connotations. Knierim is aware of this, and therefore emphasizes that "the Christian designation of the Jewish Bible as their Old Testament must not be interpreted negatively". According to him it "can only mean antecedence to the New Testament historically, even as this antecedence is not the basis for determining the relationship of the two testaments".[80] But "Old" and "New" mean, to use the words of Gunneweg, "eine theologisch nicht auflösbare Zuordnung an: das Alte ist alt nur im Verhältnis zum Neuen, das Neue neu nur in seinem Bezug zum Alten."[81] I have no doubt that Knierim does not intend any negative connotation by using this term. But I wonder why he did not use simply a term like "Hebrew Bible/Scripture", Tanak, or Mikra, in order to avoid the problematic term ("First Covenant Book" / *Erstes Bundesbuch* as well as "First Testament" / *Erstes Testament* are still Christian terminologies, since the Jewish people have only one "Covenant Book" / "Testament").[82] More

---

[79] These and similar issues have been handled by the classical and medieval Jewish exegeses as well as in modern times by some European scholars, see, for example, J. Ebach, "Der Gott des Alten Testaments – ein Gott der Rache?", *Biblische Erinnerungen – Theologische Reden zur Zeit* (Bochum: SWI Verlag, 1993), pp. 81-93; N. Lohfink, "Der gewalttätige Gott des Alten Testaments und die Suche nach einer gewaltfreien Gesellschaft", *JBTh* 2 (1987), pp. 106-136; E. Zenger, *Ein Gott der Rache? – Feindpsalmen verstehen* (Biblische Bücher 1; Freiburg / Basel / Wien: Herder, 1994); W. Dietrich und C. Link, *Die dunklen Seiten Gottes – Willkür und Gewalt* (2nd edn.; Neukirchen-Vluyn: Neukirchener Verlag, 1997).

[80] Knierim, *Task of Old Testament Theology*, p. 2 note 1.

[81] Gunneweg, *Vom Verstehen des Alten Testaments*, p. 36.

[82] For such suggestions, see R. Rendtorff und H.H. Henrix (eds.), *Die Kirchen und das Judentum: Dokumente von 1945 bis 1985* (Paderborn: Verlag

over, the designation of the Jewish Bible by the term "Old Testament" is inaccurate. These two terms are incompatible. After all, the order and the classification of the historical, prophetical and so-called hagiographical books, the number of the books included in the Old Testament, and the content of some other books are quite different from those in the Jewish Bible.[83] The sequence of the books in the Jewish Bible and in the Old Testament, for instance, has considerable theological implications, as I have illustrated in another study.[84]

III. Conclusion

In fact, I share many of Knierim's methodological premises for the task of Hebrew Bible / Old Testament theology; for instance, a far-reaching canonical and historical range of vision as a substantial methodological framework, the plurality of theologies which constitutes central issues, rejection of criteriological superiority of the New Testament. I am critical of him, nevertheless, on several cardinal points, for example, his view of election theology.

It is customary not to agree with an author on every explicit detail or distinct part of a book. In spite of some of my critical viewpoints, however, I can conclude that *The Task of Old Testament Theology: Substance, Method and Cases* as a whole is an original study, distinguished by its depth and broadness. It makes an essential contribution to Biblical scholarship in general and to Biblical theology specifically. Knierim handles the problematic issue of the plurality of Hebrew Bible theologies from comprehensive methodological viewpoints. He presents several particular interesting cases as well, showing respect for the "mother religion".

Bonifatius-Druckerei / München: Chr. Kaiser Verlag, 1988), pp. 518-519; J.A. Sanders, "First Testament and Second", *BTB* 17 (1987), pp. 47-49; Zenger, *Das Erste Testament*, pp. 152-154. Noteworthy to mention that Zenger, in spite of his suggestion, still uses the term *Altes Testament*, see for example, his *Einleitung in das Alte Testament*.

[83] For the different order and content of the Christian Old Testament in comparison with the Hebrew Bible / *Tanak*, see Zenger u.a., *Einleitung in das Alte Testament*, p. 30.

[84] See I. Kalimi, "History of Interpretation: The Book of Chronicles in Jewish Tradition – From Daniel to Spinoza", *RB* 105 (1998), pp. 5-41 esp. 24-25. See also Sweeney, "Tanak versus Old Testament", pp. 353-372.

During the preparation of this chapter the words of Rabbi Oshaia from the Babylonian Talmud (*Pesahim* 87b) several times came to mind:

אמר רבי אושעיא מאי דכתיב "צדקת פרזונו בישראל"?
צדקה עשה הקדוש ברוך הוא בישראל שפזרן לבין האומות

> Rabbi Oshaia said: What is meant by the verse, "Even the righteous act of His Ruler in Israel" [Judg 5,11]? The Holy One, blessed be He, showed righteousness / mercy unto Israel by scattering them among the nations.[85]

I seriously question this theodicy of rabbis that attempts to justify the tragic historical circumstances of the Jewish existence among the nations as the righteousness / mercy of the Almighty unto them – circumstances which caused them to pay such a high price for keeping their identity and their unique religious-cultural heritage. Nevertheless, I allow myself to paraphrase this rabbinical statement by saying: "Blessed be Professor Rolf P. Knierim, who showed his righteousness / mercy unto Biblical scholars and theologians by collecting these scattered essays from among multilingual nations as well as from many periodicals and *Festschriften* to form one comprehensive, impressive and valuable volume"!

---

[85] For the English translation, compare H. Freedman, *Pesahim – Translated into English with Notes, Glossary and Indices* (London: Soncino Press, 1938), p. 463.

Epilogue

Any religious text written some time in the past, has a unique history of its transmission, its study, its interpretation and research as well as its value, influence and application. Therefore, awareness of the origin, continuity, and development of any text is essential also for the understanding of its parts as well as its entirety.[1] The consideration should reflect the text's impact over many centuries; how it was interpreted by various authors, its development and its continuity within the religious groups. In other words, it should not be looked upon as an isolated incident, rather as a part of a long-range and against a broad internal (variety of events, opinions, sects, etc. in the Jewish world), and external (ancient Near East / Mediterranean cultures, religions, etc.) historical background. The scholar should keep in mind that generally Jewish literature – in the large meaning of the term – flourished as a result of its dialectical contacts with different encircling cultures, religious identities as well as in diversity of thoughts and beliefs among Jews themselves. He must be, too, acutely aware of the variety of literary devices applied by the distinct writers. It seems that only through this method of deep analysis and maintaining a wide perspective, one can strive to achieve a better understanding of such a text, and place it in its appropriate historical, social and religious context.

Accordingly, the first part of the volume attempts to follow the history of the location of the *Aqedah* and its association with the Jewish and Samaritan temples from its very beginning (as much as the sources allowed us) throughout numerous generations, writers and interpreters, while presenting its nuance, relevance and particularity in each source, time and group against their own inner and outer historical relatedness. The second part of the volume demonstrates that the purpose of the rabbis' homilies is not pedagogical only, that is, to encourage Jews to follow their ancestors' Law of circumcisions

---

[1] See Kalimi, "History of Interpretation", pp. 6-7.

and ethics of non-slander, betrayal, and so on. Some of them were also intended, presumably, to dispute theologically with the new religious movement – Christianity. The Midrashim concerning circumcision and slander may have been composed against this historical background and that of the Hadrianic ban on circumcision, etc. in the Land of Israel, in the second half of the first and the first half of the second centuries CE. By observing from this perspective one certainly achieves a better understanding of them. While some Christians questioned Moses' Law in general and the practicing of circumcision in particular, and some Midrashim disputed with them and sided against those slanderers who cooperated with Romans (chapters three and four), others disputed with Jews who questioned the credibility of the Biblical accounts (chapter five).

Writers react indeed to various socio-cultural, religious and political events. This is evident from the time of the Biblical authors through the Jewish and non-Jewish writers of ancient periods and onwards. All of them worked and are working not in a vacuum but in a given historical context. In order to gain more specific knowledge of them, one needs to study each of them from a wide horizon of their historical surroundings. All of them are correlated in their own time, place and circumstances. Thus, the Deuteronomist conforms to the norms of his contemporary scribal writing mode when he does not designate the precise place of the Temple. On the other hand, the Chronicler mentions this precise point in detail, probably not only to fill in a gap in his *Vorlage*, but also for polemical reasons: with some Jewish groups in the Second Temple era (who were not satisfied with the poorly built Temple) as well as with Samaritans (who opposed theologically the existence of Jerusalem's Temple). A variety of Jewish and Samaritan writers composed, expounded and interpreted against the background of the non-ending dispute with each other concerning the legitimate Temple and the holy mountain. The rabbis composed some of their homilies and expositions against the background of the struggle with the new rival religion – Christianity – as well as the struggle against the internal interrogators and slanderers in the Jewish communities and the prohibitions and persecutions by the powerful empire, Rome.

It is hoped that these studies will serve also as an example for the benefit the Biblical scholarship can gain from a comparative study of early Jewish exegesis.

The last part of the volume stresses that Biblical scholarship should indicate and define the theology of Hebrew Bible / Old Testament for its own merit and right, and not on an a priori association of it with any other post Hebrew Bible compositions or corpora, such as the New Testament. The study of the Hebrew Bible from a theological viewpoint must be carried out through defined unique methods without confusing them with those of the history of ancient Israelite religion. Instead of looking for a single theme, *die Mitte*, in the Hebrew Bible, one must recognize the plurality of several theologies in this corpus, and attempt to reveal them within their context and against their own general and particular historical background. Biblical scholarship must deal more intensively with the problem of how the variety of contradictory theological lines could coexist in one and the same corpus or even within a literary unit.

Jewish and Christian scholars can indeed cooperate not only in the investigation of the history of ancient Israelite religion, but also in the handling of the variety of the contradictory theologies included in the Hebrew Bible. They can attempt contemporaneously to represent the full viewpoints of the Scriptures, it means, the positive as well as the negative aspects of the Deity in the course of His activities in the universe as reflected in the Hebrew Bible.

Christians and Jews could draw together the theological guidelines of the Biblical authors, editors and canonists; discover the theological guidelines controlling the common Biblical corpora; read the Hebrew Bible for religious messages and moral values which may be derived from it for the benefit of all mankind. They could form a Biblical theological research as a branch of academic learning, and give preference to a 'non-confessional' presentation of Hebrew Bible theology. It could deal – as objectively as possible – with secular, academic-intellectual viewpoints of the Hebrew Bible. Then Jews as well as Christians could apply the results of such an inquiry as they see appropriate. The object of such research is theology or several forms of theology, but the research itself is not theological in nature; in other words, it is not religious or denominational. Such a cooperative theological undertaking may make more obvious the common heritage and values of the sister-religions, and contribute to mutual understanding and respect. It can indeed be done alongside the development of separate Jewish and Christian theologies, as subjective and confessional as they are, without losing their own identities and particularities.

In any case, the Christian theologians must always and everywhere avoid anti-Jewish and anti-Semitic theology, and negation of the Jewish people and Judaism in order to define their own religious principles and to show the superiority of Christianity. It is time to stop "playing with this fire"; which has generated consequences which have been, and continue to be, unfortunate for both sides, but especially for the Jewish people. It is necessary not only for the principle of doing justice to Judaism and Jewish people, but to meeting the primary concerns of Christianity and Christian theology as well.

Over thousands of years there was, and still is, a Jewish interest in the theology of the Hebrew Bible as well as Biblical theology. It is impossible to imagine lack of interest in theology on the part of Jews. Generally it is just expressed in different ways compared to the Christian literary works in this field. The main concentration of the Jewish-Israeli research on the historical and archaeological viewpoints of the Hebrew Bible is apparent against the background of the establishment of the new Jewish statehood. No less it stemmed from their focus to uncover their roots in their own ancient homeland. Nonetheless, it is a time for Jewish Biblical scholars to write comprehensive compositions, "Theology of the Hebrew Bible" / "Biblical Theology", for contemporary times, while showing their unique approach, values and identity, or, if you wish: identities.

Bibliography

ACKROYD, P.R., "The Theology of the Chronicler", *The Chronicler in His Age* (JSOT Suppl. 101; Sheffield: Sheffield Academic Press, 1991), pp. 273-289.

ALBECK, Ch., *The Mishnah, Vol. IV – Seder Nezikin* (Jerusalem: Bialik Institute / Tel Aviv: Dvir, 1953; Hebrew).

ALBERTZ, R., *Religionsgeschichte Israels in alttestamentlicher Zeit* (ATDER 8,1, Göttingen: Vandenhoeck & Ruprecht, 1992).

ALBERTZ, R., *A History of Israelite Religion in the Old Testament Period, Volume I: From the Beginning to the End of the Monarchy* (OTL; Louisville, KY: Westminster / John Knox, 1994).

ALBERTZ, R., "Religionsgeschichte Israels statt Theologie des Alten Testaments!", *JBTh* 10 (1995), pp. 3-24.

ALBRIGHT, W.F. and C.S. MANN, *Matthew* (AB 26; Garden City, NY: Doubleday, 1971).

ALBRIGHT, W.F., Review of E. TÄUBLER, *Biblische Studien: Die Epoche der Richter* (Tübingen: J.C.B. MOHR, 1958), *BO* 17 (1960), pp. 242-243.

ALON, G., *The History of the Jewish People in the Land of Israel in the Mishnah and Talmud Ages* (Jerusalem: Publishing House Hakibutz Hameuchad, 1977), vol. II (Hebrew).

ANDERSON, H., "Maccabees, Books of – Fourth Maccabees", *ABD,* vol. 4, pp. 452-454.

AULD, A.G. *Kings Without Privilege: David and Moses in the Story of the Bible's Kings* (Edinburgh: T&T Clark, 1994).

AVIGAD, N. and Y. YADIN, *A Genesis Apocryphon – A Scroll from the Wilderness of Judaea* (Jerusalem: Magnes Press & Heikhal Ha-Sefer, 1956).

BACHER, B., "Ein polemischer Ausspruch Jose b. Chalaftha's", *MGWJ* 42 (1898), pp. 505-507.

BAR-KOCHVA, B., *Judas Maccabaeus – The Jewish Struggle Against the Seleucids* (Cambridge: Cambridge University Press, 1989).

BARNARD, L.W., "Judaism in Egypt AD 70-135", *Studies in Apostolic Fathers and their Background* (Oxford: Oxford University Press, 1966), pp. 41-55.

BARR, J., *The Concept of Biblical Theology – An Old Testament Perspective* (London: SCM Press, 1999).

BARRETT, C.K., *The Gospel According to St. John* (London: SPCK, 1965).

BARTH, M. and H. BLANKE, *Colossians – A New Translation with Introduction and Commentary* (AB 34B; New York / London / Toronto / Sydney / Auckland: Doubleday, 1994).

BEASLEY-MURRAY, G.R., *John* (WBC 36; Waco, TX: Word Books, 1987).

BEATTIE, D.R.G., *The Targum of Ruth* (The Aramaic Bible 19; Edinburgh: T&T Clark, 1994).

BEN-HAYYIM, Z., *Tibåt Mårqe – A Collection of Samaritan Midrashim* (Jerusalem: The Israel Academy of Sciences and Humanities, 1988; Hebrew).

BEN-ZVI, I., *The Book of the Samaritans* (2nd edn.; Jerusalem: Yad Izhak Ben-Zvi, 1970; Hebrew).

BERGER, K. und C. NORD, *Das Neue Testament und Frühchristliche Schriften* (Frankfurt am Main & Leipzig: Insel Verlag, 1999).

BERNARD, J.H., *A Critical and Exegetical Commentary on the Gospel According to St. John* (ICC; Edinburgh: T&T Clark, 1928), vol. I.

BICKERMAN, E.J., *The Jews in the Greek Age* (Cambridge, MA: Harvard University Press, 1988).

BLACK, M., "The Recovery of the Language of Jesus", *NTS* 3 (1956-57), pp. 305-313.

BLACK, M., *The Scrolls and Christian Origins* (Toronto & New York: Thomas Nelson, 1961).

BLACK, M., *An Aramaic Approach to the Gospels and Acts* (3rd edn.; Oxford: Clarendon Press, 1967).

BLASCHKE, A., *Beschneidung – Zeugnisse der Bibel und verwandter Texte* (TANZ 28; Tübingen und Basel: A. Francke Verlag, 1998).

BLENKINSOPP, J., "Old Testament Theology and the Jewish-Christian Connection", *JSOT* 28 (1984), pp. 3-15.

BLUM, E., *Die Komposition der Vätergeschichte* (WMANT 57; Neukirchen-Vluyn: Neukirchener Verlag, 1984).

BORNSTEIN, D.J., "Nathan ha-Bavli", *Encyclopaedia Judaica* (Jerusalem: Keter, [without date]), vol. 12, p. 861.

BOWKER, J., *The Targums and Rabbinic Literature* (Cambridge: Cambridge University Press, 1969).

BRAUDE, W.G., *The Midrash on Psalms* (YJS 13; New Haven: Yale University Press, 1976), vols. I-II.

BRAUDE, W.G., *Pesikta Rabbati* (YJS 18; New Haven & London: Yale University Press, 1968), vols. I-II.

BROCKWAY, A., P. VON BUREN, R. RENDTORFF and S. SCHOON, *The Theology of the Churches and the Jewish People: Statements by the World Council of Churches and its Member Churches – A Commentary* (Geneva: World Council of Churches, 1988).

BROWN, R.E., *The Gospel According to John* (AB 29; Garden City, NY: Doubleday, 1966).

BROWN, R.E., *The Death of the Messiah* (ABRL; New York / London / Toronto / Sydney & Auckland: Doubleday, 1994).

BUBER, M., *The Prophetic Faith* (New York: Macmillan, 1949).

BUBER, M., *Der Glaube der Propheten* (Zürich: Manesse Verlag, Conzett & Huber, 1950).

BUBER, M., *Königtum Gottes* (3rd edn.; Heidelberg: Verlag Lambert Schneider, 1956).

BUBER, M., *The Kingship of God* (New York: Harper & Row, 1967).

BUBER, S., *Midrash Tehillim* (Vilna: Reem, 1891; reprinted in Jerusalem: Ch. Wagschal, 1977; Hebrew).

BUBER, S., *Yalkut Machiri zu den 150 Psalmen* (Berdyczew: Verlag von J. Scheftel, 1899).

BUDDE, K., *Die Bücher Richter und Samuel ihre Quellen und ihr Aufbau* (Gießen: J. Ricker, 1890).

BUDDE, K., *Die Bücher Samuel erklärt* (KHCAT 8; Tübingen & Leipzig: J.C.B. Mohr [Paul Siebeck], 1902).

BULTMANN, R., *Das Evangelium des Johannes* (KEKNT; 16th edn., Göttingen: Vandenhoeck & Ruprecht, 1959).

CAIRD, G.B. and L.D. HURST, *New Testament Theology* (Oxford: Clarendon Press, 1994).

CASEY, M., *Aramaic Sources of Mark's Gospel* (Cambridge / New York / Oakleigh: Cambridge University Press, 1998).

CASPARI, W.K.A., *Die Samuelbücher* (KAT 7; Leipzig: Deichter, 1926).

CASSUTO, U., "Beit El in the Bible", *Encyclopaedia Biblica* (Jerusalem: Bialik Institute, 1954), vol. 2, pp. 63-67 (Hebrew).

CASSUTO, U., "Jerusalem in the Pentateuch", *Biblical and Oriental Studies, Volume 1: Bible* (Jerusalem: Magnes Press, 1973), pp. 71-78.

CHARLESWORTH, J.H. (ed.), *The Old Testament Pseudepigrapha* (ABRL; New York / London / Toronto / Sydney / Auckland: Doubleday, 1985), vols. 1-2.

CHARLESWORTH, J.H., "Is the New Testament anti-Semitic or anti-Jewish?", *Explorations – Rethinking Relationships Among Jews and Christians,* vol. 7, number 2 (1993), pp. 2-3.

CHILDS, B.S., *Biblical Theology in Crisis* (Philadelphia: Westminster, 1970).

CHILDS, B.S., *Biblical Theology of the Old and New Testament: Theological Reflection on the Christian Bible* (Minneapolis, MN: Fortress, 1993).

CLARK, E.G. et al., *Targum Pseudo-Jonathan of the Pentateuch: Text and Concordance* (Haboken: NJ, Ktav Pulishing House, 1984).

COGAN, M., *Imperialism and Religion: Assyria, Judah and Israel in the Eighth and Seventh Centuries BCE* (SBLMS 19; Missoula, MT: Scholars Press, 1974).

COGAN, M., "'The City that I Chose' – The Deuteronomistic View of Jerusalem", *Tarbiz* 55 (1986), pp. 301-309 (Hebrew).

COGGINS, R. [J.], "Old Testament Theology – How?", *ExpTim* 107 (1996), p. 309.

COLLINS, J.J., "Historical Criticism and the State of Biblical Theology", *Christian Century* (July 28-August 4, 1993), pp. 743-747.

COÜASNON, C., *The Church of the Holy Sepulcher in Jerusalem* (The Schweich Lectures of the British Academy, 1972; London: Oxford University Press, 1974).

CROSS, F.M., "The Cave Inscriptions from Khirbet Beit Lei", in J.A. SANDERS (ed.), *Near Eastern Archaeology in the Twentieth Century: Essays in honor of Nelson Glueck* (Garden City, NY: Doubleday, 1970), pp. 299-306.

CROSS, F.M., "The Themes of the Book of Kings and the Structure of the Deuteronomistic History", *Canaanite and Hebrew Epic – Essays in the History of the Religion of Israel* (Cambridge, MA: Harvard University Press, 1973), pp. 274-289.

CROSS, F.M., "A Reconstruction of the Judean Restoration", *JBL* 94 (1975), pp. 4-18.

CROWN, A.D., R. PUMMER and A. TAL (eds.), *A Companion to Samaritan Studies* (Tübingen: J.C.B. Mohr [Paul Siebeck], 1993).

DANBY, H., *The Mishnah* (Oxford: Oxford University Press / London: Geoffrey Cumberlege, 1954).

DAUBE, D., "Jesus and the Samaritan Woman: The Meaning of *sygchraomai*", *JBL* 69 (1950), pp. 137-147.

DAUBE, D., "Samaritan Women", *The New Testament and Rabbinic Judaism* (London: The Athlone Press, 1956), pp. 373-382.

DAVIES, P.R., Review of H.D. Preuss [sic!], *Theologie des Alten Testaments. I. JHWHs erwählendes und verpflichtendes Handeln* (Stuttgart / Berlin / Köln: W. Kohlhammer, 1991), *JSOT* 59 (1993), p. 122.

DAVILA, J.R., "The Name of God at Moriah: An Unpublished Fragment from 4QGenExod^a", *JBL* 110 (1991), pp. 577-582.

DE JONGE, M., "Patriarchs, The Testaments of the Twelve", *ABD,* vol 5, pp. 181-186.

DE VAUX, R., *Ancient Israel: Its Life and Institutions* (2nd edn.; London: Darton, Longman & Todd, 1965).

DIETRICH, W. und C. LINK, *Die dunklen Seiten Gottes – Willkür und Gewalt* (2nd edn.; Neukirchen-Vluyn: Neukirchener Verlag, 1997).

DÍEZ MACHO, A., *Neophyti 1 – Tomo I: Génesis* (Madrid & Barcelona: Consejo Superior de Investigaciones Científicas, 1968).

DILLARD, R.B., "Reward and Punishment in Chronicles: The Theology of Immediate Retribution", *WTJ* 46 (1984), pp. 164-172.

DILLMANN, A., *Genesis* (Edinburgh: W.B. Stevenson, 1897).

DONNER, H. – W. RÖLLIG, *Kanaanäische und Aramäische Inschriften,* vol. I: *Texte* (3rd edn.; Wiesbaden: Otto Harrassowitz, 1971).

DONNER, H. – W. RÖLLIG, *Kanaanäische und Aramäische Inschriften,* vol. II: *Kommentar* (3rd edn.; Wiesbaden: Otto Harrassowitz, 1973).

DONNER, H., *Geschichte des Volkes Israel und seiner Nachbarn in Grundzügen* (Göttingen: Vandenhoeck & Ruprecht, 1987).

DORAN, R., "Pseudo-Eupolemus", in CHARLESWORTH, *The Old Testament Pseudepigrapha*, vol. 2, pp. 873-882.

DRIVER, S.R., *An Introduction to the Literature of the Old Testament* (ITL; 9th edn.; Edinburgh: T&T Clark, 1913).

EBACH, J., "Der Gott des Alten Testaments – ein Gott der Rache?", *Biblische Erinnerungen – Theologische Reden zur Zeit* (Bochum, SWI Verlag, 1993), pp. 81-93.

EHRLICH, A.B., *Mikrâ ki-Pheschutô*, vol. I: *Divre Tora* (Berlin: M. Poppelauer's Buchhandlung, 1899; reprinted: Library of Biblical Studies; New York: Ktav Publishing House, 1969; Hebrew).

EIßFELDT, O., "Israelitisch-jüdische Religionsgeschichte und alttestamentliche Theologie", *ZAW* 41 (1926), pp. 1-12.

EIßFELDT, O., *Kleine Schriften* (herausgegeben von R. SELLHEIM und F. MAASS; Tübingen: J.C.B. Mohr [Paul Siebeck], 1962), vol. I, 105-114.

EIßFELDT, O., *Einleitung in das Alte Testament* (3rd edn.; Tübingen: J.C.B. Mohr [Paul Siebeck], 1964).

EISSFELDT, O., *The Old Testament – An Introduction* (New York / Hagerstown / San Francisco / London: Harper & Row, 1965).

ELBOGEN, I., *Jewish Liturgy – A Comprehensive History* (Translated by R.P. SCHEINDLIN based on the original 1913 German edition, and the 1972 Hebrew edition; Philadelphia / New York / Jerusalem: The Jewish Publication Society & The Jewish Theological Seminary of America, 1993).

ENDRES, J.C., *Biblical Interpretation in the Book of Jubilees*, (CBQMS 18; Washington, DC: The Catholic Biblical Association of America, 1987).

ESHEL, H., "The Prayer of Joseph, a Papyrus from Masada and the Samaritan Temple on *APGAPIZIN*", *Zion* 56 (1991), pp. 125-136 (Hebrew).

ESHEL, H., "The Samaritan Temple on Mount Gerizim and the Historical Research", *Beit Mikra* 39 (1994), pp. 141-155 (Hebrew).

EVANS, C.A. and D.A. HAGNER (eds.), *Anti-Semitism and Early Christianity: Issues of Faith and Polemic* (Minneapolis, MN: Fortress, 1993).

FALLON, F., "Eupolemus", in CHARLESWORTH, *The Old Testament Pseudepigrapha*, vol. 2, pp. 861-872.

FELDMAN, L.H., *Jew & Gentile in the Ancient World* (Princeton: Princeton University Press, 1993).

FITZMYER, J.A., *Essays on the Semitic Background of the New Testament* (London: Geoffrey Chapman, 1971).

FITZMYER, J.A., *The Genesis Apocryphon of Qumran Cave I – A Commentary* (BibOr 18; 2nd edn., Rome: Pontifical Biblical Institute, 1971).

FLUSSER, D., "Tobit, The Book of Tobit", *Encyclopaedia Biblica*, (Jerusalem: Bialik Institute, 1958), vol. 3, pp. 367-375 (Hebrew).

FLUSSER, D., "Enoch", *Encyclopaedia Biblica* (Jerusalem: Bialik Institute, 1958), vol. 3, pp. 203-210 (Hebrew).

FLUSSER, D., "A New Commentary on Pseudo-Philo's *Liber Antiquitatum Biblicarum*", *Tarbiz* 67 (1997/98), pp. 135-138 (Hebrew).

FLUSSER, D. and S. SAFRAI, "Who Sanctified the Beloved in the Womb", *Immanuel* 11 (1980), pp. 46-55.

FOHRER, G., *Geschichte der israelitischen Religion* (Berlin: Walter de Gruyter, 1968).

FOHRER, G., *History of Israelite Religion* (Nashville, TN & New York: Abingdon Press, 1972).

FREEDMAN, H., *Pesahim – Translated into English with Notes, Glossary and Indices* (London: Soncino Press, 1938).

FREEDMAN, H., *Shabbath – Translated into English with Notes, Glossary and Indices* (London: Soncino Press, 1938), vol. I.

FREEDMAN, H. and M. SIMON (translators), *The Midrash Rabbah – Volume One: Genesis* (London / Jerusalem / New York: Soncino Press, 1977).

FREEDMAN, H. and M. SIMON (translators), *The Midrash Rabbah – Volume Two: Exodus – Leviticus* (London / Jerusalem / New York: Soncino Press, 1977).

FRETHEIM, T.E., *Deuteronomic History* (IBT; Nashville, TN: Abingdon Press, 1983).

FREUDMANN, L.C., *Anti-Semitism in the New Testament* (Lenham, MD / New York / London: University Press of America, 1994).

FRIEDLANDER, G. (ed.), *Pirke de-Rabbi Eliezer* (2nd edn.; New York: Hermon Press, 1965).

FRIEDMANN, M. (ed.), *Pesikta Rabbati* (Wien: Selbstverlag des Herausgebers, 1880; Hebrew).

FURNISH, V.P., "Colossians, Epitle to the", *ABD*, vol. 1, pp. 1090-1096.

GAGER, J.G., *The Origins of Anti-Semitism: Attitudes Toward Judaism in Pagan and Christian Antiquity* (New York & Oxford: Oxford University Press, 1983).

GAGER, J.G., *Reinventing Paul* (Oxford & New York: Oxford University Press, 2000).

GASTER, M., *The Samaritans: Their History, Doctrines and Literature* (The Schweich Lectures of the British Academy, 1923; London: Humphrey Milford and Oxford University Press, 1925).

GEIGER, J., "The Ban on Circumcision and the Bar-Kokhba Revolt", *Zion* 41 (1976), pp. 139-147 (Hebrew).

GEYER, H.G., "Zur Frage der Notwendigkeit des Alten Testaments", *EvT* 25 (1965), pp. 207-237.

GIBSON, J.C.L., *Textbook of Syrian Semitic Inscriptions, Volume 1: Hebrew and Moabite Inscriptions* (Oxford: Clarendon Press, 1973).

GINZBERG, L., *The Legends of the Jews* (Philadelphia: The Jewish Publication Society of America, 1968), vols. I-VI.

GLUECK, N., *Rivers in the Desert: A History of the Negev* (New York: Farrar, Straus and Cudahy, 1959).

GOLDIN, J., *The Fathers According to Rabbi Nathan*, (YJS 10; New Haven: Yale University Press, 1955).

GOLDIN, J., "Avot de-Rabbi Nathan", *Encyclopaedia Judaica* (Jerusalem: Keter, [without date]), vol. 3, pp. 984-986.

GOLKA, F.W., "The Aetiologies in the Old Testament", *VT* 26 (1976), pp. 410-428.

GOLKA, F.W., "Universalism and the Election of the Jews", *Theology* 90 (1987), pp. 273-280.

GOLKA, F.W., "Die Geschöpflichkeit des Menschen und die Erwählung Israels", *Jona* (CBK; Stuttgart: Calwer Verlag, 1991), pp. 25-33.

GOLLANCZ, H., "The Targum to the Song of Songs", in B. GROSSFELD (ed.), *The Targum to the Five Megilloth* (New York: Hermon Press, 1973).

GOODENOUGH, E.R., *Jewish Symbols in the Greco-Roman Period: Volume One – The Archeological Evidence from Palestine* (Bollingen Series 37; New York: Pantheon Books, 1953).

GOODENOUGH, E.R. and M. AVI-YONAH, "Dura-Europos", *Encyclopaedia Judaica* (Jerusalem: Keter Publishing House, 1971), vol. 6, pp. 279-293.

GOSHEN-GOTTSTEIN, M.H., "Jewish Biblical Theology and the Study of Biblical Religion", *Tarbiz* 50 (1980/81), pp. 37-52 (Hebrew).

GOSHEN-GOTTSTEIN, M.H., "Tanakh Theology: The Religion of the Old Testament and the Place of Jewish Biblical Theology", in P.D. MILLER, JR., P.D. HANSON, and S.D. MCBRIDE (eds.), *Ancient Israelite Religion – Essays in Honor of Frank Moore Cross* (Philadelphia: Fortress, 1987), pp. 617-644.

GRAYSON, A.K., *Assyrian Royal Inscriptions: Volume I – From the Beginning to Ashur-resha-ishi I* (Wiesbaden: Otto Harrassowitz, 1972).

GREENBERG, M., "Religion: Stability and Ferment", in A. MALAMAT (ed.), *The World History of the Jewish People: The Age of the Monarchies – Culture and Society* (Jewish History Publication; Jerusalem: Massadah Press, 1979), pp. 79-123, 296-303.

GREENBERG, M., *On the Bible and on Judaism* (Edited by A. Shapiro; Tel Aviv: Am Oved, 1984; Hebrew).

GRINTZ, Y.M., *The Book of Judith* (Jerusalem: Bialik Institute, 1957; Hebrew).

GRINTZ, Y.M., *From the Ancient Egyptian Literature* (Jerusalem: Bialik Institute, 1975; Hebrew).

GROSSFELD, B., "The Targum to Lamentations 2,10", *JJS* 28 (1977), pp. 60-64.

GUNNEWEG, A.H.J., *Vom Verstehen des Alten Testaments: Eine Hermeneutik* (Grundrisse zum Alten Testament – ATDER 5; Göttingen: Vandenhoeck & Ruprecht, 1977).

GUNNEWEG, A.H.J., *Biblische Theologie des Alten Testaments: Eine Religionsgeschichte Israels in biblisch-theologischer Sicht* (Stuttgart / Berlin / Köln: W. Kohlhammer, 1993).

GUTMAN, Y., *The Beginning of Jewish-Hellenistic Literature* (Jerusalem: Bialik Institute, 1963), vol. II. (Hebrew).

GUTMANN, J., "The Sacrifice of Isaac: Variations on a Theme in Early Jewish and Christian Art", in D. AHRENS (ed.), *Thiasos ton Mouson: Studien zu Antike und Christentum, Festschrift für Josef Fink zum 70. Geburtstag* (Köln & Wien: Böhlau Verlag, 1984), pp. 115-122.

GUTTMANN, J., "Über zwei dogmengeschichtliche Mischnastellen", *MGWJ* 42 (1898), pp. 337-345.

GUTTMANN, J., *The Philosophy of Judaism* (New York / Chicago / San Francisco: Holt, Rinehart and Winston, 1964), pp. 3-17, 413.

GUTTMANN, J., *Die Philosophie des Judentums* (München: Verlag Ernst Reinhardt, 1933).

HALL, R.G., "Circumcision", *ABD*, vol. 1, pp. 1025-1031.

HALL, R.G., "Epispasm and the Dating of Ancient Jewish Writings", *JSP* 2 (1988), pp. 71-86.

HARAN, M., "Shiloh and Jerusalem", *JBL* 81 (1962), pp. 14-24.

HARAN, M., "The Disappearance of the Ark", *IEJ* 13 (1963), pp. 46-58.

HARAN, M., "The Graded Taboos of Holiness", *Festschrift M.Z.[=H.] Segal* (Jerusalem: Kiryat-Sepher, 1965), pp. 33-41 (Hebrew).

HARAN, M., "The Priestly Image of the Tabernacle", *HUCA* 36 (1965), pp. 191-226.

HARAN, M., "The Religion of the Patriarch: Beliefs and Practices", in B. MAZAR (ed.), *The World History of the Jewish People, Volume II: Patriarchs* (Jewish History Publication; Givatayim: Peli & Rutgers University Press, 1970), pp. 219-245, 285-288.

HARAN, M., *Ages and Institutions in the Bible* (Tel Aviv: Am Oved, 1972; Hebrew).

HARAN, M., *Temples and Temple-Service in Ancient Israel: An Inquiry into Biblical Cult Phenomena and the Historical Setting of the Priestly School* (Winona Lake, IN: Eisenbrauns, 1985).

HARRINGTON, D.J., *"Pseudo-Philo – A New Translation and Introduction"*, in CHARLESWORTH, *The Old Testament Pseudepigrapha*, vol. 2, pp. 297-377.

HASEL, G., *Old Testament Theology: Basic Issues in the Current Debate* (Grand Rapids, MI: Eerdmans, 1991).

HEINEMANN, I., *The Methods of the Aggadah* (2nd edn.; Jerusalem: Magnes Press & Massadah, 1974; Hebrew).

HEINEMANN, J., *Aggadah and its Development – Studies in the Transmission of Traditions* (Jerusalem: Keter Publishing House, 1974; Hebrew).

HEINEMANN, J., "The Ancient 'Orders of Benedictions' for New Year and Fasts", *Tarbiz* 45 (1976), pp. 258-267 (Hebrew).

HEINEMANN, J., *Studies in Jewish Liturgy* (edited by A. SHINAN; Jerusalem: Magnes Press, 1981; Hebrew).

HERRMANN, S., "Das konstruktive Restauration – Das Deuteronomium als Mitte biblischer Theologie", *Gesammelte Studien zur Geschichte und Theologie des Alten Testaments* (München: Chr. Kaiser, 1986), pp. 163-178.

HERZBERG, H.W., *Die Samuelbücher – Übersetzt und erklärt* (ATD 10; 2nd edn.; Göttingen: Vandenhoeck & Ruprecht, 1960).

HERTZBERG [sic!], H.W., *I & II Samuel – A Commentary* (OTL; London: SCM Press, 1964).

HESCHEL, A.J., *Die Prophetie* (Cracow: Polish Academy of Sciences, 1936).

HESCHEL, A.J., *God in Search of Man* (New York: Farrar, Straus & Giroux, 1955), pp. 7-8.

HESCHEL, A.J., *The Prophets* (New York: Harper, 1962).

HESCHEL, A.J., "Depth Theology", *The Insecurity of Freedom* (New York: Farrar, Straus & Giroux, 1966), pp. 115-126.

HEYMEL, M., "Warum gehört die Hebräische Bibel in den christlichen Kanon?" *BTZ* 7 (1990), pp. 2-20.

HIGGER, M., "Pirke Rabbi Eliezer", *Horeb* 9 (1946/7), pp. 94-166; 10 (1948), pp. 184-294 (Hebrew).

HIRSCHFELD, H., *Book of Kuzari by Judah Hallevi — Translated from the Arabic, with Introduction, Notes and Appendix* (New York: Pardes Publishing House, 1946).

HIRSCHFELD, H., *An Argument for the Faith of Israel — The Kuzari* (New York: Schocken, 1971).

HJELM, I., *The Samaritans and Early Judaism — A Literary Analysis* (JSOT Suppl. 303 & CIS 7; Sheffield: Sheffield Academic Press, 2000).

HOFFMAN, Y., *Exodus in the Bible Belief* (Tel Aviv: Am Oved, 1983; Hebrew).

HOFFMAN, Y., "The Creativity of Theodicy", in H.G. REVENTLOW and Y. HOFFMAN (eds.), *Justice and Righteousness — Biblical Themes and Their Influence* (JSOT Suppl. 137; Sheffield: JSOT Press, 1992), pp. 117-130.

HOFFMANN, C., *Juden und Judentum im Werk Deutscher Althistoriker des 19. und 20. Jahrhunderts* (Leiden / New York / Kopenhagen / Köln: E.J. Brill, 1988), pp. 133-189.

HOFTIJZER, J., *Die Verheissungen an die drei Erzväter* (Leiden: E.J. Brill, 1956).

HOLLADAY, C.R., *Fragments from Hellenistic: Jewish Authors, Vol. I: Historians* (Chico, CA: Scholars Press, 1983).

HOLLADAY, C.R., "Eupolemus, Pseudo-", *ABD*, vol. 2, pp. 672-673.

HOLLANDER, H.W., *Joseph as an Ethical Model in the Testaments of the Twelve Patriarche* (SVTP 6; Leiden: E.J. Brill, 1981).

HOLLANDER, H.W., "The Portrayal of Joseph in Hellenistic Jewish and Early Christian Literature", in M.E. STONE and T.A. BERGREN (eds.), *Biblical Figures Outside the Bible* (Harrisburg, PA: Trinity Press International, 1998), pp. 237-263.

HOLLANDER, H.W. and M. DE JONGE, *The Testaments of the Twelve Patriarchs — A Commentary* (SVTP 8; Leiden: E.J. Brill, 1985).

HORBURY, W., *Jews and Christians in Contact and Controversy* (Edinburgh: T&T Clark, 1998).

HOROVITZ, H.S. and L. FINKELSTEIN (eds.), *Sifre on Deuteronomy* (Berlin: Gesellschaft zur Förderung der Wissenschaft des Judentums, 1889; reprinted, New York: The Jewish Theological Seminary of America, 1969; Hebrew).

HOROVITZ, H.S. and I.A. RABIN (eds.), *Mechilta d'Rabbi Ismael* (Jerusalem: Bamberger & Wahrmann, 1960; Hebrew).

HOROWITZ, V. (A.), *I Have Built You an Exalted House - Temple Building in the Bible in the Light of Mesopotamian and Northwest Semitic Writing,* (JSOT Suppl. 115; Sheffield; Sheffield Academic Press, 1992).

ISAAC, E., "1 (Ethiopic Apocalypse of) Enoch", in CHARLESWORTH, *The Old Testament Pseudepigrapha*, vol. 1, pp. 6-7.

ISSER, S., *The Dositheans — A Samaritan Sect in Late Antiquity* (Leiden: E.J. Brill, 1976).

JACOB, L., *A Jewish Theology* (London: Darton, Longman and Todd, 1973).

JAPHET, S., *The Ideology of the Book of Chronicles and Its Place in Biblical Thought* (translated by A. BARBER from the Hebrew edition of 1977, BEATAJ 9; Frankfurt am Main / Bern / New York / Paris: Peter Lang, 1989).

JOEL, M., *Blicke in die Religionsgeschichte zu Anfang des zweiten christlichen Jahrhunderts* (Breslau: S. Schottländer, 1880-83).

JOHNSTONE, W., *1 and 2 Chronicles: Vol. 1: 1 Chronicles1 – 2 Chronicles 9: Israel's Place Among the Nations* (JSOT Suppl. 253; Shieffeld: Shieffeld Academic Press, 1998).

JUNG, L., *Yoma – Translated into English with Notes, Glossary and Indices* (London: Soncino Press, 1938).

KALIMI, I., *The Books of Chronicles – A Classified Bibliography* (SBB 1; Jerusalem: Simor, 1990).

KALIMI, I., "Die Abfassungszeit der Chronik – Forschungsstand und Perspektiven", *ZAW* 105 (1993), pp. 223-233.

KALIMI, I., *Zur Geschichtsschreibung des Chronisten: Literarisch-historiographische Abweichungen der Chronik von ihren Paralleltexten in den Samuel- und Königsbüchern* (BZAW 226; Berlin & New York: Walter de Gruyter, 1995).

KALIMI, I., "Religionsgeschichte Israels oder Theologie des Alten Testaments? Das Jüdische Interesse an der Biblischen Theologie", *JBTh* 10 (1995), pp. 45-68.

KALIMI, I., "Paronomasia in the Book of Chronicles", *JSOT* 67 (1995), pp. 27-41.

KALIMI, I., "Was the Chronicler a Historian?", in M.P. GRAHAM, K.G. HOGLUND and S.L. MCKENZIE (eds.), *The Chronicler as Historian*, (JSOT Suppl. 238; Sheffield: Sheffield Academic Press, 1997), pp. 73-89.

KALIMI, I., "History of Interpretation: The Book of Chronicles in Jewish Tradition – From Daniel to Spinoza", *RB* 105 (1998), pp. 5-41.

KALIMI, I., "Könnte die aramäische Grabinschrift aus Ägypten als Indikation für die Datierung der Chronikbücher fungieren?", *ZAW* 110 (1998), pp. 79-81.

KALIMI, I., *The Book of Chronicles: Historical Writing and Literary Devices* (The Biblical Encyclopaedia Library XVIII; Jerusalem: Bialik Institute, 2000; Hebrew).

KALIMI, I., "Die Bibel und die klassisch-jüdische Bibelauslegung – Eine Interpretations – und Religionsgeschichtliche Studie", *ZAW* 114/$_2$ (2002), forthcoming.

KALIMI, I., "Die Auseinandersetzung mit den internen und äußeren Opponenten in mittelalterlicher-jüdischer Schriftauslegung", *ZAW* 114/$_3$ (2002), forthcoming.

KALIMI, I., "The Date of Chronicles: The Biblical Text, the Elephantine Papyri and the El-Ibrahimia's Aramaic Grave Inscription", in J.H. & D. ELLENS, I. KALIMI and R.P. KNIERIM (eds.), *Hebrew Bible and Related Literature – S.J. Devries Commemorative Volume* (Harrisburg, PA: Trinity Press International, 2002), forthcoming.

KALIMI, I. and J.D. PURVIS, "King Jehoiachin and the Vessels of the Lord's House in Biblical Literature", *CBQ* 56 (1994), pp. 449-457.

KALIMI, I. and J.D. PURVIS, "The Hiding of the Temple Vessels in Jewish and Samaritan Literature", *CBQ* 56 (1994), pp. 679-685.

KASHER, M.M., *Torah Shelemah (Complete Torah) – Talmudic-Midrashic Encyclopaedia of the Pentateuch* (New York: American Biblical Encyclopaedia Society, 1949), vol. 3 Tome 4 *(Genesis)*.

KAUFMANN, Y., *The Religion of Israel: From Its Beginning to the Babylonian Exile* (translated by M. Greenberg; Chicago: Chicago University Press, 1960).

KAUFMANN, Y., *The Babylonian Captivity and Deutero-Isaiah* (translated by C.W. EFROYMSON; New York: Union of American Hebrew Congregations, 1970).

KEE, H.C., "Testaments of the Twelve Patriarchs", in CHARLESWORTH, *The Old Testament Pseudepigrapha*, vol. 1, pp. 775-828.

KILIAN, R., *Isaaks Opferung: Zur Überlieferungsgeschichte von Gen. 22* (Stuttgart: Katholisches Bibelwerk, 1970).

KIMELMAN, R., "*Birkat Ha-Minim* and the Lack of Evidence for an Anti-Christian Jewish Prayer in Late Antiquity", in E.P. SANDERS, A.I. BAUMGARTEN & A. MENDELSON (eds.), *Jewish and Christian Self-Definition*, Volume II: *Aspects of Judaism in the Graeco-Roman Period* (London: SCM Press, 1981), pp. 226-244.

KINDLER, A., *Thesaurus of Judaean Coins* (Jerusalem: Bialik Institute, 1958).

KIPPENBERG, H.G., *Garizim und Synagoge – Traditionsgeschichtliche Untersuchungen zur samaritanischen Religion der aramäischen Periode* (Religionsgeschichtliche Versuche und Vorarbeiten 30; Berlin & New York: Walter de Gruyter, 1971).

KISTER, M.J., "... 'And He was Born Circumcised' – Some Notes on Circumcision in Hadith", *Oriens* 34 (1994), pp. 10-30.

KLEIN, Ch., *Theologie und Anti-Judaismus* (München: Chr. Kaiser, 1975).

KLEIN, Ch., *Anti-Judaism in Christian Theology* (Philadelphia: Fortress, 1978).

KLEIN, M.L., *The Fragment-Targums of the Pentateuch. Volume I: Texts, Indices and Introductory Essays* (AnBib 76; Rome: Biblical Institute Press, 1980).

KLONER, A., "Ancient Synagogues in Israel: An Arch[a]eological Survey", in LEVINE, *Ancient Synagogues Revealed*, pp. 11-18.

KNIERIM, R.P., *The Task of Old Testament Theology: Substance, Method and Cases* (Grand Rapids, MI: Eerdmans, 1995).

KOESTER, H. and T.O. LAMBDIN, "The Gospel of Thomas (II,2)", in J.M. ROBINSON (ed.), *The Nag Hammadi Library in English* (San Francisco: Harper Collins, 1990).

KOHN-ROELIN, J., "Antijudaismus – die Kehrseite jeder Christologie?", in D. STRAHM und R. STROBEL (eds.), *Vom Verlangen nach Heilwerden: Christologie in feministisch-theologischer Sicht* (Freiburg / Luzern: Exodus, 1991), pp. 65-80.

KOMLOSH, Y., *The Bible in the Light of the Aramaic Translations* (Tel Aviv: Bar Ilan University Press & Dvir, 1973; Hebrew).

KRAUS, H.-J., *Die Biblische Theologie: Ihre Geschichte und Problematik* (Neukirchen-Vluyn: Neukirchener Verlag, 1977).

KUENEN, A., *An Historico-Critical Inquiry into the Origin and Composition of the Hexateuch* (London: MacMillan, 1886).

KUGEL, J.L., *In Potiphar's House – The Interpretive Life of Biblical Texts* (San Francisco: Harper, 1990).

KYSAR, R., "John, The Gospel of", *ABD*, vol. 3, pp. 912-931.

KYSAR, R., "Anti-Semitism and the Gospel of John", in C.A. EVANS and D.A. HAGNER (eds.), *Anti-Semitism and Early Christianity: Issues of Faith and Polemic* (Minneapolis, MN: Fortress, 1993), pp. 113-127.

KYSAR, R., "John's Anti-Jewish Polemic", *BR 9* (1993), pp. 26-27.

LE DÉAUT, R. and S. ROBERT, *Targum des Chroniques (cod. Vat. Urb. Ebr. 1)*, (AnBib 51; Rome: Biblical Institute Press, 1971), vols. 1-2.

LEMAIRE, A., "Prières en Temps de Crise: Les Inscriptions de Khirbet Beit Lei", *RB* 83 (1976), pp. 560-561.

LEVENSON, J.D., *Sinai & Zion – An Entry into the Jewish Bible* (San Francisco: Harper & Row, 1987).

LEVENSON, J.D., "Why Jews are Not Interested in Biblical Theology", in J. NEUSNER, B.A. LEVINE, and E.S. FRERICHS (eds.), *Judaic Perspectives on Ancient Israel* (Philadelphia: Fortress, 1987), pp. 281-307.

LEVENSON, J.D., *The Hebrew Bible, The Old Testament and Historical Criticism: Jews and Christians in Biblical Studies* (Louisville, KY: Westminster / John Knox, 1993).

LEVINE, B.A., *In the Presence of the Lord – A Study of Cult and Some Cultic Terms in Ancient Israel* (Leiden: E.J. Brill, 1974).

LEVINE, L.I. (ed.), *Ancient Synagogues Revealed* (Jerusalem: Israel Exploration Society, 1981).

LEVINE, L.I., "The Inscription in the 'En Gedi Synagogue", in idem (ed.), *Ancient Synagogues Revealed* (Jerusalem: Israel Exploration Society, 1981), pp. 140-145.

LEVINE, L.I., "The Synagogue of Dura-Europos", in idem (ed.), *Ancient Synagogues Revealed* (Jerusalem: The Israel Exploration Society, 1981), pp. 172-177.

LICHTENSTEIN, H., "Die Fastenrolle – Eine Untersuchung zur jüdisch-hellenistischen Geschichte", *HUCA* 8-9 (1931/32), pp. 257-351.

LICHTHEIM, M., *Ancient Egyptian Literature – A Book of Readings,* Vol. II: *The New Kingdom* (Berkeley / Los Angeles / London: University of California Press, 1976).

LIEBERMAN, S., *Tosefta Ki-Feshutah – A Comprehensive Commentary on the Tosefta* (New York: The Jewish Theological Seminary of America, 1973), Part VIII, pp. 647-651.

LIEBERMAN, S., "On the Persecution of the Jewish Religion", in S. LIEBERMAN and A. HYMAN (eds.), *Salo Wittmayer Baron Jubilee Volume* (Jerusalem: American Academy for Jewish Research, 1974), Hebrew Section pp. 213-245.

LOEWENSTAMM, S.E., "Moriah, the Land of Moriah", *Encyclopaedia Biblica*, (Jerusalem: Bialik Institute, 1968), vol. 5, pp. 458–460 (Hebrew).

LOEWENSTAMM, S.E., "God's Property", in *Festschrift S. Deim* (Jerusalem: Kiryat-Sepher, 1958), pp. 120–125 (Hebrew).

LOHFINK, N., "Der gewalttätige Gott des Alten Testaments und die Suche nach einer gewaltfreien Gesellschaft", *JBTh* 2 (1987), pp. 106–136.

MACDONALD, J., *The Theology of the Samaritans* (NTL; London: SCM Press, 1964).

MAGEN, Y., "A Fortified Town of the Hellenistic Period on Mount Gerizim", *Qadmoniot* 19 (1986), pp. 91–101 (Hebrew).

MAGEN, Y., "The Samaritans in Shechem and the Blessed Mount Gerizim", in Z.Ch. EHRLICH (ed.), *Shomron and Benyamin – A Collection of Studies in Historical Geography* (Ophra [Israel]: haChevra leHaganat haTeva and Ophra's Sadeh School, 1987), pp. 177–210 (Hebrew).

MAGEN, Y., "Mount Gerizim – A Temple-City", *Qadmoniot* 23 (1990), pp. 70–78 (Hebrew).

MAORI, Y., *The Peshitta Version of the Pentateuch and Early Jewish Exegesis* (Jerusalem: Magnes, 1995; Hebrew).

MARCUS, R., *Josephus* (The Loeb Classical Library; Cambridge, MA: Harvard University Press / London: William Heinemann, 1963), vol. VIII.

MARGALIOT, E., *Those Who are Blamed in Mikra but Blameless in the Talmud and Midrashim* (London: Ararat Press, 1949; Hebrew).

MARGALIOT, M. (ed.), *The Encyclopaedia of Talmudic and Gaonic Sages* (2nd edn.; Tel Aviv: Yavneh Publishing House, 1995), vols. I–II.

MARGULIES, M. (ed.), *Midrash Wayyikra Rabbah – A Critical Edition Based on Manuscripts and Genizah Fragments with Variants and Notes* (Jerusalem: Central Press, 1956; Hebrew).

MARQUARDT, F.-W., *Von Elend und Heimsuchung der Theologie* (München: Chr. Kaiser, 1988).

MATTHEWS, C.D., *Palestine – Mohammedan Holy Land* (Yale Oriental Series Researches 24; New Haven: Yale University Press, 1949).

MAZAR, B., "Jerusalem in Biblical Period", *Cities and Districts in Eretz-Israel* (Jerusalem: Bialik Institute & Israel Exploration Society, 1975), pp. 11–44 (Hebrew).

MAZAR, B., "The Historical Background of the Book of Genesis", *The Early Biblical Period – Historical Studies* (Jerusalem: The Israel Exploration Society, 1986), pp. 49–62.

MCCARTER, P.K., Jr., *II Samuel – A New Translation with Introduction, Notes and Commentary* (AB 9; New York / London / Toronto / Sydney / Auckland: Doubleday, 1984).

MCCARTHY, C., *The Tiqqune Sopherim* (OBO 36; Freiburg/Schweiz: Universitätsverlag and Göttingen: Vandenhoeck & Ruprecht, 1981).

MCIVOR, J.S., *The Targum of Chronicles* (The Aramaic Bible 19; Edinburgh: T&T Clark, 1994).

MCKENZIE, S.L., "The Chronicler as Redactor", in M.P. GRAHAM and S.L. MCKENZIE (eds.), *The Chronicler as Author: Studies in Text and Texture* (JSOT Suppl. 263; Sheffield: Sheffield Academic Press, 1999), pp. 70-90.

MCNAMARA, M., *Targum Neofiti 1: Genesis – Translated, with Apparatus and Notes* (The Aramaic Bible 1A; Edinburgh: T&T Clark, 1992).

MILGROM, J., *Cult and Conscience* (Leiden: E.J. Brill, 1976).

MILGROM, J., *Studies in Cultic Theology and Terminology*. (Leiden: E.J. Brill, 1983).

MILIKOWSKY, Ch., "Gehenna and 'Sinners of Israel' in the Light of *Seder Olam*", *Tarbiz* 55 (1986), pp. 311-343 (Hebrew).

MOMIGLIANO, A., "Flavius Josephus and Alexander's Visit to Jerusalem", *Athenaeum* 57 (1979), pp. 442-448 (= idem, *Settimo Contributo alla storia degli studi classici e del mondo antico* [Edizioni di Storia e Litteratura 161; Roma 1984], pp. 319-329).

MONTGOMERY, J.A., *The Samaritans – The Earliest Jewish Sect: Their History, Theology and Literature* (Philadelphia 1907; reprinted New York: Ktav Publishing House, 1968).

MONTGOMERY, J.A., "Paronomasias on the Name Jerusalem", *JBL* 49 (1930), pp. 277-282.

MOORE, C.A., "Tobit, Book of", *ABD*, vol. 6, pp. 585-594.

MOORE, G.F., "Christian Writers on Judaism", *HTR* 14 (1921), pp. 191-254.

MOR, M., "Samaritans and Jews in the Ptolemaic Period and the Beginning of the Seleucid Rule in Palestine", *Studies in the History of the Jewish People and the Land of Israel* 5 (Haifa: University of Haifa, 1980), pp. 71-81 (Hebrew).

MOR, M., "The Samaritan Temple on Mount Gerizim", *Beit Mikra* 38 (1993), pp. 313-327 (Hebrew).

MOR, M., "The Samaritan Temple Once Again: Josephus Flavius and the Archaeological Find", *Beit Mikra* 40 (1994), pp. 43-64 (Hebrew).

NA'AMAN, N., "Migdal-Shechem and the House of El Berith", *Zion* 51 (1986), pp. 260-265 (Hebrew).

NAVEH, J., "Old Hebrew Inscriptions in a Burial Cave", *IEJ* 13 (1963), pp. 85-86.

NAVEH, J., "A Collection of Inscriptions – Canaanite and Hebrew Inscriptions", *Lešonenu* 30 (1966), 65-80 (Hebrew).

NELSON, R.D., *The Double Redaction of the Deuteronomistic History* (JSOT Suppl. 18; Sheffield: JSOT Press, 1981).

NEUMARK, D., *The Philosophy of the Bible* (Cincinnati: Ark Publishing Company, 1918).

NEUSNER, J., (ed.), *Understanding Jewish Theology* (New York: Ktav Publishing House, 1973), pp. 14-22, 24-31.

NIEHOFF, M., "The Figure of Joseph in the Targums", *JJS* 39 (1988), pp. 234-250.

NIEHOFF, M., *The Figure of Joseph in Post-Biblical Jewish Literature* (Leiden / New York / Köln: E.J. Brill, 1992).

NOTH, M., *Geschichte Israels* (3rd edn.; Göttingen: Vandenhoeck & Ruprecht, 1956).

NOTH, M., *The History of Israel* (London: Adam & Charles Black, 1959).

NOTH, M., *Überlieferungsgeschichtliche Studien* (Tübingen: Max Niemeyer Verlag, 1957).

NOTH, M., *The Deuteronomistic History* (JSOT Suppl. 15; Sheffield: JSOT Press, 1981).

NOTH, M., *The Chronicler's History* (translated by H.G.M. WILLIAMSON; JSOT Suppl. 50; Sheffield: JSOT Press, 1987).

OEMING, M., *Das wahre Israel: Die "genealogische Vorhalle" 1 Chronik 1-9* (BWANT 128; Stuttgart / Berlin / Köln: Verlag W. Kohlhammer, 1990).

PECKHAM, B., *The Composition of the Deuteronomistic History* (HSM 35; Atlanta, GA: Scholars Press, 1985).

PERDUE, L.G., *The Collapse of History – Reconstructing Old Testament Theology* (Minneapolis, MN: Fortress Press, 1994).

PERLES, P., "What is Biblical Scholarship for Us?", An Inaugural Lecture at the Institute for Jewish Studies, The Hebrew University of Jerusalem (Jerusalem: Association for the Hebrew University, 1926; Hebrew).

PERLITT, L., *Vatke und Wellhausen* (BZAW94; Berlin: Verlag Alfred Töpelmann, 1965).

PINES, S., *Moses Maimonides, The Guide of the Perplexed – Translated with an Introduction and Notes* (Chicago & London: Chicago University Press, 1963).

PREUß, H.D., *Theologie des Alten Testaments*, Band 1: *JHWHs erwählendes und verpflichtendes Handeln* (Stuttgart / Berlin / Köln: Verlag W. Kohlhammer, 1991).

PREUß, H.D., *Theologie des Alten Testaments*, Band 2: *Israels Weg mit JHWH* (Stuttgart / Berlin / Köln: W. Kohlhammer, 1992).

PREUß, H.D., *Old Testament Theology* (Edinburgh: T&T Clark, 1995), vols. I-II.

PRITCHARD, J.B. (ed.), *Ancient Near Eastern Texts Related to the Old Testament* (= *ANET*; 3rd edn.; Princeton: Princeton University Press, 1969).

PROCKSCH, O., *Theologie des Alten Testaments* (Gütersloh: C. Bertelsmann Verlag, 1950).

PUMMER, R., "*ARGARIZIN*: A Criterion for Samaritan Provenance?", *JSJ* 18 (1987), pp. 18-25.

PUMMER, R., *The Samaritans* (Iconography of Religions 5; Leiden: E.J. Brill, 1987).

PUMMER, R., "New Testament and the Samaritans", in CROWN, PUMMER and TAL, *A Companion to Samaritan Studies*, p. 170.

PUMMER, R., "Samaritan Tabernacle Drawings", *Numen* 45 (1998), pp. 30-68.

PURVIS, J.D., *The Samaritan Pentateuch and the Origin of the Samaritan Sect* (HSM 2; Cambridge, MA: Harvard University Press, 1968).

RAHMER, M., *Die hebräischen Traditionen in den Werken des Hieronymus*, Erster Teil (Breslau: H. Skutsch, 1861).

RAPPAPORT, U., "The Samaritans in the Hellenistic Period", *Zion* 55 (1990), pp. 373-396 (Hebrew).

RATNER, B. (ed.), *Midrash Seder Olam* (New York: The Talmudical Research Institute, 1966).

RENDTORFF, R., "Das 'Ende' der Geschichte Israels", *Gesammelte Studien zum Alten Testament* (TB 57; München: Chr. Kaiser, 1975), pp. 267-276.

RENDTORFF, R., "Die Hebräische Bibel als Grundlage christlich-theologischer Aussagen über das Judentum", in M. STÖHR (ed.), *Jüdische Existenz und die Erneuerung der christlichen Theologie* (München: Chr. Kaiser, 1981), pp. 33-47.

RENDTORFF, R., "Recent German Old Testament Theologies", *JR* 76 (1996), pp. 328-337.

RENDTORFF, R. und H.H. HENRIX (eds.), *Die Kirchen und das Judentum: Dokumente von 1945 bis 1985* (Paderborn: Verlag Bonifatius-Druckerei / München: Chr. Kaiser Verlag, 1988).

REVENTLOW, H.G., *Problems of Old Testament Theology in the Twentieth Century* (Philadelphia: Fortress, 1985).

ROFÉ, A., The Belief in Angels in the First Temple Period According to Biblical Traditions (Dissertation; Jerusalem: The Hebrew University, 1969).

ROFÉ, A., "Moses' Blessing, the Sanctuary at Nebo and the Origin of the Levites", in Y. AVISHUR and J. BLAU (eds.), *Studies in Bible and the Ancient Near East Presented to S.E. Loewenstamm on His Seventieth Birthday* (Jerusalem: E. Rubinstein's Publishing House, 1978), vol. I, pp. 409-424 (Hebrew).

ROLLER, D.W., *The Building Program of Herod the Great* (Berkeley / Los Angeles / London: University of California Press, 1998).

ROSENBLATT, S., *Saadia Gaon, The Book of Beliefs and Opinions – Translated from the Arabic and the Hebrew* (New Haven: Yale University Press / London: Geoffrey Cumberlege / Oxford: Oxford University Press, 1948).

ROTH, L., "Tinneius Rufus", *Encyclopaedia Judaica* (Jerusalem: Keter, [without date]), vol. 15, p. 1148.

RUETHER, R.R., *Faith and Fratricide: The Theological Roots of Anti-Semitism* (New York: Seabury, 1974).

SÆBO, M., "Johann Philipp Gabler at the End of Eighteenth Century: History and Theology", *On the Way to Canon: Creative Tradition History in the Old Testament* (JSOT Suppl. 191; Sheffield: Sheffield Academic Press, 1998), pp. 310-326.

SANDERS, J.A., *The Psalms Scroll of Qumran Cave 11* (ASOR, Discoveries in the Judaean Desert of Jordan, IV; Oxford: Clarendon Press, 1965), pp. 53-93.

SANDERS, J.A., "First Testament and Second", *BTB* 17 (1987), pp. 47-49.

SARNA, N.M., *Understanding Genesis* (2nd edn.; New York: Schocken, 1970).

SASSON, J.M., "Circumcision in the Ancient Near East", *JBL* 85 (1966), pp. 473-476.

SCHÄFER, P., *The History of the Jews in Antiquity: The Jews of Palestine from Alexander the Great to the Arab Conquest* (Luxembourg: Harwood Academic Publishers, 1995).

SCHECHTER, S. (ed.), *Avot de-Rabbi Nathan* (Wien 1889; reprinted New York & Jerusalem: The Jewish Theological Seminary of America, 1997).

SCHIFFMAN, L.H., *Who was a Jew? – Rabbinic and Halachic Perspectives on the Jewish Christian Schism* (Hoboken, NJ: Ktav Publishing House, 1985).

SCHMAUS, M., *Der Glaube der Kirche* (München: Max Hueber Verlag, 1969) vol. I, pp. 508-509.

SCHMIDT, W.H., "Das Problem des Alten Testaments in der christlichen Theologie", in *Festschrift H. Donner* (Wiesbaden: Otto Harrassowitz, 1995), pp. 243-251.

SCHREINER, J., "Das Verhältnis des Alten Testaments zum Neuen Testament", *Segen für die Völker – Gesamelte Schriften zur Entstehung und Theologie des Alten Testament* (Würzburg: Echter Verlag, 1987), pp. 392-407.

SCHÜSSLER FIORENZA, E., "Christlicher Antijudaismus aus feministischer Perspektive", in C. HURTH and P. SCHMID (eds.), *Das christlich-jüdische Gespräch* (Judentum und Christentum, 3; Stuttgart: W. Kohlhammer, 2000), pp. 56-75.

SCHWARTZ, D.R., "On Some Papyri and Josephus' Sources and Chronology for the Persian Period", *JSJ* 21 (1990), pp. 175-199.

SHINAN, A., "The Language of the Sanctuary in the Targumim of the Pentateuch", *Beit Mikra* 21 (1976), pp. 472-474 (Hebrew).

SHINAN, A. (ed.), *Midrash Shemot Rabbah Chapters I-XIV* (Jerusalem & Tel Aviv: Dvir Publishing House, 1984).

SIEGELE-WENSCHKEWITZ, L., "Antijudaismus", in E. GROSSMANN, E. MOLTMANN-WENDEL et al. (eds.), *Wörterbuch der Feministischen Theologie* (Gütersloh: Gütersloher Verlags-Haus Mohn, 1991), pp. 22-24.

SIMON, M., *Berakoth – Translated into English with Notes, Glossary and Indices* (London: Soncino Press, 1948).

SKINNER, J., *A Critical and Exegetical Commentary on Genesis* (ICC; Edinburgh: T&T Clark, 1930).

SMITH, J.Z., *To Take Place – Toward Theory in Ritual* (Chicago Studies in the History of Judaism; Chicago and London: The University of Chicago Press, 1987).

SONNE, I., "The Paintings of the Dura Synagogue", *HUCA* 20 (1947), pp. 225-362.

SPERBER, A. (ed.), *The Bible in Aramaic – Vol. I: The Pentateuch According to Targum Onkelos* (Leiden: E.J. Brill, 1959).

SPERBER, A. (ed.), *The Bible in Aramaic – Vol. IV A: The Hagiographa* (Leiden: E.J. Brill, 1968).

SPIEGEL, A., "From the *Aqedah* Legends: A Piyyut on the Slaughtering of Isaac and his Resurrection by Rab Ephraim of Buna", *The Alexander Marx Jubilee Volume* (New York: The Jewish Theological Seminary of America, 1950), pp. 471-547 (Hebrew section).

SPIEGEL, S., *The Fathers of Piyyut – Texts and Studies* (Selected from his Literary Estate and edited by M.H. SCHMELZER; New York & Jerusalem: The Jewish Theological Seminary of America, 1996; Hebrew).

STENDAHL, K., "Anti-Semitism and the New Testament", *Explorations* – *Rethinking Relationships Among Jews and Christians* vol. 7, number 2 (1993), p. 7.

STERN, M., *Greek and Latin Authors on Jews and Judaism* (Jerusalem: The Israel Academy of Sciences and Humanities), vol. I, 1974; vol. II, 1980.

STEUERNAGEL, C., "Alttestamentliche Theologie und alttestamentliche Religionsgeschichte", in K. BUDDE (ed.), *Vom Alten Testament – Festschrift Karl Marti* (BZAW 41; Gießen: Verlag Alfred Töpelmann, 1925), pp. 266-273.

STUCKENBRUCK, L.T., "Johann Philipp Gabler and the Delineation of Biblical Theology", *SJT* 52 (1999), pp. 139-157.

SUKENIK, E.L., *Ancient Synagogues in Palestine and Greece* (The Schweich Lectures of the British Academy, 1930; London: Oxford University Press, 1934).

SUKENIK, E.L., *The Synagogue of Dura-Europos and its Frescoes* (Jerusalem: Bialik Institute, 1947; Hebrew).

SWEENEY, M.A., "Tanak versus Old Testament: Concerning the Foundation for a Jewish Theology of the Bible", in H.T.C. SUN and K.L. EADES (eds.), *Problems in Biblical Theology – Essays in Honor of Rolf Knierim* (Grand Rapids, MI / Cambridge: W.B. Eerdmans, 1997), pp. 353-372.

SWEENEY, M.A., "Why Jews Should be Interested in Biblical Theology", *CCAR Journal* 46 (1997), pp. 67-75.

SWEENEY, M.A., "Reconceiving the Paradigms of Old Testament Theology in the Post-*Shoah* Period", *BI* 6 (1998), pp. 142-161.

SWEENEY, M.A., "The Emerging Field of Jewish Biblical Theology", in Z. GARBER (ed.), *Academic Approaches to Teaching Jewish Studies* (Lanham, MD / New York / Oxford: University Press of America, 2000), pp. 83-105.

SWEENEY, M.A., "Isaiah and Theodicy after the *Shoah*", in T. LINAFELT (ed.), *Strange Fire – Reading the Bible after the Holocaust* (Sheffield: Sheffield Academic Press, 2000), pp. 208-219.

TAL, A., *The Samaritan Targum of the Pentateuch – A Critical Edition, Part I – Genesis and Exodus* (Tel Aviv: Tel Aviv University Press, 1980).

TAL, A., "Samaritan Literature", in A.D. CROWN (ed.), *The Samaritans* (Tübingen: J.C.B. Mohr [Paul Siebeck], 1989), pp. 462-465.

TAL, A., "*Tibât Mârqe*", in CROWN, PUMMER and TAL, *A Companion to Samaritan Studies*, pp. 235-236.

TALMON, S., "Biblical Traditions on the Early History of the Samaritans", in J. AVIRAM (ed.), *Eretz Shomron – The Thirtieth Archaeological Convention – September 1972* (Jerusalem: Israel Exploration Society, 1973; Hebrew).

TALMON, S. "Fragments of Scrolls from Masada", *Eretz-Israel* 20 (1989), pp. 278-286 (Hebrew).

TALSHIR, Z., "The Reign of Solomon in the Making: Pseudo-Connections between 3 Kingdoms and Chronicles", *VT* 50 (2000), pp. 233-249.

THACKERAY, H.St.J., *Josephus in Nine Volumes* (The Loeb Classical Library; Cambridge, MA: Harvard University Press / London: William Heinemann), vol. II (1961); vol. III (1976).

THEODOR, J. (ed.), *Bereschit Rabba mit kritischem Apparat und Kommentar* (Veröffentlichungen der Akademie für die Wissenschaft des Judentums; Berlin: H. Itzkowski, 1903; 2nd edn. with additional corrections by Ch. Albeck, Jerusalem: Wahrmann Books, 1965).

THOMA, C., *Das Messiasprojekt: Theologie Jüdisch-christlicher Begegnung* (Augsburg: Pattloch Verlag, 1994).

TOWNSEND, J.T., "The New Testament, the Early Church, and Anti-Semitism", in J. NEUSNER, E.S. FRERICHS and N.M. SARNA (eds.), *From Ancient Israel to Modern Judaism* (BJS 159; Atlanta, GA: Scholars Press, 1989), pp. 171-186.

TOWNSEND, J.T., "Anti-Judaism in the New Testament", *Mercer Dictionary of the Bible* (Macon, GA: Mercer University Press, 1990), pp. 33-34.

TOWNSEND, J.T., *Midrash Tanḥuma – Translated into English with Introduction, Indices and Brief Notes: Volume I – Genesis* (S. Buber Recension; Hoboken, NJ: Ktav Publishing House, 1989).

TOWNSEND, J.T., *Midrash Tanḥuma – Translated into English with Indices and Brief Notes: Volume II – Exodus and Leviticus* (S. Buber Recension; Hoboken, NJ: Ktav Publishing House, 1997).

UFFENHEIMER, B., *Early Prophecy in Israel* (Jerusalem: Magnes Press, 1973; Hebrew).

VANDERKAM, J.C., "Jubilees, Book of", *ABD*, vol. 3, pp. 1030-1032.

VANDERKAM, J.[C.] and J.T. MILIK, *Qumran Cave 4, VIII* (Discoveries in the Judaean Desert XIII; Oxford: Clarendon Press, 1994), pp. 141-155.

VERMES, G., "New Light on the Sacrifice of Isaac", *JJS* 47 (1996), pp. 140-146.

VILNAY, Z., "Gerizim", *Ariel – The Encyclopaedia of the Land of Israel* (Tel Aviv: Sifriyat ha-Sadeh, 1974), pp. 1432-1434 (Hebrew).

VINCENT, L.H., "Abraham à Jerusalem", *RB* 58 (1951), pp. 366-371.

VON CAMPENHAUSEN, H., "Das Alte Testament als Bibel der Kirche", *Aus der Frühzeit des Christentums: Studien zur Kirchengeschichte des ersten und zweiten Jahrhunderts* (Tübingen: J.C.B. Mohr [Paul Siebeck], 1963), pp. 152-196.

VON GALL, A.F. (ed.), *Der Hebräische Pentateuch der Samaritaner* (Giessen: Verlag Alfred Töpelmann, 1918).

VON RAD, G., *Genesis – A Commentary* (OTL; 2nd edn.; London: SCM Press, 1963).

WACHOLDER, B.Z., "Pseudo-Eupolemus – Two Greek Fragments on the Life of Abraham", *HUCA* 34 (1963), pp. 83-113.

WALTER, N., *Fragmente jüdisch-hellenistischer Historiker,* in W.G. KÜMMEL (ed.), *Jüdische Schriften aus hellenistisch-römischer Zeit* (Gütersloh: Gütersloher Verlaghaus Gerd Mohn, 1976), Band I, Lieferung 2.

WATSON, F., "The Old Testament as Christian Scripture", *SJT* 52 (1999), pp. 227-232.

WEINFELD, M., "God the Creator in Genesis 1 and in Deutero-Isaiah", *Tarbiz* 37 (1968), pp. 105-132 (Hebrew).

WEINFELD, M., "The Work of the Israeli Molech and his Background", *Proceedings of the Ninth World Congress of Jewish Studies* (The World Union of Jewish Studies; Jerusalem: Magnes Press, 1969), pp. 37-61, 152 (Hebrew).

WEINFELD, M., "Theological Trends in Torah Literature", *Beit Mikra* 16 (1971), pp. 10-22 (Hebrew).

WEINFELD, M., *Deuteronomy 1-11* (AB 5; New York / London / Toronto / Sydney / Auckland: Doubleday, 1991).

WEISS, M., "The Origin of the 'Day of the Lord' – Reconsidered", *HUCA* 37 (1966), pp. 29-60.

WEISS, M., "Psalm 23: The Psalmist on God's Care", in M. Fishbane and E. TOV (eds.), *Sha'arei Talmon – Studies in the Bible, Qumran, and the Ancient Near East Presented to Shemaryahu Talmon* (Winona Lake, IN: Eisenbrauns, 1992), pp. 31*-41*.

WELLHAUSEN, J., *Die Composition des Hexateuchs und der historischen Bücher des Alten Testaments* (Berlin: Georg Reimer, 1889).

WELLHAUSEN, J., *Prolegomena zur Geschichte Israels* (6th edn.; Berlin & Leipzig: Walter de Gruyter, 1927)

WELLHAUSEN, J., *Prolegomena to the History of Ancient Israel* (Gloucester, MA: Peter Smith, 1973).

WENHAM, G.J., *Genesis 16-50* (WBC 2; Dallas, TX: Word, 1994).

WESTERMANN, C., *Genesis – 2. Teilband, Genesis 12-36* (Neukirchen-Vluyn: Neukirchener Verlag, 1981).

WESTERMANN, C., *Die Joseph-Erzählung* (Calwer Taschenbibliothek 1; Stuttgart: Calwer Verlag, 1990).

WHITE, R.T., "Genesis Apocryphon", *ABD*, vol. 2, pp. 932-933.

WILLIAMSON, C.M., *Has God Rejected His People? – Anti-Judaism in the Christian Church* (Nashville, TN: Abingdon Press, 1982).

WILLIAMSON, C.M., *A Guest in the House of Israel – Post-Holocaust Church Theology* (Louisville, KT: Wesmister / John Knox Press, 1993).

WILLIAMSON, H.G.M., *1 and 2 Chronicles* (NCBC; Grand Rapids, MI: Eerdmans / London: Marshall, Morgan & Scott, 1982).

WINTER, P., "Note on Salem – Jerusalem", *NovT* 2 (1957-58), pp. 151-152.

WINTERMUTE, O.S., *Jubilees – A New Translation and Introduction*, in CHARLESWORTH, *The Old Testament Pseudepigrapha*, vol. 2, pp. 35-142.

WRIGHT, G.E., "The Biblical Traditions of Shechem's Sacred Area", *BASOR* 169 (1963), pp. 30-32.

WRIGHT, G.E., *Shechem – The Biography of a Biblical City* (New York: McGraw-Hill, 1965).

YADIN, Y., "The First Temple", in M. AVI-YONAH (ed.), *The Book of Jerusalem* (Jerusalem & Tel Aviv: Bialik Institute and Dvir, 1956), vol. 1, pp. 176-190.

YERKES, R.K., "The Location and Etymology of יהוה יראה, Gn. 22,14", *JBL* 31 (1912), pp. 136-139.

YOHANNAN, J.D. (ed.), *Joseph and Potiphar's Wife in World Literature* (New York: A New Directions Book, 1968).

ZENGER, E., *Das Erste Testament: Die jüdische Bibel und die Christen* (4th edn.; Düsseldorf: Patmos Verlag, 1994).

ZENGER, E., *Ein Gott der Rache? – Feindpsalmen verstehen* (Biblische Bücher 1; Freiburg / Basel / Wien: Herder, 1994).

ZENGER, E. u.a., *Einleitung in das Alte Testament* (SBT 1,1; 3rd edn.; Stuttgart / Berlin / Köln: W. Kohlhammer, 1998).

ZUCKERMANDEL, M.S. (ed.), *Tosephta Based on Erfurt and Vienna Codices* (Trier 1881; reprinted: Jerusalem: Bamberger & Wahrmann, 1937; Wahrmann Books, 1963).

Indexes

(1) Index of Sources

1. Hebrew Bible References

2. Ancient Biblical Versions

3.   Apocrypha and Pseudepigrapha

10. Jewish Medieval Writings

12. Early Christian Writings

(2) General Index – Names and Topics

(3) Index of Modern Authors

C. Thoma 84
W.S. Towner 137
J.T. Townsend 48, 58, 68, 84, 85, 87, 116, 117

B. Uffenheimer 128

J.C. VanderKam 35, 66
J.[C.] VanderKam and J.T. Milik 35, 36
G. Vermes 36
Z. Vilnay 52
L.H. Vincent 13
H. von Campenhausen 148
A.F. von Gall 49
G. von Rad 9, 11, 13, 14, 123, 135, 140

B.Z. Wacholder 40
N. Walter 39
F. Watson 148

M. Weinfeld 122, 128, 129
M. Weiss 6, 123, 128
J. Wellhausen 13, 24, 80, 125, 126
G.J. Wenham 14
C. Westermann 13, 14, 91
R.T. White 36
C.M. Williamson 116
H.G.M. Williamson 12, 14, 15, 26, 27, 34
J.A. Wilson 99
P. Winter 38
O.S. Wintermute 66
G.E. Wright 21

Y. Yadin 20
R.K. Yerkes 10
J.D. Yohannan 99

E. Zenger 117, 124, 157, 158
M.S. Zuckermandel 37, 63, 85, 98